BASIC PRINCIPLES

OF THE

ISLAMIC
WORLDVIEW

BASIC PRINCIPLES
OF THE
ISLAMIC
WORLDVIEW

SAYYID QUTB

TRANSLATED BY RAMI DAVID
PREFACE BY HAMID ALGAR

Islamic Publications International
North Haledon, New Jersey

Published and distributed by
Islamic Publications International
5 Sicomac Road, Suite 302, North Haledon, NJ 07508, USA
Telephone: 800-568-9814   Fax: 800-466-8111
Email: ipi@onebox.com
Website: www.IslamPub.com

First Edition 2006

Library of Congress Cataloging-in-Publication Data
Qutb, Sayyid, 1903–1966.
[Muqawwimāt al-tassawwur al-Islāmī. English]
    Basic Principles of the Islamic Worldview / Sayyid Qutb ; translated by Rami David.
    p. cm.
    ISBN 1-889999-34-2 — ISBN 1-889999-35-0
    1. Islam—Doctrines. 2. God (Islam) 3. Theological anthropology—Islam.
    4. Philosophy, Islamic.   I. David, Rami. II. Algar, Hamid. III. Title.
    BP165.5.Q8313 2005
    297.2--dc22

                                                              2005033286

Director of Publications: Moin Shaikh
Book design: Chris Alaf

CONTENTS

PREFACE

Sayyid Qutb has long been recognized as one of the most influential writers and activists of the Arab world in the past fifty years.[1] Although his career was cut short by execution at the hands of the regime of Abdel Nasser in 1966, he left behind an abundant body of work that continues to be studied and varyingly appreciated down to the present. Attention has been paid in particular to al-'Adalat al-Ijtima'iyya fi 'l-Islam ("Social Justice in Islam"), the first of his works to appear in English translation); Fi Zilal al-Qur'an ("In the Shade of the Qur'an"), a complete commentary on the Qur'an; and Ma'alim fi 't-Tariq ("Milestones"), a manifesto for change which, together with the flimsiest of forensic evidence, was used by the Egyptian government to serve as a pretext for his execution. Qutb saw himself above all, however, as a thinker called upon to articulate Islam in its purest, simplest, and most imperative form, to free it from the host of misconceptions, which, in his opinion, had obscured it for centuries, and several of his most important books were dedicated to that purpose. The book now presented to the reader in English translation is one such book; it may serve as a key to the understanding of some of his better known writings.

The text entitled Khasa'is at-Tasawwur al-Islami wa Muqawwimatuhu ("The Characteristics and Fundamentals of the Islamic Concept") is said to have been first published in either 1960 or 1962, at a time when its author was in jail.[2] The printing used for this translation is described

---

[1] On the life of Sayyid Qutb, see the present writer's introduction to Social Justice in Islam, revised translation by John B. Hardie (Oneonta, NY, 2000), pp. 1-17, and the sources cited there.

[2] For 1960, see Gilles Keppel, Muslim Extremism in Egypt (Berkeley and Los Angeles, 1985), p. 69; for 1962, see Shahrough Akhavi, "Sayyid Qutb: the Poverty of Philosophy and the Vindication of Islamic Tradition," Serif Mardin, ed., Cultural Transitions in the Middle East (Leiden, 1994), p. 131, n.1. It may not be irrelevant to note that Keppel, now transatlantically famed as an expert on "Islamism," fails both to transliterate accurately and to translate correctly the title of Sayyid Qutb's work.

on the frontispiece as the "ninth legitimate edition" (Dar al-Shuruq, Beirut and Cairo, 2000), "legitimate" in that it has been authorized by Sayyid Qutb's heirs and is not a pirate edition. Several of Qutb's works, above all *al-'Adalat al-Ijtima'iyya fi 'l-Islam*, changed significantly in content from one edition to the next, and short of locating a copy of the 1960 or 1962 edition of *Khasa'is* and comparing it with the ninth, it is impossible to tell whether changes were ever made between the first edition and any of its successors. Probably, however, the text did not undergo any major revision, for it was intended as the first in a two-part series, and Sayyid Qutb spent part of the time left to him in completing the sequel, *Muqawwimat al-Tasawwur al-Islami* ("The Fundamentals of the Islamic Concept"). At numerous points in the *Khasa'is*, where he senses, perhaps, that he has not dealt with matters in adequate detail, he refers the reader precisely to his forthcoming *Muqawwimat* for a fuller discussion of the topic in question; it is therefore unlikely that he should have thought it necessary to rework the *Khasa'is*. As for the *Muqawwimat*, he was unable to finish writing it before his execution, and it was not until 1986 that his brother, Muhammad Qutb, published the five chapters that were complete together with his notes for two final chapters, prefacing the book with a lengthy introduction. The work entitled *Khasa'is at-Tasawwur al-Islami wa Muqawwimatuhu* ("The Characteristics and Fundamentals of the Islamic Concept"), both in the first and in the ninth edition, here offered in translation, deals in fact only with the "Characteristics," not at all with the "Fundamentals"; our retention of the title is simply a matter of fidelity to Sayyid Qutb's choice.

It has often been remarked by admirers and detractors alike that Sayyid Qutb was not a scholar of Islam, an *'alim*, in the formal and traditional sense. From his point of view, this was an advantage, in that it enabled him, he believed, to encounter the Qur'an directly, free of the extraneous elements that had come to cloud Islamic scholarship over the centuries. He was particularly critical of the philosophical tradition represented by such luminaries as Ibn Sina and Farabi, denying it the attribute of "Islamic" because of its obvious debt to the Greeks, whose concepts, he rightly remarked, were indelibly marked by mythology. Scholastic theology (*kalam*) was hardly preferable, for it, too, bore the signs of external influence and caused the Muslims to dissipate their energies on vain and arcane matters. The correct understanding of the Qur'an and, as he put it, the "Islamic concept" was dependent on engagement in struggle and effort to create the society mandated by revelation. This had been the case with the first generation of Muslims, whom Qutb idealized to a unprecedented extent and effectively exempted from all the complexities of history, both before and after. Then, as a result of the conquests, Muslims began to make contact with other cultures, and the contamination set in. One might well ask why Islamic civilization, at such an early and vigorous period in its history, was so easily contaminated, and how it might shake off the consequences at a time when its resources are far fewer. These questions remained unasked by Sayyid Qutb. His urgent concern was rather to reconstitute, after a more than millennial lapse, the environment of struggle in which the revelation had first been received and to achieve thereby a new, exemplary era, mirroring the first. This concern accounts for the hortatory and insistent tone, often involving the repetition of one and the same sentence in a single paragraph, which pervades the whole book.

The present work should, then, be read as a document of struggle, not of theological or historical analysis. This feature serves to explain, perhaps, a curious and even paradoxical feature of the book: that while ostensibly devoted to expounding the thoroughly unique features of the Islamic revelation, it accords a great deal of space to the refutation of a wide array of religions and philosophies. Such attention to what-is-not-Islam while setting forth what-is-Islam is not, of course, peculiar to Sayyid Qutb. All too many works by modern Muslim writers, *'ulama* for the most part excepted, give the impression of having been written with the awareness of a censorious Westerner peering over the shoulder of the writer. Insofar as the works in question function as a counteroffensive against current or traditional Western attitudes and criticisms of Islam, the practice of blending the exposition of Islam with the refutation of contemporary ideologies is understandable. The range of targets addressed by Sayyid Qutb is, however, unusually broad—Judaism, Christianity, Brahmanism, Zoroastrianism, many schools of philosophy, both ancient and modern, Marxism, Darwinism—all come under his rubric of "debris", and in some cases they receive greater analytical attention than the characteristics of Islam that form the subject matter of each chapter. Those chacteristics are spelled out only in the most general terms, to the accompaniment of relevant Qur'anic verses cited without interpretation or comment. Particularly remarkable is that the exposition of the scope of *tawhid*, placed for some reason at the very end of the book, is preceded by a critique of Brahmanism (in terms virtually identical to those used earlier in the text), Platonism, and even the para-monotheistic cult of Iton in Pharaonic Egypt. It is as if the veritable uniqueness of Islam can be seen only by way of stark contrast with all that preceded and followed it.

It has been correctly remarked that Sayyid Qutb for the most part lacked—or at least failed to demonstrate—direct textual acquaintance with the traditions and philosophies he criticized.[3] The principal sources on which he drew for the purpose were *Allah*, a work by his longtime associate, the littérateur Mahmud 'Abbas al-'Aqqad (d.1964), and *al-Fikr al-Islami al-Hadith wa Silatuhu bi 'l-Isti'mar al-Gharbi* ("Modern Islamic Thought and Its Relation to Western Imperialism") by Muhammad al-Bahi. He also made use of writings by Abu 'l-A'la Mawdudi (d. 1979), Abu 'l-Hasan Nadwi (d. 1999), and Muhammad Asad (d. 1992), regularly identified as "the former Leopold Weiss" in order to highlight his status as an eminent convert. Sayyid Qutb's lack of access to original sources and dependence on works which already carried a polemical intent definitely placed him at a disadvantage, although he cannot for the most part be said to have distorted the creeds and philosophies he reviews.

A more serious problem is, perhaps, that he occasionally disregarded his own chosen methodology, defined negatively as the avoidance of themes, emphases and terms alien to Islam and its own distinctive vocabulary. He criticizes two of his predecessors, Muhammad 'Abduh (d. 1905) and Muhammad Iqbal (d. 1938), for doing precisely that. He correctly remarks of the former that as a reaction to Western polemics against Islam as a passive and fatalistic creed, he has attempted to make reason the judge of revelation, and of the latter, that under the influence of Nietzsche he has massively exaggerated the role of the ego. Sayyid Qutb's own use of terms such as "positivism" (*al-ijabiyya*) and "realism" (*al-waqi'iyya*) to describe characteristics of the Islamic concept also represents, however, a terminological borrowing from an

---

[3] Akhavi, *"Sayyid Qutb,"* p. 132.

alien vocabulary. It seems that he was aware of this himself, for in the case of "realism" he found it necessary to append a footnote clarifying the sense in which he used the word and distancing himself from other senses. Similarly, his proclamation that the establishment of a truly Islamic society will result in "the liberation of man" and "the birth of man" owes little to the terminology of the Qur'an and much to the ideological climate in which the book was written. Most significant of all is the key word in the title, *tasawwur* ("concept"), the unmistakeable lexical sense of which is an idea, something formed in the mind. Sayyid Qutb's reliance on it throughout the work as his organizing theme is at odds with the "divine nature" (*rabbaniya*) which he correctly emphasizes as a leading feature of Islam; something possessing divine nature can hardly be a mental construct. What is underway here is clearly the construction of an Islamic ideology (not that Qutb himself ever, to my knowledge, used that word).

None of the foregoing is intended to invalidate the substance of what Sayyid Qutb puts forth in his book, but only to clarify the purposes for which he wrote it, the method he espoused, and the climate of struggle which he both experienced and aspired to cultivate. For whatever else may be said about the man and his work, he remained utterly faithful to his central belief: that proper comprehension of the "Islamic concept" depends on living out its implications in the actuality of existence, individual and collective. To this, he bore powerful testimony with his pen and his life.

In the aftermath of 9/11, a malodorous flood of pseudo-scholarly writing on Islam, "Islamism," "political Islam," "Islamic extremism," "Islamic fundamentalism," etc. has gushed forth across America, in such proportions that one might imagine there to be one expert on Islamic and Middle Eastern affairs per hundred head of the population. This body of literature, to use the word loosely, is in many ways heir to the musings of British, French and Russian scholar-imperialists in earlier times on the wellsprings of "Mohammadan fanaticism" and to their search for a single, malevolent source of their troubles. And according to several of the freshly minted experts with whom we are blessed, none other than Sayyid Qutb is the villain of the age. To the plaintive question, "Why do they hate us?" we now have an answer: "Because Sayyid Qutb told them to.

The campaign against him began as early as the fall of 2001 but picked up steam with a piece published in the *New York Times Magazine* on March 23, 2003, "Al-Qaeda's Philosopher: How an Egyptian Islamist Invented the Terrorist Jihad from his Jail Cell," by a certain Paul Berman. This was yellow journalism at its most lurid, both literally and figuratively, literally in the sense that the front cover of the magazine bore a picture of Sayyid Qutb composed of alternating dots of yellow and black, for no apparent aesthetic purpose. The attempt to merge Osama bin Laden with Sayyid Qutb continued on the inside with a picture of bin Laden superimposed on a page from Sayyid Qutb's Qur'an commentary, *Fi Zilal al-Qur'an*, and another, showing the blackened silhouette of a fighter taking aim, similarly mounted on a page from that work. The heading to the article promised that it would show how "the roots of Al Qaeda are not in poverty or in anti-Americanism but in Sayyid Qutb's ideas about how Christianity went wrong and how martyrdom could change the world." In fact, it failed to show any line of filiation from Sayyid Qutb, who died in 1966, to al-Qa'ida, which emerged in the 1980's; the mere fact that while in Saudi Arabia bin Laden is said to have studied with Muhammad Qutb, the brother of Sayyid Qutb, is hardly decisive. Neither Sayyid Qutb or his brother advocated at any point the indiscriminate slaughter of civilians, nor are the intellectual, cultural and social concerns Sayyid Qutb manifested in many of his works reflected in the published communiques of al-Qa'ida. True, both men speak of Crusaders and Zionists as enemies of Islam, but this cannot be dismissed as a fantasy originating in either or both of their minds, given the fervid support of Evangelical Christians for the invasions of Iraq and Afghanistan, the ugly manifestations of Islamophobia in and around both of those wars, and the apocalyptic fantasies of the Christian Zionists.

Berman's article was the prelude to a book that appeared later in the year, *Terror and Liberalism*, fully fifty pages of which were devoted to Sayyid Qutb. Again Sayyid Qutb's largely unhappy sojourn in Greeley, Colorado, was portrayed as important for his growing disdain for the West, and this disdain, Berman suggests, was magnified several decades later into murderous form by al-Qa'ida: the reader might almost conclude that had Sayyid Qutb not witnessed dancing he regarded as lascivious in the church halls of Greeley back in the 1940's, the Twin Towers might still be standing. All that Berman can muster by way of evidence for his thesis is that bin Laden's "presentation of political issues" is made "in a spirit close to Qutb's theology of the absolute," and that his analysis of the world is comparable to the depiction of Medina in the time of the Prophet made by Sayyid Qutb in *Fi Zilal al-Qur'an*.[4] Running through the book like a thread is the insistence that Sayyid Qutb and other troublesome Arabs and Muslims were formatively influenced by Nazism and Fascism; hence the irreducible clash between the "terror" they espoused and the "liberalism" so dear to Berman's heart.[5] His understanding of "liberalism" can be gauged from his benign conjoining of United States influence in Pahlavi Iran with "liberal civilization."[6] Imperialism is completely absent from Berman's purview, and Zionism is close to flawless; he even finds something to admire in the murderous Israeli assault on Jenin.[7]

A similar tack is taken by Ian Buruma and Avishai Margalit in an opuscule entitled *Occidentalism: The West in the Eyes of its Enemies* (New York, 2004). Here Sayyid Qutb and his real or imaginary cohorts are presented as retrograde enemies of the modern urban civilization of the West, lusting destructively after an unattainable alternative and sharing with pre-World War Two Japan a fascination with the ideas of extreme German nationalism.[8] A year later, Stephen Schwartz, an ex-Spartacist who migrated to neo-conservatism via a stint as a pseudo-Sufi, guided throughout by the Zionist lodestar, added his voice to the cacophony with a tome entitled *The Two Faces of Islam*. Here, the main emphasis is on Wahhabism as the source of all evil, but Sayyid Qutb also comes in for the condemnation that was by now becoming obligatory. Sayyid Qutb, Schwartz impudently intoned, "never grew

---

[4] *Terror and Liberalism*, pp. 116–118.

[5] As the present writer suggested in a rejoinder to Berman's article, belatedly published in the *New York Times Magazine* on April 20, 2003, "it is elsewhere in the contemporary Middle East that one might look for a closer analogue" with Fascists and Nazis. For some of the evidence, see Norman G. Finkelstein, *Image and Reality of the Israel-Palestine Conflict* (London and New York, 1995), pp. 88–120.

[6] *Terror and Liberalism*, p. 107.

[7] *Terror and Liberalism*, p. 136.

[8] *Occidentalism*, pp. 31–32, 117–121.

beyond the mental horizon of an isolated and impoverished peas-
ant," but his "hostility to the West expressed itself in an exaltation of
his concept of *jihad*. This *jihad* embodied a guerilla ethos of radical
assault, from below, on Western societies."[9] What precisely is meant
by "from below" is unclear, but somewhat later Schwartz managed a
slightly greater degree of coherence: "Wahhabi intolerance, metasta-
sized through Mawdudi and Sayyid Qutb," led to the rise of "Islamic
terrorism."[10] His case thus stated although entirely unproven, Schwartz
confidently speculated that Sayyid Qutb "would likely have been proud
of bin Laden."[11]

In view of these precedents, it is not surprising that the *The 9/11
Commission Report*, while signally failing to answer a host of questions concerning that tragic day, was able sagely to pinpoint Sayyid
Qutb as a source of inspiration for bin Laden, who, we are informed,
"relies heavily" on him. For Sayyid Qutb, the report asserts, those
Muslims who rejected his vision of an ideal Islamic society were like
"nonbelievers worthy of destruction."[12] None of the sources adduced
in the three footnotes to the relevant sentences of the report bear out
these contentions.

Two other recent authors, Haneef James Oliver and Natania Long-
Bas, also portray Sayyid Qutb as the ultimate source of inspiration for
al-Qa'ida and all its murderous activities.[13] Their vantage point is, however, diametrically opposed to that of the writers reviewed above, for
unlike Schwartz who condemns Sayyid Qutb as an agent of Wahhabi
metastasis, they disconnect him from Wahhabism and thereby seek
to exculpate that creed from even remote and general responsibility
for 9/11 and, indeed, much else besides. In a sense, they are correct:

---

9 *The Two Faces of Islam*, p. 134.

10 *The Two Faces of Islam*, p. 178.

11 *The Two Faces of Islam*, p. 182. Lest anyone doubt Schwartz's credentials as a scholar
of Islam, let us draw attention to his remarkable discovery that the Qur'an itself
endorses or even mandates the Zionist project, a fact that has until now somehow
eluded the attention of the entire Islamic *umma* (see pp. 19-20 of his book).

12 *The 9/11 Commission Report* (Washington, DC, 2004), p. 51.

13 Haneef James Oliver, *The "Wahhabi" Myth: Dispelling Prevalent Fallacies and the
Fictitious Link with Bin Laden*, Toronto; The Reign of Islamic Da'wah Centre (*sic*),
2004; Natana Delong-Bas; *Wahhabi Islam: From Revival and Reform to Global
Jihad*, Oxford: Oxford University Press, 2004.

for better or for worse, Qutb was an original thinker and owed little if anything to Wahhabism, although his conviction that Islamic history had for long been perverted was not entirely dissimilar to one of Muhammad ibn 'Abd al-Wahhab's basic contentions. As for Wahhabi responsibility for 9/11 or more generally the activities of al-Qa'ida, the most that can reasonably be said is that Osama bin Laden came from a Wahhabi background, and that some Wahhabi preachers glorified the attack on New York; others, closer to the royal family, condemned it, as Oliver points out.[14] Moreover, as he does not point out, Wahhabi violence has traditionally been directed against Muslims, not against non-Muslims.

Oliver's evidence for the ideological dependence of al-Qa'ida on Sayyid Qutb consists mostly of ill-informed articles appearing in the same Western newspapers that he otherwise excoriates for their attacks on Wahhabism.[15] Mirroring the professional anti-Wahhabis who label as Wahhabi all who arouse their displeasure, he maintains that "Qutbism" is a widespread and pernicious phenomenon, exemplified by groups and personages as diverse as Hamas, the Islamic Salvation Front of Algeria, 'Ali Shari'ati of Iran, and the Saudi oppositionist groups led from London by Sa'd al-Faqih and Muhammad Mis'ari. These last are plainly the worst offenders, for they aim to displace the Saudi regime, a government which according to a communique approvingly cited by Oliver is "the only country that has Islamic legislation (even though it is not perfect) and is actually built upon the foundation of *Tawheed* (true monotheism)."[16] For Oliver, all these variegated "Qutbists" are the "Khawaarij of the Era," or alternatively a "wing of the Khawaarij."[17] The charge of neo-Kharijism stems from Sayyid Qutb's condemnation of contemporary Muslim societies as *jahili* in light of their acceptance of non-Islamic laws, which is, however, a different matter from denouncing individual Muslims as non-believers and declaring their

---

[14] For the supportive declarations, see the present writer's *Wahhabism: A Critical Essay* (Oneanta, NY, 2002), p. 66, and for a sample of the condemnations, Oliver, *The "Wahhabi" Myth*, p. 138

[15] Oliver, *The "Wahhabi" Myth*, pp. 18, 30–32. Among the luminaries he invokes is David Forte of the same *National Review* that opened its columns to the proposal that Mecca should be nuked.

[16] Oliver, *The "Wahhabi Myth,"* p. 40, n. 73.

[17] Oliver, *The "Wahhabi" Myth*, pp. 29, 37.

lives forfeit, as did the original Khariijites.[18] Many centuries later, the Kharijite example was indeed resurrected, but by none other than the early Wahhabis, in their campaigns of slaughter in Arabia and beyond; the Ottoman authorities of the time accordingly saw fit to condemn them as neo-Kharijites. It is in any event one of the curiosities of our peculiar times that Wahhabis and anti-Wahhabis are in agreement on one point: the posthumous criminality of Sayyid Qutb.

Delong-Bas's work is more temperate and scholarly in nature, if ultimately unconvincing. She portrays Muhammad ibn 'Abd al-Wahhab as a careful exegete of the Qur'an, a gentle soul, thoughtfully concerned with preserving, or even advancing, the rights of women and much inclined to ecumenical harmony; if some later Wahhabis conducted themselves more ferociously, this cannot be laid at his doorstep. Indicting Sayyid Qutb rather than Wahhabism, in any of its forms or elements, as the source of bin Laden's worldview and activities, Delong-Bas is obliged to admit that the Egyptian's influence on him is not "stated directly," and like Berman she can cite little more than the hardly decisive circumstance that bin Laden studied with Muhammad Qutb while in Saudi Arabia.[19] In a further effort to distance bin Laden from Wahhabism with its hallmark dislike of Sufism, she suggests additionally that he came under "Sufi influence" while in Afghanistan, and Ayman al-Zawahiri, his close associate, is "a major Sufi shaykh."[20] However, a choice has to be made, for Sayyid Qutb is entirely unfavorable to Sufism: bin Laden cannot be both a Qutbist and a Sufi.[21]

It is time now to invite the reader to proceed to Sayyid Qutb's text and to form his own estimate of the man, his thoughts, and his posthumous impact. The translation made by Rami David has been extensively revised to bring it into closer although not perfect, word-for-word

---

18 In his introduction to Sayyid Qutb's *Muqawwimat al-Tasawwur al-Islami* (Cairo, 1986), pp. 9–12, Muhammad Qutb argues convincingly that his brother cannot be classified as a neo-Kharijite.

19 Delong-Bas, *Wahhabi Islam*, pp. 273–274.

20 Delong-Bas, *Wahhabi Islam*, p. 274.

21 HOliver also suggests that Osama bin Laden is connected to Sufism, the conclusive evidence being that his family originated in the Hadramawt, an area where Sufi traditions are strong (*The "Wahhabi" Myth*, pp. 15–16)

alignment with the original; many of Sayyid Qutb's repetitive phrases have been excised. For citations from the Qur'an, the translation of Muhammad Asad (*The Message of the Qur'ân*, Gibraltar: Dar al-Andalus, 1980) has been used.

—Hamid Algar

A WORD ABOUT THE METHODOLOGY

"Verily, this Qur'an shows the way to all that is most upright."

Defining "The Characteristics and Fundamentals of The Islamic Concept"[1] is an essential matter for several reasons:

First, because a Muslim must have a comprehensive interpretation for existence, on the basis of which he deals with this existence. He needs an interpretation which will permit him to perceive the nature of the great truths with which he interacts and the nature of relationships and connections between these truths: the true nature of divinity, the true nature of worship (which includes the true nature of the universe, the true nature of life and the true nature of man).

Second, because a Muslim must understand the centrality of man in this cosmic existence and the purpose of his own existence. From this understanding, the role of man within the universe can be deduced, in addition to the boundaries of his functions as determined by his relationship with his Maker and the Creator of the universe.

Third, because on the basis of this comprehensive interpretation, this knowledge of centrality of man within the cosmic existence and the purpose of human existence, the Muslim determines his pattern of life and the system that permitrs its realization. The system that rules human life is dependent on and responsible to such a comprehensive interpretation; it must be derived from it in all essentials, failing which

---

[1] I earlier promised to publish this work with the title, "Islam's Concept of God, the Universe, Life and Man."

it would be an artificial system, with shallow and rapidly wilting roots. The short life allotted such a system is a period of misery for mankind, of conflict between it and human nature and the true needs of mankind. Today, this remark applies to all systems on the face of the earth—with no exceptions—especially the so-called "progressive" nations![2]

Fourth, because this religion of Islam came to create a people with a unique and distinctive character, a community that was to lead humanity, achieve the purposes of God on earth, and rescue humanity from the suffering it had endured at the hands of misguided leaders, methodologies and concepts. When a Muslim realizes the nature of the concept of Islam, its characteristics and fundamentals, he is guaranteed to become a sound element in building this community with a unique and distinctive character, an element that is able to lead and to rescue. The creedal concept of Muslims is the major guiding force in their life, together with the actual system derived from it and established on its basis. It deals with all individual and collective activity in the various fields of human activity.

The Noble Qur'an presents this comprehensive explanation to the people in a complete form that deals with all the elements of human existence, addresses all its aspects, and discusses all its fundamentals. It deals with all matters related to the senses, the mind, the imagination, and sagacity, and with all the elements of human perception and human existence. It also deals with the material reality of mankind, the reality that is created by his position within the cosmos, by addressing and directing all the elements of this existence as it came forth from the hand of the Creator.

With this concept derived directly from the Qur'an, the first Islamic community came into being in a unique manner, being entrusted with the leadership of humanity in a manner never known to mankind before. Both in matters pertaining to the heart and mind, and in those pertaining to the world of actions and reality, that community established an unprecedented and ideal system for mankind. The Qur'an was the first source of reference for that community, and it was from it that it arose: a truly wondrous phenomenon in the history of mankind, the emergence of a people from the text of a book! They lived by it and

---

[2] See Alexis Carrel, *Man the Unknown,* and the present author's *Islam and the Problems of Civilization.*

placed their reliance upon it. The *Sunnah* is nothing other than the complete and exemplary fruit of Qur'anic guidance. Aisha—may God be pleased with her—expressed the matter succinctly, accurately, and profoundly: when asked about the character of the Messenger of God (peace be upon him), she answered : "His character was the Qur'an." (narrated by al-Nasa'i).

However, people drifted away from the Qur'an, from its distinctive style, from living in its shade, from adhering to the criteria that had predominated in the environment in which it had been revealed. It was adherence to those criteria and breathing in that environment that alone had enabled the Qur'anic revelation to be understood. It cannot be fully comprehended by those who abstain from struggle and effort to establish a truly Islamic life: who do not endure the sacrifice, pain and anguish that accompanied the confrontation with *Jahiliyyah* in whatever age it may be.

The issue here, in comprehending the meanings of the Qur'an, is not the understanding of its words and phrases, because they are not a *Tafsir* (interpretation) of the Qur'an, as we are accustomed to saying. It is rather to equip the soul with emotions, perceptions and experiences similar to those that accompanied the revelation of the Qur'an, that prevailed in the life of Muslims as they received it in the course of battles, war against one's own sinful tendencies and against the outer enemy; as they experienced effort and sacrifice, fear and hope, weakness and strength, error and awakening. This took place first in the environment of Mecca, where the call first went forth and the Muslims were few in number and weak, isolated among people, suffering hunger and fear, persecution and pursuit, with devotion to God their only recours. Then came Medina and the establishment of the first Muslim society, a period of confrontation with trickery and hypocrisy, of organization and struggle. This was the era of the battles of Badr, Uhud, al-Khandaq, and al-Hudaibiyyah, of Fath, Hunayn and Tabuk, the era in which emerged the Islamic people together with their social system, in which emotions, interests and principles vitally interacted with each other.

In this environment where the Qur'anic verses were revealed as living, pulsating realities, every word and phrase conveyed meaning and inspirations. A similar environment must accompany any attempt to resume the Islamic life; then the Qur'an will open up its treasures for men's hearts, reveal its secrets, and spread its brilliance, guidance and light.

In that first environment, they understood the true meaning of these divine words:

"Many people think that they have bestowed a favour upon thee [Oh Prophet] by having surrendered to thee. Say thou: "Deem not your surrender a favour unto me: nay, but it is God who bestows a favour upon you by showing you the way to faith—if you are true to your word!"   (Al-Hujurat: 17)

And of these:

"O you who have attained to faith! Respond to the call of God and the Apostle whenever he calls you unto that which will give you life; and know that God intervenes between man and [the desires of] his heart, and that unto Him you shall be gathered.

And beware of that temptation to evil which does not befall only those among you who are bent on denying the truth, to the exclusion of others; and know that God is severe in retribution.

And remember the time when you were few [and] helpless on earth, fearful lest people do away with you—whereupon He sheltered you, and strengthened you with His succour, and provided for you sustenance out of the good things of life, so that you might have cause to be grateful."   (Al-Anfal: 24–26)

And of these:

"For, indeed, God did succour you at Badr, when you were utterly weak. Remain, then, conscious of God, so that you might have cause to be grateful."   (Al-'Imran: 123)

And of these:

"Be not, then, faint of heart, and grieve not: for you are bound to rise high if you are [truly] believers.

If misfortune touches you, [know that] similar misfortune has touched [other] people as well; for it is by turns that We apportion unto men such days [of fortune and misfortune]: and [this] to the end that God might mark out those who have attained to faith, and choose from among you such as [with their lives] bear witness to the truth—since God does not love evildoers—and that God might render pure of all dross those who have attained to faith, and bring to nought those who deny the truth.

Do you think that you could enter paradise unless God takes cognizance of your having striven hard [in His cause], and takes cognizance of your having been patient in adversity? For, indeed, you did long for death in God's cause before you came face to face with it; and now you have seen it with your own eyes!"

(Al-'Imran: 139–143)

And of these:

"Indeed, God has succoured you on many battlefields, [when you were few]; and [He did so, too], on the Day of Hunayn, when you took pride in your great numbers and they proved of no avail whatever to you—for the earth, despite all its vastness, became [too] narrow for you and you turned back, retreating: whereupon God bestowed from on high His [gift of] inner peace upon His Apostle and upon the believers, and bestowed [upon you] from on high forces which you could not see, and chastised those who were bent on denying the truth: for such is the recompense of all who deny the truth!"

(At-Tawbah: 25–26)

And of these:

"You shall most certainly be tried in your possessions and in your persons; and indeed you shall hear many hurtful things from those to whom revelation was granted before your time, as well as from those who have come to ascribe divinity to other beings beside God. But if you remain patient in adversity and conscious of Him—this, behold, is something to set one's heart upon."

(Al-'Imran: 186)

They understood the true meaning of these words because God was speaking to them of realities they lived through, of memories etched in their souls, of experiences not distant in time.

Those who endure today and tomorrow similar experiences are those who understand the meanings of the Qur'an. They can taste the truths of the Islamic concept as it appears in the Qur'an, because it exists in their emotions and experiences; they interpret and perceive all things in its light. Those people are but few.

Since people have drifted away from the Qur'an as they have from living in a world comparable to that which saw its revelation, it is now necessary to provide them with the truths of the Islamic concept concerning God, the universe, life and mankind, by means of the relevant verses of the Qur'an, accompanied by explanation and commentary, coordinated with each other and classified. Such supplementary material is not intended to substitute for the Qur'an in addressing men's hearts and minds, but to enable them to connect with the Qur'an as much as possible, to aid them in touching and tasting the supreme Islamic concept.

Here, a major fact has to be pointed out. By expounding the truths of the Islamic concept, we are not aiming at purely cultural knowledge. We do not wish to create a new section in the Islamic library, to be added to what used to be known as "Islamic philosophy." No, our aim is not some frigid knowledge that deals only with men's minds and adds to the accumulation of "culture." Such an aim does not deserve pain and effort, for it is a cheap and foolish aim. We seek "movement" as a stage beyond "knowledge." We want knowledge to transform itself into a motivating power for realizing its meaning in the real world. We seek to enlist the conscience of man to achieve the purpose of his existence, as traced out by this divine concept. We seek to return humanity to its Lord, to the plan He had drawn up for it, and the noble and elevated life that conforms to the nobility that God prescribes for mankind, the life that was achieved once in history, when the Islamic concept became a reality embodied in a people leading mankind towards goodness, righteousness and growth.

In the history of Islam, there came a time when the original Islamic way of life, derived from the correct Islamic concept, came in contact with other ways of life and cultures predominating in the conquered lands.

When the life of the Muslims became free of the concerns of *jihad,* and they surrendered to comfort and affluence; and when at the same time different opinions and schools of thought came into existence, largely because of political problems going back to the well-known conflict between 'Ali and Mu'awiya, they began to concern themselves with Greek philosophy and theological discussions relating to Christianity, which were then translated into Arabic. From such concern, which can be characterized as a kind of intellectual indulgence during the Abbasid period and in Andalusia, there emerged deviations and tendencies alien to the original Islamic concept. That concept had come precisely in order to rescue humanity from such deviations and tendecies, to bring it back to the positive and realistic understanding which orients all of man's energies towards life, constructive action, cultivation, advancement and purity; to preserve his energies from being wasted on prattle that results from man's intellect wandering in the wilderness without a guide.

Many Muslim scholars found themselves compelled to deal with the results of interaction with alien cultures and the consequent deviations. They started responding, explaining and arguing about the essence and attributes of God, about fate and divine decree, about the actions of mankind, his punishment and reward, his sin and repentance. Various sects, such as Khawarij, Shi'a, Murji'ah, Qadariyyah, Jabriyyah, Sunniyyah and Mu'tazilah, emerged as a result of this process.

Some of these Muslim scholars and thinkers became infatuated with Greek philosophy, especially the commentaries on Aristotle (who was referred to as "the first teacher"), and theological and metaphysical discussions. They imagined that Islamic thought could not attain perfection and maturity, glory and distinction, unless it clothed itself in the garb of philosophy or philosophizing. Just as some people today are fascinated by the garb of Western thinking today, so too were the people of the past fascinated by the garb of Greek thought, and they tried to develop an "Islamic philosophy" similar to the Greek philosophy. They also tried to establish a science of theology based on Aristotelian logic.

Instead of moulding the Islamic concept in its own independent format, and in accordance with its overall nature that addresses human existence with all its fundamentals and concerns, not the human intellect alone, people borrowed the philosophical mould and poured the Islamic concept into it. They also borrowed some philosophical concepts and tried to reconcile them with the Islamic concept, but almost all their terminology was borrowed.

There is a basic disagreement between the philosophical approach or method and faith, between the sublime truths of Islamic belief and the petty and confused endeavors that belong in the category of human philosophies and theological schemes. So-called "Islamic philosophy" is manifestly out of harmony with the coherent scheme of Islamic belief. These endeavors have resulted in abundant confusion tainting the purity of the Islamic concept, narrowing its scope, and polluting it with superficiality. With all the intricacies, dryness and confusion, "Islamic philosophy" and theology alike became completely alien to the nature, truth, method and style of Islam.

Of course, these remarks will shock many of those working in the field of "Islamic philosophy" or philosophical research in general. However, the "Islamic concept" cannot be purified from distortion, deviation and falsification until it is cleansed from everything related to so-called "Islamic philosophy" and theology, from all the arguments that were raised among the various Islamic sects across the centuries. Once this is done, we can go back to the Qur'an and directly obtain the fundamentals of the Islamic concept and demonstrate the characteristics that distinguish it from all other concepts. There is no harm in making a few comparisons in order to clarify those characteristics, but the fundamentals of this concept should be obtained directly from the Qur'an and presented in a complete and independent manner.

In order to understand the aforementioned method, it becomes important to realize the following three facts:

First, whatever the Islamic world took from Greek philosophy and Christian theology had an effect on shaping the arguments that occurred among the various sects. Those arguments were nothing more than latter day commentaries on the Greek philosophy, conveyed in a distorted and disrupted manner and a defective language.

Second, the attempt to reconcile the commentaries of Greek philosophy with the Islamic concept was simplistic in the extreme and and based on ignorance of the nature of Greek philosophy, of its profoundly pagan elements, lack of a unified intellectual system and a unified methodological base, in all of which respects it contrasts with the Islamic notion and its authentic sources. Greek philosophy arose in a pagan environment replete with mythology and its roots were nourished by an all-pervading paganism. It was therefore foolish and pointless to attempt a reconciliation between Greek philosophy and the Islamic concept based on the principle of absolute and profound belief in the Oneness of God. Under the spell of Christian-influenced, late commentaries on the Greek philosophers, Muslim philosophers and polemicists believed erroneously that the Greek "sages" could not have been pagan and could not have denied the Oneness of God. Based on this fallacy, they undertook the task of reconciliation, and the result was what came to be called "Islamic philosophy."

Third, the problems arising in the Islamic world—those that provoked discussions since the murder of 'Uthman, may God be pleased with him—led people to interpret the verses of the Qur'an in their own way, deviating from its meanings and concepts. When arguments were set forth to support the various viewpoints, each sect sought support in philosophical and theological discussions. Such resources were not fit to be used as a foundation for pure Islamic thought, the fundamentals and concepts of which can be drawn only from the established text of the Qur'an, in an atmosphere, moreover, free of the contamination of these historical disputes. It will be fitting to separate this entire heritage from our genuine understanding of Islam, and to subject it to a thorough historical study in order to demonstrate the various deviations existing within it and the reasons for them. Then we will be able to avoid falling into similar traps today when we are outlining the meaning of the Islamic concept and its constituent elements.

Western ways of thought followed their own particular paths, drawing first on Greek thought with all its pagan contamination, and then on an enmity to the church that resulted in ecclesiastical anathema.

From the Renaissance onwards, the general tendency was to oppose the Catholic Church and its concepts, then to oppose the church as such, and finally to oppose religious concepts in general. The doctrines of the church never represented true Christianity. The environment accompanying first the establishment of Christianity under the rule of the pagan Roman Empire and then the entry of the Roman Empire to Christianity deformed Christianity with the residue of paganism. Then, the Church and its councils joined with the divine principle of Christianity various interpretations and additions that were intended to confront the political issues of the day and the sectarian differences that arose as well as to gather together all the feuding segments of the empire in a religion acceptable to them all. The result was a Christianity that expressed ecclesiastical thought rather than the Christian faith as it had been revealed by God.

When the Church adopted these distorted concepts and embraced false or defective notions about the universe—something inevitable in human research and experimentation—it adopted a harshly adversarial stance to the natural scientists who were trying to correct this false or defective knowledge. The Church did not only attack them verbally, but also utilized its secular power in a rather ugly manner, in order to punish all those who opposed its religious and scientific concepts.

From then on, European thought took an adversarial stance not only to the prevailing doctrines and concepts of the Church, but also to all religious doctrines and concepts at large. This enmity went beyond particular religious doctrines and concepts to embrace religious mode of thought as such. European thinkers established methodologies and schools of thought the main purpose of which was to oppose religious thought and to eliminate the authority of the Church by eliminating its God and all modes of thought related to Him. Enmity to religion and its ways of thought continued to exist not only within the issues, philosophies and beliefs established by European thinkers, but also within the core of their thought and their methods for appropriating knowledge.

Consequently, a basis for Islamic thought can no longer be found within the modes of European thought, nor can it be revived on the basis of European thought, as the matter has been put by some Muslim thinkers. Once he has finished perusing this book, the reader will understand that it is impossible to borrow Western modes of thought or any of its products.

The method we have used in this research on "The Characteristics and Fundamentals of the Islamic Concept" is to obtain inspiration directly from the Qur'an, after having lived for a long time in its shade, and to demonstrate, as far as possible, the environment in which the words of God were revealed to mankind; a mass of confused religious, social and political conditions, a wilderness in which humanity was wandering after deviating from divine guidance.

Our method of seeking inspiration from the Qur'an means that we do not approach it with pre-existing criteria, whether intellectual or emotional, derived from the remnants of other cultures; we do not judge its meanings according to such criteria.

First and foremost, the verses of the Qur'an were revealed in order to establish the correct criteria on which God wishes the concepts of humans as well as their life to be based. The least that human beings can do is to thank God Almighty by receiving the Qur'an wholeheartedly and with minds clear of all impurities, so that their new concepts are clear of all the impurities of ignorance, whether old or new, and are derived solely from the teachings of God rather than the speculations of human beings.

There are, therefore, no pre-established criteria to judge the Book of God Most High. Our criteria are derived from the Qur'an at the very outset, and it is on that basis that we establish our concepts. This, and only this, is the correct methodology in approaching the Noble Qur'an and in deriving from it the Characteristics and Fundamentals of the Islamic Concept.

We are not trying to borrow a philosophical framework in order to demonstrate the realities of the Islamic concept, for we are convinced that there is a close connection between the nature of the subject and the nature of the framework in which it is discussed: the subject will be affected by the framework, and its nature may change and be distorted if presented in a framework that has a history of enmity to the subject. This is definitely the case with the Islamic concept and the philosophical framework, as can be realized by whoever experiences the reality of this concept as demonstrated in the verses of the Qur'an.

We are in disagreement with Iqbal in his attempt to demonstrate the Islamic concept in a philosophical framework borrowed from the well-known formulations of Hegel concerning idealistic rationalism or those of August Comte concerning materialistic objectivism.

Belief in general, and Islamic belief in particular, addresses the nature of mankind in its own style, one that is distinguished by vigor, harmony, immediacy and inspiration. This inspiration reveals great truths which cannot be expressed through words, although they may be addressed by words. The style of belief is also distinguished by the way it addresses human nature in all its aspects, capacities and modes of knowledge, not simply the intellect.

Philosophy, on the other hand, has a different style. It attempts to confine the truth in verbal formulae. However, the truths which it attempts to grasp refuse such confinement, and they are in their essential nature beyond the sphere in which human thought operates. The result is that philosophy ends up as a complex, arid, and confused affair.

Furthermore, philosophy has not had a significant role in the general life of mankind, and has not moved humanity forward. Religion, on the other hand, has advanced humanity through the wilderness of time and along dark roads.

Belief must be presented in a religious style, because attempting to present it in a philosophical style, kills its entire meaning, extinguishes its luminous rays, and confines it to a single one of the many aspects of human existence. Distortion and deviation will beset any attempt to present religion in a style alien to it.

We are not eager to have an "Islamic philosophy" as a chapter in Islamic thought. We do not want this framework to be an Islamic mode of expression because, in our opinion, neither Islam nor Islamic thought are lacking in anything, which is a strong proof of its authenticity, purity and uniqueness.

Another word about the methodology followed in this research:

We are not about to deal with a particular deviation that has infected Islamic thought or Islamic reality and allow it to consume all our attention, so that refuting and correcting it becomes our main motive for the efforts we invest in clarifying "The Characteristics and Fundamentals of the Islamic Concept." What we are trying to do is to present the truth about this concept, as revealed in the Holy Qur'an, in a comprehensive, balanced and coordinated manner that is harmonious with the universe and its equilibrium, and with human nature and its equilibrium.

Presenting a particular deviation or imperfection, attempting to refute it by formulating the truths of the Islamic concept as a way of response, is a very dangerous methodology, among its consequences being the establishing of a new deviation taking the place of the old.

Instances of this danger are found in researches conducted with the intention of "defending" Islam from those who attack and contest it, such as Orientalists of the past and present and atheists. We also find this danger in researches written in response to a certain deviation within a certain environment and during a certain time.

Some Crusaders and Zionists, for example, doggedly accuse Islam of being the religion of the sword, claiming that it was spread by the edge of the sword. Consequently, some of us defend Islam and refute this accusation by invoking the idea of "defence." Thereby they lessen the value of jihad in Islam, narrow its scope, and apologise for each of its instances, claiming that they were undertaken only for the purpose of "defence," in its present shallow meaning. These people forget that Islam, being the last divine path for humanity, has an essential right to establish its own system on earth so that all humanity can enjoy its blessings, while every individual enjoys the liberty to follow his chosen creed, for "there is no compulsion in religion." Establishing the "Islamic system" to have beneficial sway over all humanity, those who embrace Islam and those who do not, does indeed require Jihad as does the liberty of men to follow their own beliefs. This goal can only be accomplished with the establishment of a virtuous authority, a virtuous law and a virtuous system that calls to account whoever attempts to attack freedom of worship and and belief.

This is only one example of distorting the Islamic concept while intending to defend it against a cunning attack.

Works written in response to one deviation generate another. Examples close at hand are some of the arguments made by the Imam Sheikh Muhammad 'Abduh, and the lectures of Iqbal on the issue of "The Reconstruction of Religious Thought in Islam."

Sheikh Muhammad 'Abduh was confronted with a difficult intellectual situation: the gate of Ijtihad had been closed and reason had been denied its role in understanding the laws of God and deriving wisdom from them. The environment was full of books written by authors during the era of intellectual stagnation, books relying on superstitions and popular notions of religion.

He also confronted a time when reason was worshiped and considered as a god by the people of Europe, especially following the scientific achievements that won great victories for science, a time when rationalist philosophy accorded great authority to the mind. At the same time, the Orientalists attacked the Islamic concept and the belief in fate and divine decree it contains for allegedly hampering the human mind and dissuading man from optimism and exertion.

Sheikh Muhammad 'Abduh confronted this particular situation by affirming the value of the mind in encountering the revealed text, by reviving the concept of *Ijtihad*, by attacking superstition, ignorance and illiteracy, by proving that Islam accords value to the mind and its function within religion and life, rather than destroying Muslims through fatalism and the denial of free will as the Europeans claim. However, when Sheikh Muhammad 'Abduh wanted to address the stagnancy of the mind in the East, and the anarchy of the mind in the West, he elevated the human mind to a position of equality to revelation in guiding human beings rather than being a tool for the understanding of revelation. He tried to prevent all conflict between what the mind understands and divine revelation, not contenting himself with permitting the mind to pereceive what it can and to submit to what it cannot, for the intellect, like every other aspect of man, is inevitably partial and limited by time and space. Divine revelation, by contrast, deals with absolute realities such as the divine truth and the manner in which the divine will attaches to the creation of contingent beings. The mind has to recognize these absolute principles as lying beyond its understanding.[3]

Sheikh Muhammad 'Abduh provided us with arguments which appear to be logical, but go back to his desire to correct the deviation that denigrates the role of the mind. In his *Risalat al-Tauhid* he stated:

"The revelation of a divine message is an act of God, as is the bestowal of human intellect. The acts of God must cohere with each other, not contradict each other."

In a general sense, this is true, but revelation and reason are not coequal; one of them is greater and more comprehensive than the other, and one was destined to be the source to which the other refers, the balance on which it weighs its concepts and ideas. This forms the basis of coherence and agreement between them, not equivalence or parity, so that one is equal to the other. Furthermore, a reason free from imperfections and faults does not exist on earth.

The commentary provided by Sheikh Muhammad 'Abduh on the thirtieth part of the Qur'an clearly demonstrates the impact of this perspective, as does the commentary on the Qur'an authored by 'Abduh's pupil, the late Sheikh Rashid Rida. As for Dr. al-Shaikh al-Maghribi's commentary on *Tabarak* (the twenty-ninth part of the Qur'an), he explicitly declares the need for forced interpretation in order to align the text with human reason. This is a rather dangerous principle because the word "reason" does not in itself refer to anything actually existing, as mentioned earlier. I have a reason of my own, you have a reason of your own, he has a reason of his own, etc. There is no abso-

---

[3] Refer to Chapter Four for further clarification.

lute mind, free from faults, imperfections, lust and ignorance, able to judge the Qur'anic text. If we were to interpret the texts of the Qur'an to suit the vast diversity of minds, we will only end up in chaos.

All this came about as the result of preoccupation with confronting a certain deviation. If the matter were considered on its own, reason would of course be granted its rights and sphere of activity, with neither excess nor deficiency. the mind can realize its space and task without immoderation or complication or default and remissness, and the relationship between it and revelation would be unimpaired.

Divine revelation does not deny, exclude or neglect reason. It is reason that receives revelation, understands and comprehends it, as well as accepts what is beyond its scope, but it cannot have the last word. Whenever the Qur'anic text is firm and unambiguous, its straightforward meaning without interpretation is decisive. Reason must derive signification from the meanings of this straightforward text and build its methodology on this basis (further on, we will provide compete details of the correct Islamic method).

Muhammad Iqbal confronted an intellectual environment in the East that was lost in the so-called "illuminations" of Persian Sufism, as he calls it. The mystic effacement that does not recognize the human self disturbed him, as did the negativity which leaves no role for human activity on earth. Obviously enough, this is not in any way the true nature of Islam. At the same time, he realized that in the West, emphasis on experience and the sensory were in the ascendant, and he confronted too Nietzsche's declaration in *Thus Spake Zarathustra* of the birth of Superman and the death of God, words which he wrote while in the throes of epilepsy and are nonetheless regarded by some people as philosophy.

Iqbal wanted to purify Islamic thought and Islamic life of negativism, bewilderment and mystic effacement. He also wanted to prove to Islamic thought the reality of sensory experience.

The result however, was an exaggerated promotion of the human self, which compelled him to interpret some of the Qur'anic verses in a manner contrary to their nature and that of the Islamic concept. He wished to prove that neither death nor even resurrection brings an end to experience, not even an end to the Day of Resurrection. Experience and growth of the human self continue even after Paradise and Hell, according to Iqbal. The Islamic concept, however, is that this world is the realm of testing and deed, while the Hereafter is the realm of accounting and reward. There is no place other than this world for the human soul to engage in deeds, or a place in the Hereafter to engage in new deeds after accounting and reward have taken place. This exaggeration on the part of Iqbal arose from his desire to affirm the existence and continuity of the self, or the ego, as he termed it in a borrowing from Hegelian terminology.

At the same time, Iqbal was compelled to provide the term "experience" with a much wider meaning than it possessed in Western thought, by including in its scope the spiritual experience that Muslims realize and through which they taste the supreme reality. In its Western philosophical meaning, "experience" can never include the spiritual aspect because in the first place, it was established to exclude all means for the acquisition of knowledge that do not rely on sensory experience.

The attempt to borrow a Western term is what led to this further attempt characterised by a dryness that contrasts with the vibrant and lively poetic side of Iqbal.

I do not wish to belittle these great and fruitful efforts for reviving and stimulating Islamic thought that were undertaken by Imam Muhammad 'Abduh and his pupils, and by the poet Iqbal, may God have mercy on their souls. I only wish to point out that an enthusiastic attempt to resist a certain deviation might itself trigger another deviation. What should be a priority in the methodology of Islamic research is demonstrating the truth of the Islamic concept in its complete, comprehensive and harmonious nature and specific style.

Finally, this research is not a book of philosophy, theology or metaphysics. It is a work dictated by reality and addressing reality.

Islam came to save the entirety of humanity from the accumulated debris that was distorting and burdening their thoughts and their lives, from the wilderness in which they were wandering. Islam came to provide humanity with a special and unique concept, and a distinctive way of life conforming to God's straight path. But today, all humanity has regressed to the wilderness and the debris.

Islam came to establish a community to which the leadership of humanity was entrusted, to bring people forth from the wilderness and away from the mountains of debris. Today, this community is abandoning its position of leadership, instead falling in behind those who are lost.

This book is an attempt to define the characteristics and fundamentals of the Islamic concept, from which an actual mode of life can be derived, as willed by God, as well as guidance for the intellectual, scientific and artistic activities that derive from the comprehensive explanation presented by the concept.

Reason and heart, life and reality, Muslims and all mankind—all are in need of the clarity of the Islamic concept.

The first part of this research deals with the characteristics of the Islamic concept, while the second part deals with its fundamentals.

"And from God is success, guidance, and aid."

1

THE WILDERNESS AND
THE DEBRIS

"But then, is he that goes along with his face close to the ground better guided than he who walks upright on a straight way?"

(Al-Mulk: 22)

When Islam came, the world was full of accumulated debris: beliefs, concepts, philosophies, myths, thoughts, doubts, superstitions, customs and traditions. Truth was mixed with falsehood, right with wrong, religion with superstition, and philosophy with mythology. The human mind, buried beneath this debris, was flailing around in darkness and doubt, unable to find certitude. Human life was drifting into corruption and dissolution, into tyranny and humiliation, hardship and misery, a life unfit even for animals!

The wilderness was without a shepherd; it lacked guidance and light, certainty and stability. It was this wilderness that surrounded man's thinking about God and His attributes, His relationship with the universe and the latter's relationship with Him, the true nature of man, his position within the universe, the purpose of his existence, the manner in which he attains this purpose, and most particularly, the connection between God and mankind. Everything evil was being injected into humanity and all the structures on which it depended.

The human mind was unable to attain any clarity regarding the universe or regarding itself, the purpose of existence, the relationship between man and the universe and between an individual and his society. The human mind could not settle any of these issues without settling issues concerning its faith or its conception of God, before attaining some clarity in the midst of so much blindness, misguidance and confusion.

The matter was based on two basic truths concomitant with the life and nature of man, in every situation and at all times:

The first truth: man, by his innate nature, cannot reside in this huge world simply as an isolated and straying particle. He must establish a certain connection with this universe, guaranteeing him stability and allowing him to discern his place in the world. He needs to believe in something that will explain his environment and his place within that environment. This is a natural and conscious need, unconnected with the peculiarities of a given time or place. In the course of this research, we will discover the extent of man's unhappiness and misery, his bewilderment and aberration, when he fails to understand the truth about that fundamental connection.

The second truth: there is a firm link between the nature of the creedal concept and that of the social order; this, too, is independent of the peculiarities of time or place. In fact, it is not so much a question of linkage as of spontaneous derivation. The social system is derived from the comprehensive explanation for this universe, the place of man within it, as well as his role and the fundamental purpose of his existence. Any social system that is not based on this concept is short-lived and artificial, but while it exists, man will suffer and be miserable, because a collision between such a system and human nature is inevitable.

God's messengers, may peace and blessings be upon them, from Noah to Jesus, revealed this truth to mankind, informed it truthfully about its God, and clarified the position of man within this universe and the very purpose of his existence. However, the constant deviations from this truth, under pressure from political circumstances, human lusts and weaknesses, masked this truth and drove human beings into aberration, and dumped heavy loads of debris upon them, which could be removed only by a new comprehensive and complete message. Such a message would remove all the debris, dissipate the darkness, and light up the wilderness. It would also announce the truth of the Islamic concept and build a stable life for humanity. Those who throughout the world were plagued by their deviant thoughts could not have freed themselves by any means other than this message and this Messenger. God, Most High, proclaimed the truth:

> "It is not [conceivable] that such as are bent on denying the truth— [be they] from among the followers of earlier revelation or from among those who ascribe divinity to aught beside God—should ever be abandoned [by Him] ere there comes unto them the [full] evidence of the truth: an apostle from God, conveying [unto them] revelations blest with purity."   (Al-Bayyinah: 1–2)

People did not realize the importance of this message and the importance of detaching themselves from these aberrations that led human beings into darkness. They did not realize the importance of making a clear decision on the issue of faith, thus recognizing the extent of the debris and becoming able to avoid the wilderness. Man was unable to understand this message until he discarded the beliefs and concepts, philosophies and myths, thoughts and illusions, customs and traditions, situations and circumstances, which, at the time of the emergence of Islam, had settled in the minds of humans. He was unable to see the truth amidst all the babbling, bewilderment and difficulties that had infected the remnants of previous revelations—distortions, deviations, and additions, drawn from philosophies of the ancient world, paganism and myths.

This research does not intend to present these concepts, but to present the Islamic concept, its characteristics and fundamentals. It will discuss some examples from the religious concepts of Judaism and Christianity, as they reached the Arabian Peninsula, and others taken from the *Jahiliyyah* of the Arabs which Islam found itself confronting.

Judaism, the religion of the Children of Israel, was polluted with pagan concepts as well as racial arrogance. The Children of Israel, i.e., Jacob, the son of Isaac, the son of Abraham, may peace be upon them, had messengers sent to them, beginning with their ancestor Israel, who delivered the message of monotheism which he had learned from Abraham. Then came their greatest messenger Moses, may peace be upon him, again with the message of monotheism as well as the Mosaic Law based on that belief. However, as time went by, the Children of Israel went astray, and their beliefs degenerated into paganism. In their

'holy' books and the Old Testament, they included myths and concepts about the Almighty that are as debased as those of the Greeks
and other pagan peoples who never received a heavenly message or
were given a divine book.

The belief in the oneness of God, established by their ancestor
Abraham, peace be upon him, was a pure, comprehensive and complete
belief that took a firm stance in confronting paganism, as depicted in
the Holy Qur'an. Before his death, Jacob, the son of Isaac, conveyed
this belief to his children:

> "And convey unto them the story of Abraham—[how it was] when
> he asked his father and his people, "What is it that you worship?"
>
> They answered: "We worship idols, and we remain ever devoted
> to them."
>
> Said he: "Do [you really think that] they hear you when you
> invoke them, or benefit you or do you harm?"
>
> They exclaimed: "But we found our forefathers doing the
> same!"
>
> Said [Abraham]: "Have you, then, ever considered what it is
> that you have been worshiping—you and those ancient forebears of
> yours?"
>
> "Now [as for me, I know that], verily, these [false deities] are
> my enemies, [and that none is my helper] save the Sustainer of all the
> worlds, who has created me and is the One who guides me, and is
> the One who gives me to eat and to drink, and when I fall ill, is the
> One who restores me to health, and who will cause me to die and
> then will bring me back to life—and who, I hope, will forgive me my
> faults on judgment day!"
>
> "O my Sustainer! Endow me with the ability to judge [between
> right and wrong], and make me one with the righteous, and grant
> me the power to convey the truth unto those who will come after me,
> and place me among those who shall inherit the garden of bliss!"
>
> "And forgive my father—for, verily, he is among those who have
> gone astray—and do not put me to shame on the Day when all shall
> be raised from the dead: the Day on which neither wealth will be of
> any use, nor children, [and when] only he [will be happy] who comes
> before God with a heart free of evil!"   (Ash-Shuʻara: 69–89)

"And who, unless he be weak of mind, would want to abandon
Abraham's creed, seeing that We have indeed raised him high in

this world, and that, verily, in the life to come he shall be among the righteous?"

When his Sustainer said to him, "Surrender thyself unto Me!"— he answered, "I have surrendered myself unto [Thee], the Sustainer of all the worlds."

And this very thing did Abraham bequeath unto his children, and [so did] Jacob: "O my children! Behold, God has granted you the purest faith; so do not allow death to overtake you ere you have surrendered yourselves unto Him."

Nay, but you [yourselves, O children of Israel], bear witness that when death was approaching Jacob, he said unto his sons: "Whom will you worship after I am gone?"

They answered: "We will worship thy God, the God of thy forefathers Abraham and Ishmael and Isaac, the One God; and unto Him will we surrender ourselves."   (Al-Baqarah: 130–133)

The descendants of the Children of Israel moved away, however, from this pure monotheism, this clear belief and faith in the Hereafter, until Moses, may peace be upon him, brought to them anew the concept of the Oneness of God and invigorated the concept of pure faith. The Holy Qur'an refers as follows to the principles of this message brought by Moses, may peace be upon him, to the Children of Israel, and mentions as well their recalcitrance:

"And lo! We accepted this solemn pledge from [you] the children of Israel: "You shall worship none but God; and you shall do good unto your parents and kinsfolk, and the orphans, and the poor; and you shall speak unto all people in a kindly way; and you shall be constant in prayer; and you shall spend in charity."

And yet, save for a few of you, you turned away: for you are obstinate folk!

And lo! We accepted your solemn pledge that you would not shed one another's blood, and would not drive one another from your homelands—whereupon you acknowledged it; and thereto you bear witness [even now]. And yet, it is you who slay one another and drive some of your own people from their homelands, aiding one another against them in sin and hatred; but if they come to you as captives, you ransom them—although [the very act of] driving them away has been made unlawful to you!

Do you, then, believe in some parts of the divine writ and deny the truth of other parts? What, then, could be the reward of those among you who do such things but ignominy in the life of this world and, on the Day of Resurrection, commitment to most grievous suffering? For God is not unmindful of what you do."

(Al-Baqarah: 83–85)

"And indeed, there came unto you Moses with all evidence of the truth—and thereupon, in his absence, you took to worshipping the [golden] calf, and acted wickedly."

And, lo, We accepted your solemn pledge, raising Mount Sinai high above you, [saying], "Hold fast with [all your] strength unto what We have vouchsafed you, and hearken unto it!"

[But] they say, "We have heard, but we disobey" for their hearts are filled to overflowing with love of the [golden] calf because of their refusal to acknowledge the truth.

Say: "Vile is what this [false] belief of yours enjoins upon you— if indeed you are believers!"

(Al-Baqarah: 92–93)

This deviance arose when Moses was still among the Children of Israel: they worshipped a calf that was presented to them by the Sumerians, made from the gold of Egyptian women's jewellery. It is the same calf referred to in these Qur'anic verses. Previously, after their exodus from Egypt, when encountering a group of people who worshiped idols, they had asked Moses, may peace be upon him, to create an idol for them to worship:

"And we brought the children of Israel across the sea; and thereupon they came upon people who were devoted to the worship of some idols of theirs." Said [the children of Israel]: "O Moses, set up for us a god even as they have gods!"

He replied: "Verily, you are people without any awareness [of right and wrong]! As for these here—verily, their way of life is bound to lead to destruction; and worthless is all that they have ever done!"

(Al-A'raf: 138–139)

In addition, the Holy Qur'an speaks a great deal about the deviations of the Children of Israel, their misconception of God Most High, their idolatry and their paganism:

"And the Jews say, "Ezra is God's son."   (Al-Tawbah: 30)

"And the Jews say, "God's hand is shackled!" It is their own hands that are shackled; and rejected [by God] are they because of this their assertion. Nay, but wide are His hands stretched out: He dispenses [bounty] as He wills."
(Al-Ma'idah: 64)

"God has indeed heard the saying of those who said, "Behold, God is poor while we are rich!" We shall record what they have said, as well as their slaying of prophets against all right, and We shall say [unto them on Judgment Day]: "Taste suffering through fire."
(Al-'Imran: 181)

"And remember when you said, 'O Moses, indeed we shall not believe thee unto we see God face to face'—whereupon the thunderbolt of punishment overtook you before your very eyes."
(Al-Baqara: 55)

They were characterized by racial arrogance, and believed that their god is a tribal deity who holds them morally accountable only when they commit offences against each other. They are not called to account for offences to strangers, i.e., non-Jews:

"And among the followers of earlier revelation there is many a one who, if thou entrust him with a treasure, will [faithfully] restore it to thee; and there is among them many a one who, if thou entrust him a tiny gold coin, will not restore it to thee unless thou keep standing over him—which is an outcome of their assertion. 'No blame can attach to us [for anything that we may do] with regard to these unlettered folk': and [so] they tell a lie about God, being well aware [that it is a lie]."
(Al-'Imran: 75)

Their corrupted books depicted God in a manner no higher than that evinced by the Greeks with their pagan ideas about their gods.

Chapter Three of *Genesis* paints the following picture of what happened after Adam ate from the forbidden tree, which was supposedly the tree of good and evil:

"The man and his wife heard the sound of the Lord God walking in the Garden at the time of the evening breeze and they hid from the Lord God among the trees of the Garden. But the Lord called and said to him, 'Where are you?' He replied, 'I heard the sound as you were walking in the Garden and I was afraid, because I was naked and I hid myself.' God answered, 'Who told you that you were naked?' Have you eaten from the tree which I forbade you?"

(Genesis: 3: 8–11)

"And God said, 'The man has become like one of us, knowing good and evil; what if he now reaches out his hand and takes fruit from the tree of life also, eats it, and lives forever?' So the Lord God drove him out of the Garden of Eden to till the ground from which he had taken. He cast him out, and to the east of the Garden of Eden he stationed the cherubim and a sword whirling and flashing to guard the way to the tree of life."

(Genesis: 3: 22–24)

In the same Chapter, the following reason for the Flood is given:

"When mankind began to increase and to spread all over the earth and daughters were born to them, the sons of the gods saw that daughters of men were beautiful, so they took for themselves such women as they chose. But the Lord said, 'My life giving spirit shall not remain in man forever; he for his part is mortal flesh; he shall live for a hundred and twenty years.' In those days, when the sons of gods had intercourse with the daughters of men and got children by them, the Nephilium were on earth. They were the heroes of old, men of renown. When the Lord saw that man had done much evil on earth and that his thoughts and inclinations were always evil, he was sorry that he had made man on earth and he was grieved at heart. He said, 'This race of men whom I have created I will wipe off the face of the earth—man and beast, reptiles, and birds. I am sorry that I ever made them.' But Noah had won the Lord's favour."

(Genesis: 6: 1–8)

Chapter Eleven of the Book of Genesis describes how the world was filled with descendants of Noah:

"Once upon a time all the world spoke a single language and used the same words. As men journeyed in the east, they came upon a plain in the land of Shinar and settled there. They said to one another, 'Come, let us make bricks and bake them hard.' They used bricks for stone and bitumen for mortar. Come, they said, 'let us build ourselves a city and a tower with its top in the heavens, and make a name for ourselves; or we shall be dispersed all over the earth.' Then the Lord came down to see the city and tower, which mortal men had built, and He said, 'Here they are, one people with a single language, and now they have started to do this. Henceforward nothing they have a mind to do will be beyond their reach. Come, let us go down there and confuse their speech, so that they will not understand what they say to one another.' So the Lord dispersed them from there all over the earth, and they left off building the city."   (Genesis: 11: 1–8)

Chapter Twenty-Four from the Second Book of Samuel states:

Then the angel stretched out his arm toward Jerusalem to destroy it; but the Lord repented of the evil and said to the angel who was destroying the people, 'Enough! Stay your hand.'   (Samuel 2: 24: 16)

Christianity was no better than Judaism; it was even worse. It was conveyed to the Roman Empire when it was passing through a period of extreme idolatry and dissoluteness, then it was able to have Constantine made emperor in 305 C.E. Subsequently, the Empire adopted Christianity, not, however, in order to conform to it, but rather to make it conform to its own deeply rooted and widespread paganism. In his *History of the Conflict Between Religion and Science*, the American author Draper states:

"Place, power and profit—these were in view of whoever now joined the conquering sect. Crowds of worldly persons, who cared nothing about its religious ideas became its warmest supporters. Pagans at heart, their influence was soon manifested in the paganization of Christianity that soon ensued. The Emperor, no better than they, did nothing to check their proceedings. But he did not personally conform to the ceremonial requirements of the Church until the close of his evil life in A.D. 337.

Though the Christian party had proved itself sufficiently strong to give a master to the Empire, it was never sufficiently strong to destroy its antagonist, paganism. The issue of struggle between them was an amalgamation of the principles of both. In this, Christianity differed from Mohammedanism which absolutely annihilated its antagonist and spread its own doctrines without adulteration.

To the Emperor, a mere worldling and a man without any religious convictions, doubtless it appeared best for himself, best for the Empire, and best for the contending parties, Christian and pagan, to promote their union or amalgamation as much as possible. Even sincere Christians do not seem to have been averse to this; perhaps they believed that the new doctrines would diffuse most thoroughly by incorporating in themselves ideas borrowed from the old, the Truth would assert herself in the end, and the impurity be cast off."[4]

But the new religion did not cast off the impurities and contaminations of paganism, nor its mythical concepts, as the Christians had hoped it would. It became embroiled in political, racial and sectarian disputes, and steeped in pagan myths and philosophical concepts. As a result, its basic creed splintered into innumerable fragments:

One group stated: "Christ is simply man," while another maintained that: "The Father, the Son and the Holy Ghost are only different forms that God has displayed to mankind." According to this group, God is made up of three hypostases, the Father, the Son and the Holy Ghost: God, the Father, in the form of the Holy Ghost, descended onto the Virgin Mary as a human being, and was then born from her in the form of Jesus. Yet another group claimed: "The Son is not eternal like the Father, for he is a created being; he is therefore beneath the Father and should submit to Him." Another group again denied that the Holy Ghost was part of the Trinity. At the Council of Nicaea in 325 C.E. and the Constantinople Convocation in 381 C.E., it was decided that the Son and the Holy Ghost are equal to the Father in divinity; that the Son was born to the Father before the creation of the world and man; and that the Holy Ghost is derived from the Father. At the Toledo Convention of 589 C.E., it was decided that the Holy Ghost is additionally derived from the Son. At this juncture, the Eastern and Western Churches were in disagreement and separated as a result.

Some churches praised and glorified the Virgin Mary as well as Jesus Christ, may peace be upon him.

In his book *The Arab Conquest of Egypt*, Alfred Butler states:

"This is not the place for a discussion upon either the facts or the sources of Egyptian history during the last two centuries of the Empire: but when that record comes to be fully written, it will prove a record of perpetual feud between Romans and Egyptians—a feud of race and a feud of religion—in which, however, the dominating motive was religious rather than racial. The key to the whole of this epoch is the antagonism between the Monophysites and the Melkites.

---

[4] Draper, William, *History of the Conflict Between Religion and Science*, pp. 34–35. [Sayyid Qutb cites this extract not from the original text, but from its translation by Abu 'l-Hasan Nadwi in his work *Ma Dha Khasar al-'Alam bi Inhitat al-Muslimin*].

The latter, as the name implies, were the imperial or the Court party in religion, holding the orthodox opinion about the two natures of Christ: but this opinion the Monophysite Copts, or native Egyptians, viewed with an abhorrence and combated with a frenzy difficult to understand in rational beings, not to say followers of the Gospel."[5]

In *The Preaching of Islam*, T.W. Arnold describes this conflict and the attempt made by Heraclius to settle it through an intermediate faith:

"A hundred years before, Justinian had succeeded in giving some show of unity to the Roman Empire, but after his death it rapidly fell asunder, and at this time there was an entire want of common national feeling between the provinces and the seat of government. Heraclius had made some partially successful efforts to attach Syria again to the central government, but unfortunately the general methods of reconciliation which he adopted had served only to increase dissension instead of allaying it. Religious passions were the only existing substitute for national feeling, and he tried, by propounding an exposition of faith, that was intended to serve as an eirenicon, to stop all further disputes between the contending factions and unite the heretics to the Orthodox Church and to the central government. The Council of Chalcedon (451) had maintained that Christ was 'to be acknowledged in two natures, without confusion, change, division, or separation; the difference of the natures being in nowise taken away by reason of their union, but rather the properties of each nature being preserved and concurring into one person and one substance, not as it was divided or separated into two persons, but one and the same Son and only begotten, God the Word.' This council was rejected by the Monophysites, who allowed only one nature in the person of Christ, who was said to be a composite person, having all attributes divine and human, but the substance bearing these attributes was no longer a duality, but a composite unity. The controversy between the orthodox party and the Monophysites, who flourished particularly in Egypt and Syria and in countries outside the Byzantine Empire, had been hotly contested for nearly two centuries, when Heraclius sought to effect a reconciliation by means of the doctrine of Monotheletism: while conceding the duality of the natures, it secured unity of the person in the actual life of Christ, by

---

[5] Butler, Alfred, *The Arab Conquest of Egypt*, Oxford University Press, 1978, P. 29.

rejection of two series of activities in this one person; the one Christ and Son of God effectuates that which is human and that which is divine by one divine human agency, i.e. there is only one will in the Incarnate Word.

But Heraclius shared the fate of so many would-be peace-makers: for not only did controversy blaze up again all the more fiercely, but he himself was stigmatized as a heretic and drew upon himself the wrath of both parties."[6]

Some of these deviations are referred to in the Holy Qur'an, where the People of the Book are called upon to abandon deviations and correct their beliefs. The Qur'an also clarifies the origins of Christianity as it was revealed by God and before it fell prey to distortion and misinterpretation:

"Indeed, the truth deny they who say, "Behold, God is the Christ, son of Mary"—seeing that the Christ [himself] said, "O children of Israel! Worship God [alone], who is my Sustainer as well as your Sustainer." Behold, whoever ascribes divinity to any being beside God, unto him will God deny paradise, and his goal shall be the fire; and such evildoers will have none to succour them!

Indeed, the truth deny they who say, 'Behold, God is the third of a trinity'—seeing that there is no deity whatever save the One God. And unless they desist from this their assertion, grievous suffering is bound to befall such of them as are bent on denying the truth. Will they not, then, turn towards God in repentance, and ask His forgiveness? For God is much forgiving, a dispenser of grace.

The Christ, son of Mary, was but an apostle: all [other] apostles had passed away before him: and his mother was one who never deviated from the truth; and they both ate food [like other mortals].

Behold how clear We make these messages unto them: and then behold how perverted are their minds! Say: "Would you worship, beside God, aught that has no power either to harm or to benefit you—when God alone is all-hearing, all-knowing?"

Say: "O followers of the Gospel! Do not overstep the bounds [of truth] in your religious beliefs; and do not follow the errant views of people who have gone astray aforetime, and have led many others astray, and are still straying from the right path."   (Al-Ma'idah: 72–77)

---

6 T. W. Arnold, *The Preaching of Islam*,.pp. 52–54.

"And the Jews say, "Ezra is God's son," while the Christians say, "The Christ is God's son." Such are the sayings which they utter with their mouths, following in spirit assertions made in earlier times by people who denied the truth! [They deserve the imprecation:] "May God destroy them!" How perverted are their minds!"

(At-Tawbah: 30)

"And Lo! God said: "O Jesus, son of Mary! Didst thou say unto men, 'Worship me and my mother as deities beside God'?"

[Jesus] answered: "Limitless art Thou in Thy glory!

It would not have been possible for me to say what I had no right to [say]! Had I said this, Thou wouldst indeed have known it! Thou knowest all that is within myself, whereas I know not what is in Thy Self. Verily, it is Thou alone who fully knowest all the things that are beyond the reach of a created being's perception.

Nothing did I tell them beyond what Thou didst bid me [to say]: 'Worship God, [who is] my Sustainer as well as your Sustainer.' And I bore witness to what they did as long as I dwelt in their midst; but since Thou hast caused me to die, Thou alone hast been their keeper: for Thou art witness unto everything.

If thou cause them to suffer—verily. they are Thy servants; and if Thou forgive them—verily. Thou alone art almighty, truly wise!"

(Al-Ma'idah: 116–118)

Thus we see the extent of the deviations that entered Christianity through all these historical associations, resulting in mythical and pagan concepts around which disputes and massacres raged for many centuries.

The Noble Qur'an was revealed in the Arabian Peninsula, where false beliefs, concepts and deviations were widespread, transmitted there from Persia, Judaism, and Christianity, on top of the paganism already existing there and the false interpretations and distortion of all that had been taught by Abraham. One example of the indigenous paganism is that for all their disdain of daughters, the Arabs claimed that the angels are the daughters of God, and then they worshiped the angels, or the idols representing angels, believing them to be reliable mediators between them and God. The Noble Qur'an clearly condemns all this nonsense:

"And yet, they attribute to Him offspring from among some of the beings created by Him! Verily, most obviously bereft of all gratitude is man!

Or [do you think], perchance, that out of all His creation He Has chosen for Himself daughters, and favoured you with sons?

For [thus it is:] if any of them is given the glad tiding of [the birth of] what he so readily attributes to the Most Gracious, his face darkens, and he is filled with suppressed anger: "What! [Am I to have a daughter-] one who is to be reared [only] for the sake of ornament?"—and thereupon he finds himself torn by a vague inner conflict.

And [yet] they claim that the angels—who in themselves are but beings created by the Most Gracious—are females: [but] did they witness their creation?

This false claim of theirs will be recorded, and they will be called to account [for it on Judgment Day]!

Yet they say, "Had [not] the Most Gracious so willed, we would never have worshipped them!"

[But] they cannot have any knowledge of [His having willed] such a thing: they do nothing but guess."   (Zukhruf: 15–20)

"Is it not to God alone that all sincere faith is due? And yet, they who take for their protectors aught beside Him [are wont to say]. "We worship them for no other reason than that they bring us nearer to God."

Behold, God will judge between them [on Resurrection Day] with regard to all wherein they differ [from the truth]: for, verily, God does not grace with His guidance anyone who is bent on lying [to himself and is] stubbornly ingrate!

Had God willed to take unto Himself a son. He could have chosen anyone that He wanted out of whatever He has created—[but] limitless is He in His glory! He is the One God, the One who holds absolute sway over all that exists!"   (Az-Zumar: 3–4)

"And [neither will] they [who] worship, side by side with God, things or beings that can neither harm nor benefit them, saying [to themselves], "These are our intercessors with God!"

Say: "Do you [think that you could] inform God of anything in the heavens or on earth that He does not know? Limitless is He in His glory, and sublimely exalted above anything to which men may ascribe a share in His divinity!"   (Yunus: 18)

They also claimed that God—may He be exalted!—had carnal relations with the jinn: He took a woman from among the jinn and had children from her, these being the angels. In *Kitab al-Asnam* ("The Book of Idols") al-Kalbi states: "The Banu Malih clan of the tribe of Khuza'a used to worship the jinn."

The Qur'an refers to this matter as follows:

"And now ask them to enlighten thee: Has thy Sustainer daughters, whereas they would have [only] sons?—Or is it that We have created the angels female, and they [who believe them to be divine] have witnessed [that act of creation]?

Oh, verily, it is out of their own [inclination to] falsehood that some people assert, "God has begotten [a son]"; and, verily, they are lying [too, when they say], "He has chosen daughters in preference to sons!"

What is amiss with you and your judgment? Will you not, then, bethink yourselves? Or have you, perchance, a clear evidence [for your assertions]? Produce, then, that divine writ of yours, if you are speaking the truth!

And some people have invented a kinship between Him and all manner of invisible forces—although [even] these invisible forces know well that, verily, they [who thus blaspheme against God] shall indeed be arraigned [before Him on Judgment Day: for] limitless is God in His glory, above anything that men may devise by way of definition!"   (As-Saffat: 149–159)

"And [as for those who now deny the truth,] one Day He will gather them all together, and will ask the angels, "Was it you that they were wont to worship?"

They will answer: "Limitless art Thou in Thy glory! Thou [alone] art close unto us, not they! Nay, [when they thought that they were worshipping us,] they were but [blindly] worshipping forces concealed from their senses: most of them believed in them."   (Saba': 40–41)

Worshipping idols was widespread among the Arabs. Some of their idols represented angels, others their ancestors, and still others which were worshipped in their own right. The Ka'ba, which had been built for the sole purpose of worshipping God, was saturated with 360 deities, quite apart from the major deities that were scattered in various areas. Some of these deities, such as Al-Lat, Al-'Uzza and Manat, are mentioned by name in the Qur'an. During the Battle of Uhud, Abu Sufyan called upon a deity known as Hubal.

The following verses of the Qur'an indicate that Al-Lat, Al-'Uzza and Manat were deities representing angels:

> "Have you, then, ever considered [what you are worshipping in] Al-Lat and Al-'Uzza, as well as [in] Manat, the third and last [of this triad]?
>
> Why—for yourselves [you would choose only] male offspring, whereas to Him [you assign] female: that, lo and behold, is an unfair division!
>
> These [allegedly divine beings] are nothing but empty names which you have invented—you and your forefathers—[and] for which God has bestowed no warrant from on high. They [who worship them] follow nothing but surmise and their own wishful thinking—although right guidance has now indeed come unto them from their Sustainer.
>
> Does man imagine that it is his due to have all that he might wish for, despite the fact that [both] the life to come and this present [one] belong to God [alone]?
>
> For, however many angels there be in the heavens, their inter-cession can be of no least avail [to anyone]—except after God has given leave [to intercede] for whomever He wills and with whom He is well–pleased.
>
> Behold, it is [only] such as do not [really] believe in the life to come that regard the angels as female beings; and [since] they have no knowledge whatever thereof, they follow nothing but surmise: yet, behold, never can surmise take the place of truth."
>
> (An-Najm: 19–28)

They sank to such depths in their idolatry that they even started to worship stones!

Bukhari relates Aba Raja'a al-'Utaridi to have said: "We used to worship stones. If we found one stone to be better than the other, we threw away the old one and started to worship the new one. If we could not find a stone, we would collect dirt, milk a goat over it, and then circumambulate it."[7]

In the *Kitab al-Asnam* ("The Book of Idols"), al-Kalbi said: "When a man travelled, he would pick four stones and choose the best one out of them to make it his god, while the three remaining stones became a

---

[7] Al-Bukhari, *"Kitab al-Maghazi."*

resting place for his food. When he left the place, he would also leave the stones behind."[8]

They also worshipped the planets, just as the Persians did. Sa'id said: "The Himyar tribe used to worship the sun, while Kananah used to worship the moon. Tamim worshipped the Hyades and Lakhm and Jutham worshipped Jupiter. The Tay tribe worshipped Canopus, Qays worshipped Sirius, and Asad worshipped Mercury."[9]

This phenomenon is mentioned in several verses of the Qur'an:

> "Now among His signs are the night and the day, as well as the sun and the moon: [hence,] adore not the sun or the moon, but prostrate yourselves in adoration before God, who has created them—if it is Him whom you [really] worship."   (Fussilat: 37)

> "And that it is He alone who sustains the brightest star."
>   (An-Najm: 49)

Many references are made to the creation of the stars and planets and to God's sovereignty over them, together with the rest of His creations, in order to refute the divinity of the planets and their suitability for worship.

In general, polytheistic beliefs permeated the lives of the pre-Islamic Arabs. Corrupt customs were based upon these beliefs, and these, too, are referred to in many parts of the Qur'an. Examples are the dedication to their gods of part of the harvest or of newly born animals, without keeping a share for God or even depriving themselves of them at certain times, or denying them to women. Some of the Arabs also made it forbidden to ride on certain animals or slaughter them. On other occasions, they would sacrifice their children to please their gods. It was said that 'Abd Al-Muttalib made a vow to slaughter his tenth son if he was granted ten sons to protect him. The tenth son happened to be 'Abdullah, but his father ransomed him from the gods by slaughtering a hundred camels in his place. Likewise, fortune-telling and the recourse to oracles were extremely common. All of this is referred to in the Qur'an:

---

[8] Al-Kalbi, *Kitab al-Asnam*.

[9] Sa'id, *Tabaqat al-Umam*, p. 430, as cited in Nadwi's *Ma Dha Khasar al-'Alam bi Inhitat al-Muslimin*.

"And out of whatever He has created of the fruits of the field and the cattle, they assign unto God a portion, saying. "This belongs to God"—or so they [falsely] claim—"and this is for those beings who we are convinced, have a share in God's divinity." But that which is assigned to the beings associated in their minds with God does not bring [them] closer to God—whereas that which is assigned to God brings [them but] closer to those beings to whom they ascribe a share in His divinity. Bad, indeed, is their judgment!

And, likewise their belief in beings or powers that are supposed to have a share in God's divinity makes [even] the slaying of their children seem goodly to many of those who ascribe divinity to aught beside God, thus bringing them to ruin and confusing them in their faith.

Yet, unless God had so willed, they would not be doing all this: stand, therefore, aloof from them and all their false imagery!

And they say, "Such–and–such cattle and fruits of the field are sacred; none may eat thereof save those whom we will [to do so]"—so they [falsely] claim; and [they declare that] it is forbidden to burden the backs of certain kinds of cattle; and there are cattle over which they do not pronounce God's name—falsely attributing [the origin of these customs] to Him. [But] He will requite them for all their false imagery.

And they say, "All that is in the wombs of such–and–such cattle is reserved for our males and forbidden to our women; but if it be stillborn, then both may have their share thereof." [God] will requite them for all they [falsely] attribute [to him]: behold, He is wise, all–knowing.

Lost, indeed, are they who, in their weak-minded ignorance, slay their children and declare as forbidden that which God has provided for them as sustenance, falsely ascribing [such prohibitions] to God: they have gone astray and have not found the right path."

(Al-An'am: 136–140)

The concepts of the absolute oneness of God and the resurrection were utterly alien to them. They believed in God, the Creator of the heavens and the earth and whatever is between them, but did not want to admit or acknowledge His Oneness, by virtue of which only He controls their lives and their matters, only He determines what is permitted and what is prohibited, only He answers to their concerns in this life and in the Hereafter, and only His laws should be followed when making judgments among themselves. Without acknowledgement of all of this, faith and religion cannot exist.

The Noble Qur'an refers to their strong opposition to these two truths, the oneness of God and the resurrection:

> "Now these [people] deem it strange that a warner should have come unto them from their own midst—and [so] the deniers of the truth are saying: "A [mere] spellbinder is he, a liar! Does he claim that all the deities are [but] one God? Verily, a most strange thing is this!"
>
> And their leaders launch forth [thus]: "Go ahead, and hold steadfastly onto your deities: this, behold, is the only thing to do! Never did we hear of [a claim like] this in any faith of latter days! It is nothing but [a mortal man's] invention!"   (Sad: 4–7)

> "As against this, they who are bent on denying the truth say [unto all who are of like mind]: "Shall we point out to you a man who will tell you that [after your death,] when you will have been scattered in countless fragments, you shall—lo and behold!—be [restored to life] in a new act of creation? Does he [knowingly] attribute his own lying inventions to God—or is he a madman?"   (Saba': 7–8)

Such were the distorted concepts prevalent in the Arabian Peninsula. When we add them to the pile of debris that had been spread in the East and West at the advent of Islam, we gain a clear idea of the heavy burden that everywhere weighed down the human mind. It was this debris that determined the systems, situations, morals and ethics of people.[10]

As a result, the major efforts of Islam were directed to liberating faith, to defining the correct manner in which the human mind might lay hold of the truth about the Divinity, its relationship with the creation and creation's relationship with it. This bestows stability on the various aspects of men's lives, their social, economical and political relationships, and their ethics and morals. All these things cannot be settled unless the truth about the Divinity is settled, and its concepts and functions are made plain. Islam paid special attention to clarifying the nature of the divine characteristics and attributes relating to the divine will, power, and sovereignty, planning, as well as the

---

[10] The concepts, philosophies and beliefs that arrived after Islam, especially those upon which the Western thought and Western way of life was established, lived by people today in Western and Eastern Europe, are no better than the piles of debris that existed in the past. Some of these will be dealt with in later chapters.

nature of the connection between God and man. These are precisely the grave matters over which false beliefs and philosophies stumble, matters that have profound effects on the human mind and the entire life of mankind.

What deserves our attention and consideration is that Islam has served as a correction to all the chaos and confusion, to all the deviations and faults into which all the distorted religions and clashing philosophies have blindly fallen, whether before or after the emergence of Islam. Precisely this remarkable phenomenon is a proof of the source from which this religion has sprung, the source that is aware of whatever passes through the human mind and then corrects and refines it.

Islam has expended, then, continuous effort to state definitively the truth concerning God's essence, as well as His relationship with the creation, and creation's relationship with Him. This effort is manifest in many parts of the Qur'an, especially its Meccan verses.

If one does not take into consideration the debris that had accumulated before the emergence of Islam, he might fail to appreciate the efforts expended by Islam or the need for the emphatic and repetitive nature of the Qur'anic mode of exposition, its insistence on pursuing all the habits of the minds and the customs of life. Awareness of the debris reveals the importance of these efforts and the great role played by this faith in liberating and emancipating the mind and life of mankind, for in all cases life is based upon belief. We are enabled to realize the value of this liberation for establishing a life on a strong and correct basis, from which corruption and contradiction, darkness and humiliation, have been eliminated. We will realize the value of the words uttered by 'Umar—may God be pleased with him: *"Whoever is born in Islam without having known Jahiliyyah will loosen its ties, one after the other."* For whoever has known Jahiliyyah will realize the value of Islam and will know how to maintain the mercy of God within him and the blessing of God bestowed upon him.

The beauty of this faith, its perfection and symmetry, and the simplicity of the great truth it represents, become evident to the heart and mind only when the debris of Jahiliyyah—both that preceding Islam and that following—is taken into consideration. Then this faith will appear as a mercy, a true mercy for the heart and the mind, a mercy for life and the living, a mercy with all its beauty and simplicity, clarity, harmony, nearness and deep agreement with human nature:

> "But then, is he that goes along with his face close to the ground better guided than he who walks upright on a straight path?"
>
> (Al-Mulk: 22)

2

CHARACTERISTICS OF THE ISLAMIC CONCEPT

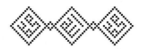

Say: "Our life takes its] hue from God! And who could give a better hue [to life] than God, if we but truly worship Him?"

(Al-Baqarah: 138)

The Islamic concept enjoys unique characteristics that distinguish it from all other concepts, giving it an independent character and a special nature of its own. This nature cannot take on diverse forms or be derived from other concepts.

Although these characteristics are numerous and various, they are all integrated into a single property from which they all emerge and to which they all return, the property of Divinity.

The concept of Divinity, with all its characteristics and fundamentals, comes to men from God with the purpose of their assimilating it and adhering to its implications in their lives without adding anything to it or subtracting anything from it. It is therefore not a concept subject to development in and of itself; what develops is rather human life once placed within its framework by perceiving its meaning and responding to it. For the source that established the concept is the same source that created man, the omnipotent Creator Who knows well the nature of man and the needs of his life as they evolve across time and Who placed within the concept the qualities that respond to those needs.

If the concepts, creeds and systems that people have established for themselves have required a constant change of their bases and modification of their principles, or even a complete reversal when they are seen to fall short of the evolving needs of humanity, it is precisely because those concepts are unconnected to divine guidance; they are the creations of human beings whose perspectives are necessarily limited. They can envision only the circumstances and situations that are disclosed to them in a given period and in a given region of the earth. Their vision is affected by man's limitations, his ignorance, passion and emotions. On the other hand, the Islamic concept of Divinity, is utterly distinct from man's, with respect to both its origin and its characteristics, and therefore it does not need to develop or change. The One Who established this concept can envision without limits of time or space; His knowledge is immune to the obstacles of ignorance and deficiency; and He chooses without being influenced by passion or emotion. Therefore, He has established for the entirety of humanity, in all places and at all times, a firm principle within the framework of which human life freely advances and develops.

The law of motion is one of the laws of this universe, as is apparent, and it is likewise a law for human life insofar as it is a part of existence. However, it is not a motion that is free of restraints, nor can there be motion without norms and regulations. If every star and every planet has its own orbit, its own sphere and axis around which it rotates, human existence must similarly have an axis and a sphere within which it rotates. If that were not the case, disorder and disaster would ensue. The same would occur if a star fell from its orbit or changed direction without regulation or any control. Similarly, the concept of Divinity has to be constant for human life to evolve around it and move within it. This concept was created to support and sustain humanity at all times as it grows, develops and advances. Therefore the concept is complete and whole in itself; it is not liable to expansion or supplementation, and it does not accept "spare parts" added to it from outside itself. It is God's creation and therefore utterly disparate from what any other than God may have created. Man can neither add anything to this concept nor modify it. It came to man to augment him, to help him mature, progress and move forward, to augment his heart and mind, his life and reality. It came to awaken all his capacities and talents, to release them to operate positively and with guidance, enabling them to yield their finest fruits, instead of being squandered and left idle, or falling prey to deviance and corruption. Thus, the concept of Divinity does not require external support, a different pathway or a nature other than its own. It plays a unique role in human life with all its concepts, methods, instructions, and tools, thus bringing human life into harmony with the universe, preventing its movement from clashing with that of the universe and the damage that would result.

Therefore, the concept is complete and balanced, taking into consideration all aspects of human life and the correct balance among those aspects. It further considers all the stages through which the human race passes, for the One Who created this concept is also the Creator of man, the One Who infuses knowledge into His creation. He is All-Knowing; there is nothing unknown to Him concerning the life of mankind and the various circumstances that surround it. He was thus able to establish for him a correct, comprehensive, balanced and realistic concept embracing all aspects and stages of his life.

This concept is, therefore, the only criterion to which man should refer, at all times and in all places, with respect to his concepts and values, his modes of conduct, his morals and deeds. It is by means of it that man knows where he stands in relation to God and the truth. There is no other criterion, no standard, ancient or modern, to which he might refer. It is from this concept alone that he derives his values and standards; it is by means of it that he forms his reason and his heart; it is its imprint that he fixes on his consciousness and his conduct; and it is his source of reference in whatever confronts him:

> "O you who have attained to faith! Pay heed unto God, and pay heed unto the Apostle and unto those from among you who have been entrusted with authority; and if you are at variance over any matter, refer it unto God and the Apostle, if you [truly] believe in God and the Last Day. This is the best [for you], and best in the end."
>
> (An-Nisa': 59)

From these basic characteristics of the Islamic concept, those that determine its nature, together with the other characteristics deriving from it, it is plain that this concept is unique and its distinguishing features are unparalleled. It is therefore a methodological error to try to borrow criteria from the various schools of human thought now current in the world and to have them interact with this utterly unique and independent concept.

We will understand this issue more clearly as we proceed with this research. We content ourselves at this point with establishing the principle just outlined as an essential rule to follow in every area of Islamic thought or research. It is here that the roads diverge.

Now let us look in more detail at this basic concept and the characteristics that derive from it.

3

DIVINITY

"Say: Surely God has guided me to the way that is most straight"
(Al-An'am: 161)

Divinity is the first characteristic and the source of the Islamic concept. It is a concept of belief that is revealed by God, unique to
this source and not derived from any other. This distinguishes it from
the philosophical concepts established by the human mind concerning the nature of God, the universe, and mankind, and the relations
between them. It is also distinct from pagan beliefs that arise from
emotion, imagination, and illusions.

One can confidently affirm that the Islamic concept is the only
creedal concept that has retained its divine origin and nature. Concepts
by earlier heavenly religions had been subjected to distortion in one
form or another, as we have previously seen. Commentaries, interpretations, additions were introduced into the very substance of those
concepts, so that their divine character was changed. Islam is the only
religion to have retained its principles in uncontaminated integrity,
truth remaining clearly separate from falsehood.

God's truthful words in this regard are:

"Behold, it is We Ourselves who have bestowed from on high, step
by step, this reminder: and, behold, it is We who shall truly guard it
[from all corruption]." (Al-Hijr: 9)

It is this indisputable truth that provides the Islamic concept with
its unique value.

In general, the crucial distinction between a philosophical concept and a creedal concept is that the former arises in the human mind as an attempt to interpret existence and man's relationship with it. This concept remains within the boundaries of cold, intellectual knowledge. A creedal concept, on the other hand, is one that is derived from the conscience, that interacts with man's emotions and life. It is a living bond between man and existence, or between man and the Creator.

The Islamic concept is distinct from such a creedal concept of belief because, as we mentioned earlier, it is a divine concept derived from God and delivered to mankind, not one created by man. Human beings received this concept exclusively from their Creator; it is not a concept invented by mankind as both the pagan and philosophical concepts were, whatever differences separated them from each other. Man's role with respect to it is to receive it, comprehend it, and act in accordance with it.

The divine source of this concept, which is the Noble Qur'an, states that everything comes from God, is a gift and a mercy from Him. Human thought, as represented in the Prophet—upon whom be peace and blessings—and all the Messengers of God who received this Islamic concept in its original form, had no part in its creation. They received it as guidance for themselves, and a means for guiding others. This guidance was a gift from God to be received with an open heart. The duty of the Prophet, or any other Messenger, with respect to the concept, was simply to convey it accurately, to transmit it faithfully without mingling with revelation any human thought, that which God calls "fancy" (*hawa*). As for the guiding of hearts and opening them to acceptance of the message, this was not part of the Prophet's responsibility, being God's concern alone:

> "And thus, too, [O Muhammad,] have We revealed unto thee a life—giving message, [coming] at Our behest.
> [Ere this message came unto thee,] thou didst not know what revelation is, nor what faith [implies]: but [now] We have caused this [message] to be a light, whereby We guide whom We will of Our servants: and, verily, [on the strength thereof] thou, too, shalt guide [men] onto the straight way—the way that leads to God, to whom all that is in the heavens and all that is on earth belongs.
> Oh, verily, with God is the beginning and the end of all things!"
> (Ash-Shura: 52–53)

"Consider this unfolding [of God's message], as it comes down from on high!

This fellow—man of yours has not gone astray, nor is he deluded, and neither does he speak out of his own desire: that [which he conveys to you] is but [a divine] inspiration with which he is being inspired."   (An-Najm: 1–4)

"Now if he [whom we have entrusted with it] had dared to attribute some [of his own] sayings unto Us, We would indeed have seized him by his right hand, and would indeed have cut his life-vein, and none of you could have saved him!"   (Al-Haqqah: 44–47)

"O APOSTLE! Announce all that has been bestowed from on high upon thee by thy Sustainer: for unless thou doest it fully, thou wilt not have delivered His message [at all]. And God will protect thee from [unbelieving] men: behold, God does not guide people who refuse to acknowledge the truth."   (Al-Ma'idah: 67}

"VERILY, thou canst not guide aright everyone whom thou lovest: but it is God who guides him that wills [to be guided]; and He is fully aware of all who would let themselves be guided."   (Al-Qasas: 56)

"And whomsoever God wills to guide, his bosom He opens wide with willingness towards self-surrender [unto Him]; and whomsoever He wills to let go astray, his bosom He causes to be tight and constricted, as if he were climbing unto the skies: it is thus that God inflicts horror upon those who will not believe."   (Al-An'am: 125)

This emphasis on the source of the Islamic concept is what provides it with its fundamental and supreme value. It is the sole trustworthy source, free of the imperfection, ignorance and fallibility which accompany all human action, and which we see manifested in concepts of human origination, whether they be pagan or philosophical in nature, or the concepts with which man has subverted originally heavenly beliefs. This source is also reliable because it is suitable to human nature, responds to all its aspects, and fulfills all its needs. It is therefore from this concept that the firmest and most comprehensive way of life is derived.

Although the Islamic concept did not arise in the human mind, the mind is not banished from its domain nor is it forbidden to work on it, "work" meaning in this context to receive and comprehend the concept, to apply in the actualities of life. The concept should be received without recourse to pre-conceived notions derived from other sources or from one's own mental categories in the light of which one then proceeds to weigh and evaluate the concept. On the contrary, all thoughts and criteria should be derived from the concept itself, and one should orient oneself accordingly. The objective truths contained in the concept should be derived from the divine source that is at the origin of the concept, not from any source external to it. The concept is the balance in which are weighed all perceptions and thoughts, all values and ideas, in order to distinguish the true from the false and the right from the wrong.

> "O you who have attained to faith! Pay heed unto God, and pay heed unto the Apostle and unto those from among you who have been entrusted with authority; and if you are at variance over any matter, refer it unto God and the Apostle, if you [truly] believe in God and the Last Day. This is the best [for you], and best in the end."
>
> (An-Nisa: 59)

At the same time, precisely as weighed in the balance of this concept, human thought is considered a valuable tool, responsible for understanding the characteristics and fundamentals of the Islamic concept as derived from its divine source, and deducing the values and norms that surround it, without adding anything to them or distorting them in any way. The Islamic system of education devotes great effort and attention to strengthening and rectifying thought by way of preparation for the tasks with which it is entrusted.[11]

It is not thought alone, however, that receives the concept; it simply shares in receiving it. For the distinguishing characteristic of this concept, which springs from its divine origin, is that it addresses human nature as an integrated whole. Moreover, there are matters that thought cannot comprehend in their essential nature or in causative or qualitative terms, and thought can in good conscience submit to them unquestioningly. For logic dictates acceptance of the simple truth that the domain covered by the concept is greater and vaster than the entirety of human reality, including as it does such subjects as the nature of the divine essence and attributes, as well as the manner in which God's power connects to His creation. This is the domain of

---

11 See Muhammad Qutb, *Manhaj al-Taribiyat al-Islamiyya.*

the Ultimate, the Pre- and Post-Eternal, the Universal, the Absolute. Humans are mortal creatures constrained in time and space, and cannot comprehend the Universal and Absolute.

"O you who live in close communion with [evil] invisible beings and humans! If you [think that you] can pass beyond the regions of the heavens and the earth, pass beyond them! [But] you cannot pass beyond them, save by a sanction [from God]!"   (Ar-Rahman: 33)

No human vision can encompass Him, whereas He encompasses all human vision: for He alone is unfathomable, all–aware."
(Al-An'am: 103)

Man with his entire nature, not simply with thought, is incapable of acting beyond these boundaries. His duty is to receive the concept from the absolute divine essence that encompasses all existence and to do so within the limits and responsibilities of human nature. Let us add, by way of clarification, that human beings are in thrall to their natures as created beings, neither universal nor absolute, neither pre- nor post-eternal. Their perceptions are therefore as limited as their nature. Man is further limited by his designated function as divine vice-regent on earth in order to realize there the true meaning of worshipping God; he has been endowed with a degree of perception appropriate to that function, neither more nor less. There are many matters that he does not need to know for fulfilling that function, and he has not therefore been given the means for perceiving them with respect to their essence or quality; he can simply perceive their possibility. For on the one hand, humans know that God's will is absolute, and on the other, that they are created beings, neither universal nor absolute; hence they acknowledge it is impossible for them to comprehend the attributes of the Pre- and Post-Eternal, the One Who encompasses all things.

The Noble Qur'an refers to some of the matters for the comprehension of which man was not endowed with the necessary power, either because they lie beyond the limited scope of human nature or because he has no need of them for fulfilling his assigned function. The Qur'an also points out how the sound disposition of the true believer accepts these matters and how a deviant person rejects them. One of these matters is the fundamental nature of the divine essence; man cannot comprehend it, nor does he have any basis for comparison or analogy.

No human vision can encompass Him, whereas He encompasses all human vision: for He alone is unfathomable, all–aware."

(Al-An'am: 103)

"AND ON WHATEVER you may differ, [O believers,] the verdict thereon rests with God.
[Say, therefore:] "Such is God, my Sustainer: in Him have I placed my trust, and unto Him do I always turn!"   (Ash-Shura: 10)

"Hence, do not coin any similitudes for God! Verily, God knows [all], whereas you have no [real] knowledge."   (An-Nahl: 74)

Furthermore, there is the relationship of God's Will with His creation:

"[Zachariah] exclaimed: "O my Sustainer! How can I have a son when old age has already overtaken me, and my wife is barren?"
Answered [the angel]: "Thus it is: God does what He wills."

(Al 'Imran: 40)

"Said she:"O my Sustainer! How can I have a son when no man has ever touched me?"
[The angel] answered: "Thus it is: God creates what He wills: when He wills a thing to be, He but says unto it, 'Be'—and it is."

(Al 'Imran: 47)

"Thus it is:" i.e., no explanation is given of the modality of the affair, for it lies beyond human comprehension. Whoever seeks for an explanation falls into error and confusion, for he is bound to make a comparison with human acts, despite the great disparity involved.[12]

Another matter belonging to this category is the nature of the spirit (ruh), whether by it life, Gabriel or revelation be intended.

"AND THEY will ask thee about [the nature of] divine inspiration. Say: "This inspiration [comes] at my Sustainer's behest; and [you cannot understand its nature, O men, since] you have been granted very little of [real] knowledge."   (Al-Isra': 85)

---

[12] Aristotle, Plato and others were mistaken when they tried to explain the connection of the act of the creator with creation, because they drew a false analogy with the connection of man's act with its object.

The realm of the unseen is also veiled from human knowledge except for what God has granted to whom He pleases:

"For, with Him are the keys to the things that are beyond the reach of a created being's perception: none knows them but He.

And He knows all that is on land and in the sea; and not a leaf falls but He knows it; and neither is there a grain in the earth's deep darkness, nor anything living or dead, but is recorded in [His] clear decree."   (Al-An'am: 59)

"He [alone] knows that which is beyond the reach of a created being's perception, and to none does He disclose aught of the mysteries of His Own unfathomable knowledge, unless it be to an apostle whom He has been pleased to elect [there-for]: and then He sends forth [the forces of heaven] to watch over him in whatever lies open before him and in what is beyond his ken."   (Al-Jinn: 26–27)

"Say [O Prophet]: "I do not say unto you, 'God's treasures are with me'; nor [do I say], 'I know the things that are beyond the reach of human perception'; nor do I say unto you, 'Behold, I am an angel': I but follow what is revealed to me."

Say: "Can the blind and the seeing be deemed equal? Will you not, then, take thought?"   (Al-An'am: 50)

"Verily, with God alone rests the knowledge of when the Last Hour will come; and He [it is who] sends down rain; and He [alone] knows what is in the wombs: whereas no one knows what he will reap tomorrow, and no one knows in what land he will die.

Verily, God [alone] is all-knowing, all-aware."   (Luqman: 34)

Another unseen reality is the promise of the Last Hour:

"THEY WILL ASK thee [O Prophet] about the Last Hour: "When will it come to pass?"

[But] how couldst thou tell anything about it, [seeing that] with thy Sustainer alone rests the beginning and the end [of all knowledge] thereof?

Thou art but [sent] to warn those who stand in awe of it.

On the Day when they behold it. [it will seem to them] as if they had tarried [in this world] no longer than one evening or [one night, ending with] its morn!"   (An-Nazi'At: 42–46)

"Nay, but [the Last Hour] will come upon them of a sudden, and will stupefy them: and they will be unable to avert it, and neither will they be allowed any respite."   (Al-Anbiya': 40)

God Almighty expounds how these matters, which lie beyond the awareness of human beings, should be received:

"He it is who has revealed to you the Book wherein are verses clear. They are the essence of the Book, and still others are allegorical. As for those in whose heart is crookedness, they pursue the allegorical part, seeking dissension, and seeking its hidden interpretations. But no one knows its hidden interpretations except God. And those of firm knowledge say "We believe in it; all of it is from our Lord." But no one will truly grasp the Message except men of understanding. Our Lord, make not our hearts swerve after You have guided us, and bestow upon us mercy from Yourself, indeed You are the Bestower of all things."   (Al-'Imran: 7–8)

With the exception of these matters, human thought or human perception is invited to contemplate and consider, to examine and investigate, to adopt and assimilate, and then to apply, both in the realm of the mind and in that of outer reality, all the implications of the divine concept.

No religion has celebrated as Islam has done the fully awakened human mind, refined its mode of operation, mobilized it for positive activity, liberated it from delusion and superstition, and at the same time protected it from overstepping its bounds and wandering guideless in the wilderness. Furthermore, no religion has equalled Islam in drawing attention to the divine norms that govern men's souls and the world in which they live, to the nature of the universe and of man, to the capacities potential within man, and to the norms of God as they affect human life and are recorded in the annals of history.

The following Qur'anic verses bear on cultivating man's perceptions and refining his method of thought and judgement:

"And never concern thyself with anything of which thou hast no knowledge: verily, thy hearing, and sight, and heart-all of them-will be called to account for it [on Judgement Day]!"   (Al-Isra': 36)

"O you who have attained to faith! Avoid speculation as much as possible, for speculation in some cases is a sin."   (Al-Hujurat: 12)

"Most of them follow nothing but conjecture. Assuredly conjecture can never be a substitute for the truth."   (Yunus: 36)

"They have no knowledge whatsoever of that; they do merely conjecture."   (Zukhruf: 20)

Drawing attention to the signs of God revealed in man's own being and on the horizons, the Qur'an states:

"Say: "Consider whatever there is in the heavens and on earth!"
                                                                   (Yunus: 101)

"AND ON EARTH there are signs [of God's existence, visible] to all who are endowed with inner certainty, just as [there are signs thereof] within your own selves: can you not, then, see?"
                                                        (Adh-Dhariyat: 20–21)

"In time We shall make them fully understand Our messages [through what they perceive] in the utmost horizons [of the universe] and within themselves, so that it will become clear unto them that this [revelation] is indeed the truth. [Still,] is it not enough [for them to know] that thy Sustainer is witness unto everything?"   (Fussilat: 53)

As for observing the operation of God's norms in human life and their history, as well as the destinies of past peoples:

"Say: Travel in the land and see how He originated creation, then will God bring forth a later creation. Verily, God is able to do all things."   (Al-'Ankabut: 20)

"Have they, then never journeyed about the earth and beheld what happened in the end to those [deniers of the truth] who lived before their time? Greater were they in power than they are; and they left a stronger impact on the earth, and built it up even better than these [are doing]; and to them [too] came their apostles with all evidence of the truth: and so, [when they rejected the truth and thereupon perished,] it was not God who wronged them, but it was they who had wronged themselves.

And once again: evil is bound to be the end of those who do evil by giving the lie to God's messages and deriding them."
                                                              (Ar-Rum: 9–10)

"Have, then, they [who deny the truth] never yet seen how We visit the earth [with Our punishment], gradually depriving it of all that is best thereon?
For, [when] God judges, there is no power that could repel His judgment: and swift in reckoning is He!"   (Ar-Ra'd: 41)

There are a great many such examples to be found in the Noble Qur'an; a complete methodology for educating, empowering and directing the human mind can be derived from them.[13] Many such examples will be referred to in later chapters.

God, the Creator of man, knows the nature and the extent of human capabilities, for He bestowed on him the ability to deduce the laws of matter in order to subjugate matter to himself as the divine vicegerent on earth. God also knows, however, that some of the secrets of life are hidden from man, the mysteries of his spiritual and rational formation, and even those aspects of his physical composition that touch on his spiritual and mental functioning. All of this is still hidden from man's knowledge and perception. One of the greatest scientists of the twentieth century, Dr. Alexis Carrel, stated this point in complete sincerity and honesty. He writes in his book, *Man the Unknown*:

"Indeed, mankind has made a gigantic effort to know itself. Although we possess the treasure of the observations accumulated by the scientists, the philosophers, the poets, and the great mystics of all times, we have grasped only certain aspects of ourselves. We do not comprehend man as a whole. We know him as composed of distinct parts. And even these parts are created by our methods. Each one of us is made up of a procession of phantoms, in the midst of which strides an unknowable reality.

"In fact, our ignorance is profound. Most of the questions put to themselves by those who study human beings remain without answer. Immense regions of our inner world are still unknown. How do the molecules of chemical substances associate in order to form the complex and temporary organs of the cell? How do the genes contained in the nucleus of a fertilized ovum determine the characteristics of the individual deriving from the ovum? How do cells organize themselves by their own efforts into societies, such as the tissues and organs? Like

---

13 See Muhammad Qutb, *Manhaj al-Tarbiyat al-Islamiyya*.

the ants and the bees, they have advance knowledge of the part they are destined to play in the life of the community. And hidden mechanisms enable them to build up an organism both complex and simple. What is the nature of our duration, of psychological time, and of physiological time? We know that we are a compound of tissues, organs, fluids, ad consciousness. But the relations between consciousness and cerebrum are still a mystery. We lack almost entirely knowledge of the physiology of nervous cells. To what extent does will power modify the organism? How is the mind influenced by the state of the organs? In what manner can the organic and mental characteristics, which each individual inherits, be changed by the mode of life, the chemical substances contained in food, the climate, and the physiological and moral disciplines?

"We are very far from knowing what relations exist between skeleton, muscles, and organs, and mental and spiritual activities. We are ignorant of the factors that bring about nervous equilibrium and resistance to fatigue and to diseases. We do not know how moral sense, judgment, and audacity could be augmented. What is the relative importance of intellectual, moral, and mystical activities? What is the significance of aesthetics and religious sense? What form of energy is responsible for telepathic communications? Without any doubt, certain physiological and mental factors determine happiness or misery, success, or failure. But we do not know what they are. We cannot artificially give to any individual the aptitude of happiness. As yet, we do not know what environment is the most favourable for the optimum development of civilized man. Is it possible to suppress struggle, effort, and suffering from our physiological and spiritual formation? How can we prevent the degeneracy of man in modern civilization? Many other questions could be asked on subjects that are to us of utmost interest. They would also remain unanswered. It is quite evident that the accomplishments of all these sciences having man as an object remain insufficient, and that our knowledge of ourselves is still most rudimentary."

This is the extent of our ignorance of the true nature of man, one of the truths required for any comprehensive scheme of belief. Indeed, we are ignorant of some of the smallest and most obvious aspects of our own nature. This is what is affirmed by one of the greatest scholars of the twentieth century whose learning, authority and rank no one disputes.

The reasons for this ignorance are many according to Carrel, who bases himself on the scientific methods known in the West; he was trained there in an atmosphere of scientific research and was in fact surrounded by science, as he states in the introduction to his book. We agree with him on some of the reasons he proposes for our ignorance, but not on all of them:

"Our ignorance may be attributed, at the same time, to the mode of existence of our ancestors, to the complexity of our nature, and to the structure of our mind."

He speaks about the first two reasons in depth, but we are concerned only with the third reason, which he describes as follows:

"There is another reason for the slow progress of the knowledge of ourselves. Our mind is so constructed as to delight in contemplating simple facts. We feel a kind of repugnance in attacking such a complex problem as that of the constitution of living beings and of man. The intellect, as Bergson wrote, is characterized by a natural inability to comprehend life. On the contrary, we love to discover in the cosmos the geometrical forms that exist in the depths of our consciousness. The exactitude of the proportions of our monuments and the precision of our machines express a fundamental character of our mind. Geometry does not exist in the earthly world. It has originated in ourselves. The methods of nature are never so precise as those of men. We do not find in the universe the clearness and accuracy of our thought. We attempt, therefore, to abstract from the complexity of phenomena some simple systems whose components bear to one another certain relations susceptible to being described mathematically."

"This power of abstraction of the human intellect is responsible for the amazing progress of physics and chemistry. A similar success has rewarded the physiochemical study of living beings. The laws of chemistry and of physics are identical in the world of living things and in that of inanimate matter, as Claude Bernard thought long ago. This fact explains why modern physiology has discovered, for example, that the constancy of the alkalinity of the blood and of the water of the ocean is expressed by identical laws, that the energy spent by the contracting muscle is supplied by the fermentation of sugar, etc. The physiochemical aspects of human beings are almost as easy to investigate as those of the other objects of the terrestrial world. Such is the task that general physiology succeeds in accomplishing."

"The study of the truly physiological phenomena, that is, of those resulting from the organization of living matter—meets with more important obstacles. On account of the extreme smallness of things to be analysed, it is impossible to use the ordinary techniques of physics and of chemistry. What method could bring to light the chemical constitution of the nucleus of the sexual cells, of its chromosomes, and of the genes that compose these chromosomes? Nevertheless, those very minute aggregates of chemicals are of capital importance, because they contain the future of the individual and of the race. The fragility of certain tissues, such as the serious substance, is so great that to study them in the living state is almost impossible. We do not possess any technique capable of penetrating the mysteries of the brain, and of the harmonious association of its cells. Our mind, which loves the simple beauty of mathematical formulas, is bewildered when it contemplates the stupendous mass of cells, humours, and consciousness that make up the individual, we try, therefore, to apply to this compound the concepts that have proved useful in the realm of physics, chemistry, and mechanics, and in the philosophical and religious disciplines. Such an attempt does not meet with much success, because we can be reduced neither to a physiochemical system nor to a spiritual entity. Of course, the science of man has to use the concepts of all the other sciences. But it must also develop its own. For it is as fundamental as the sciences of the molecules, the atoms, and the electrons."

"In short, the slow progress of the knowledge of the human being, as compared with the splendid ascension of physics, astronomy, chemistry, and mechanics, is due to our ancestors' lack of leisure, to the complexity of the subject, and to the structure of our mind. Those obstacles are fundamental to be overcome at the cost of strenuous effort. The knowledge of ourselves will never attain the elegant simplicity, the abstractness, and the beauty of physics. The factors that have retarded its development are not likely to vanish. We must realize clearly that the science of man is the most difficult of all sciences."[14]

This, in the view of a great Western scientist, is the reason for our ignorance of the nature of man, even the smallest and most evident

---

[14] Alexis Carrel, *Man the Unknown*, pp 4–5.

aspects of his nature. No matter how much we may differ with his approach to the issue as a whole, we take heed of his witness, for we see that he has put his finger on the main reason, which is the formation of our intellect, a formation suited to man's function on earth as the divine vice-regent. It enables him to progress in understanding the laws of matter, in bringing them under his control and even in understanding more and more aspects of the nature of man. However, the mysteries of his creation will remain eternally hidden from him, as will the mysteries of life and death and of what constitutes man's own spirit, for none of this is needed by man to fulfil his basic function.

From the testimony of Carrel, two self-evident truths emerge:

The first is the truth of God's mercy to mankind. God did not leave man alone with the ignorance to which our twentieth century scientist bears witness, compelling him to construct his own creedal concept. This concept includes a comprehensive interpretation, not only of the true nature of man which is unknown to him, but also of the nature of divinity, the universe, and life, as well as the interconnections among all these. Since man is ignorant of his own reality, God did not leave it to him to establish the modes of his life and the laws governing it, for such matters require complete and comprehensive knowledge not only of man's nature but also of the universe in which man lives, as well as the very essence of life itself and the supreme power that creates and administers the universe.

The second truth is the arrogance of those who, in past times and present, have attempted themselves to put forward a comprehensive interpretation of the universe, life and mankind, and to lay down paths, systems and laws for regulating the lives of mankind. The ignorance underlying these endeavours can lead only to bewilderment and the accumulated debris of corrupt and deficient concepts and methodologies, to misery and wretchedness. Such are the bitter fruits of arrogance and ignorance!.[15]

The divine concept is a pure gift of God to mankind. It exempts weak and ignorant humanity from the need to struggle with these concerns and protects them from squandering their energies in a domain where they are ill equipped to venture. Further, it frees them to receive and assimilate this gift, to take it as a basis on which to found their

---

[15] See the present writer's *al-Islam wa Mushkilat al-Hadara*.

lives, as a criterion for their values, and as a guide to accompany them. If men move away from this path, they wander in misguidance and confusion, a prey to concepts that make one either laugh or weep. They fall into wretchedness thanks to all the systems that are erected on the basis of profound ignorance.

In his valuable book *What the World Lost with the Decline of the Muslims,* Professor Abul Hasan al-Nadwi has the following to say:

"The Prophets had imparted to man the true knowledge of God's existence and His attributes and actions. They had laid the foundations upon which man could erect the edifice of his own spiritual conduct without getting involved in the fruitless metaphysical discussions on "being" and "knowing." But man heeded not. Instead of being grateful for Divine guidance, he allowed the ship of his thought to drift on uncharted seas. He behaved like an explorer who, setting aside the geographical charts and maps, tries to scale every height, fathom every depth, and measure every distance on his own initiative. The results of such endeavours can at best be a few sketchy notes and incomplete hints picked up here and there. So when the people tried to reach God with the help of reason alone and without the aid of light furnished by the Prophet's teachings, the knowledge of God gathered by them consisted of little else besides random thoughts, conflicting theories, and haphazard conclusions."

Those who have tried to establish creedal concepts drawing on their own resources, or elaborate philosophical concepts to interpret existence, are in fact more severely misguided than those whom Nadwi describes and cause greater danger to humanity than they do. Still graver was the distortion of messages revealed by God, particularly in the case of Christianity. The Church in Europe came to exercise authority in the name of a distorted Christianity, imposing by force its false concepts and its erroneous and defective teachings about the physical world, and barbarically opposing scientific research. All this was done in the name of religion, but religion had no part in it.

Such situations arose as a result of the human mind distorting and polluting the divine origin of the Christian faith and the Christian concept, attributing its own products to the faith as such.

Let us remind ourselves that all the tendencies that arose in Europe in opposition to religion and religious thought actually owed their origin to this deviation and the circumstances to which it gave birth. Examples are idealist rationalism, sensory objectivism and dialectical materialism. We can therefore conclude that all the unparalleled misery that encompasses mankind today derives from the consequences of man's polluting the original divine concept with his own thought.

In order to clarify this point in a manner befitting its supreme importance, it will be appropriate to provide a brief summary of the trajectory followed by European thought, insofar as it is a direct and natural result of the distortion of the religious concept by subjecting it to human tampering, to political factors and racial and sectarian clashes.

This summary will reveal the wisdom of God and the care that He has shown for preserving the principles of the Islamic concept from distortion by human beings, as well as the dangers implicit in attempts made to infuse a human element into the divine concept while invoking slogans such as "religious renewal" or "the development of religious thought." For it is this concept alone that has remained untouched by the ignorance and defectiveness of human beings, and it alone is the refuge where man can count on finding guidance, tranquillity and assurance.

It will be enough for our purposes to cite excerpts from the chapter "Religion is a Narcotic" in Dr. Muhammad al-Bahi's *al-Fikr al-Islami al-Hadith wa Silatuhu bi 'l-Isti'mar al-Gharbi* ("Modern Islamic Thought and its Relation with Western Imperialism"), for there he describes the way in which European thought came to oppose the Church and its teachings.

"The conflict between religion, reason and sense perception in the history of Western thought: Since the fourteenth century, the Western mind has gone through four stages of intellectual conflict centred on the justification of one or another of the sources of knowledge that have been known to mankind throughout its history, these being religion, reason, and sense perception. At each of the four stages the value of one of these three has been questioned for its value as a source of certain knowledge, and either positive or negative answers have been given. The answer to this question might be negative or positive. Philosophical schools have formed as a result of these controversies, privileging one or other of the three sources.

The supremacy of the authoritative text or of religion: During the Middle Ages, religion predominated in directing mankind with respect to human conduct, organizing the community and understanding nature. Religion meant Christianity, Christianity virtually meant Catholicism, and Catholicism, the Papacy, an ecclesiastical system in which supreme power was vested in the pope, who had the sole right to interpret the scriptures, together with the upper echelons of the priesthood. The text of the scriptures and the understanding of them by the Catholic Church were made equally valid, so that belief in the trinity became a fundamental doctrine of Christianity, and the confession of sins and the granting of indulgences became incorporated into Catholic practice.

This situation persisted until the fifteenth century when the Crusades began to have positive results for the European mentality [thanks to the contacts established with Muslim civilization]. Martin Luther (1453–1546) rose up in struggle against the "satanic teachings," as he called them, of the Pope and the Catholic Church. He fought against the granting of indulgences, which he regarded as tools of enslavement. He also opposed the concept of the Trinity, as well as the authority of the Pope, with the aim of making the Bible, the word of God, the sole authority for Christianity. He called for freedom in studying the scriptures, but not total freedom of thought. He made the Bible the true source of faith, and regarded faith as superior to all else, whether it be the intellect or nature.

Calvin (1509–1564) followed the same path of Martin Luther, affirming that the Bible is the sole source for true Christianity and that authentic Christianity does not accept the doctrine of the Trinity.

Thanks to the reform movements of Luther and Calvin, Christianity—meaning Catholicism and the Papacy—entered on a period of intellectual controversy; it became a topic for rational discussion and philosophical debate. Any philosopher who denied the authority of religion necessarily denied also the authority of the Pope. Whoever posited a relationship between religion and reason as two opposing or contradictory things thereby limited the relationship between Catholicism—including the doctrine of the Trinity and the granting of indulgences—and the human intellect. If a philosopher like Hegel later rose in defence of Christianity, he would do so in the name of the "pure teachings of Christianity" as expounded by Luther, not the teachings of the Catholic Church.

Religion thus became a topic of intellectual debate in Europe, but a particular kind of religion. A certain set of doctrines was accepted in the name of philosophy, and another set was rejected, again in the name of philosophy.

The Sovereignty of Reason: The validity of revelation as the ultimate source of knowledge, persisted—despite differences in doctrine—until the second half of the eighteenth century, the period of what is known as the Age of Enlightenment in the history of European philosophy. The Age of Enlightenment has its own unique character that distinguishes it from both previous and later centuries. It owed its distinctive stamp to German, French and British philosophers of the time, each acting in their own sphere. The following were its important features:

It praised and exalted human reason and its ability to take control of the future destiny of humanity, after first eliminating all forms of inherited slavery in order to remove any obstacle that stood in the way of clear planning.[16]

It had the courage and daring to subject every historical event to the test of reason, as well as to create new states, societies, economies, laws, religions and educational systems, each of them based on correct and pure foundations.

It asserted belief in the compatibility of all interests and benefits and in human brotherhood, basing itself on a constantly developing rational culture.

"The meaning of all this was the supremacy of reason over other sources of knowledge, which at the time meant religion, in other words, Catholicism and perhaps Protestantism as well.

"Reason was entitled to supervise all aspects of life, including politics, law and religion, humanity being the supreme goal of all life.

"This period of time is referred to as the Age of Enlightenment, as well as the Age of Humanism and the Age of Deism, i.e. the age when philosophers believed in a god that is neither the sender of revelations nor the creator. All these names betray certain qualities. The purpose of Enlightenment was nothing other than distancing religion from its directive role and having reason take its place. The Humanism proclaimed in this age was nothing but an attempt to serve as a substi-

---

[16] Dr. Alexis Carrel explained the extent of true knowledge of the mind in humanity, not only in the eighteenth century, but also in the twentieth century.

tute for nearness to God as the goal of mankind in the conduct of its life. As for the god who neither creates nor sends revelations, this is a concept that accords perfectly with affirming the sole authority of the intellect and its sovereignty over all aspects of life.

Hence, in the age of Enlightenment religion and reason were antithetical, and thought which was inclined to subject reason to religion moved in the direction of subjecting religion to reason. It was therefore the era in which reason reigned supreme, just as the previous age had belonged to religion.

It becomes evident then that the conflict between reason and religion is in fact a conflict between human thought and the Christianity of the Church. What motivated this conflict were the conditions the Church had created in European life, whether in respect of scholarship, or politics, or doctrine and faith.

"The Supremacy of Sense Perception": the Age of the Enlightenment came to a close by around the end of the eighteenth century, and a new period in European thought began with the advent of the nineteenth century. The theme of the conflict remained the same: it was a contest among religion, reason, and nature. However, the nineteenth century was characterized by a particular philosophy, given the fact that thought now became inclined to the "supremacy of nature"—i.e., sense perception—over religion and reason, and the autonomy of "objective reality" as a source of certain knowledge. The philosophy in question which came to define the age "Positivism," a theory that emerged in the arena of epistemology. It arose in a particular environment and on a particular basis. The environment was formed by the dominant wish of certain scholars and philosophers to oppose the Church with its claims to a specific type of knowledge which it exploited in its confrontation with those who would deny its influence. As previously mentioned, the knowledge in question might be described as Christian or Catholic knowledge, or more generally as religious or metaphysical knowledge. Moreover, in addition to their intense hostility to the Church and its claims, the Positivists were convinced that the rationalist or idealist philosophy of the Age of Enlightenment had proven bankrupt and unable to deflect the Church from its directive role in human life and the organization of human society. Indeed, in the age of Hegel this philosophy was inclined to advocate revelation and religion anew.

The principal aim of the positivist school, in its logic, is to oppose the Church and its system of knowledge in the name of science, or, to put it differently, to oppose metaphysics and rationalist idealism. While denying the religion of the Church, the positivist school substitutes for it a new religion, the religion of "supreme humanity," which is based on forms of worship and rituals, just like Christianity, and embraces the concepts of sanctity and veneration, just like Catholicism.

As for the distinctive foundation on which positivism was based, it was the veneration and respect of nature, external and immediate actuality, the entirety of the sensory realm, these all being synonymous in the view of the positivists. Moreover, the Positivists venerated nature not simply as an independent source of knowledge but as the sole and unique source of certain or true knowledge. The meaning of this is that it is nature itself which delineates reality in the human mind, by means of a type of revelation with its own clear signs and indications; it is nature, indeed, which forms the human mind. And the significance of venerating nature in this way is that nature is what imprints reality on the human mind, and it is what engenders and portrays its clear features. Nothing comes to man from beyond nature, and nothing comes to him from within his own essence. Indeed, anything that comes to him from beyond nature is falsehood and deceit, and whatever conceptions his own intellect forms are fantasy and imagination. Therefore, religion, which is revelation originating from "beyond nature" can be nothing other than deceit, coming from a being indefinable in terms of the natural realm. Rationalist idealism also has no link with the natural realm and has no relationship with the truth; it consists of nothing more than human musings and imaginings uninspired by nature.

Thus, whatever a person has to say, as an individual entity, about humanity as a describable subject, or whatever he opines about the nature in which he lives—if it be derived from religious knowledge or idealistic rationalism—is necessarily untrue and relates to something that is necessarily unreal. is about something that is unreal, and is not about a real thing. The person will have been deceived either by religious tradition or the illusions that arise from man's own pride in himself.

The human mind, together with the knowledge it contains, is the product of nature as represented by heredity, environment, economic and social life. The mind is therefore created, but its creator is sensory existence. It thinks, but as a result of its interaction with the surrounding environment that both dominates and restricts it. Domination and restriction are the concomitants of material life. Man has no pre-existing intellect and no pre-existing knowledge; both intellect and knowledge are subordinate to man's material existence, and are like impresses made on his sensory being.

Nature speaks of itself, and humans must rely on its logic if they are to live in its realm. Only its logic can delineate the straight path of human life, not that of the theists, that of the rationalists, or that of the proponents of the psychological theory of human knowledge.

Moreover, the path of the human in his natural life begins with the individual and culminates in society. Hence, the individual is not an end in himself nor can his own life be the goal for all of his striving. In fact, the final aim for which he must strive, just like the Sufi devotee who believes in the essential identity of God and His creation, is the collectivity. Insofar as the collectivity is the ultimate goal of the individual, it is also the object of worship to which he sacrifices his liberty so that it, the collectivity, may remain free, and to which he devotes his life in order that it might endure.[17]

Marxism: Dialectical materialism. Marx conceived his materialist theory under the influence of Comte, one of the Positivist philosophers. He does not deny the existence of the mind as does the mechanistic school of materialism. Equally, however, he does not claim that matter existed prior to the existence of reason, simply that matter is more important than the mind, since the mind is existentially contingent on matter. The consequence of this is that Marx rejects not only the assertion made by religion that the mind (or the spirit) will endure after the body, but also the fundamental belief of religion—God as an everlasting being utterly independent of material existence. As an explicit fact: each religion, in principle, according to Marx, is therefore in and of itself a curse, and functions as "the opium of the people."

The dependence of mind on reason is depicted by Marx as follows: reason is a reflection of matter, contrary to what Hegel affirmed, namely, that matter is a reflection of reason. This connotes that reason is a kind of mirror that reflects material existence. This Marxian con-

---

17 And hence the degradation of the individual in the systems which were erected on the basis of this school, and the violation of all his individual and human fundamentals.

ceptualisation of material reality, namely, that it is the basis of every-thing, encompasses in Marxist logic all natural phenomena together with the multiplicity of standpoints to which they give rise; it is also the major material force. As for political, social and moral phenomena, they are a reflection of current economic phenomena. Although Marx and Engels discerned the meaning of history in social phenomena generally, they focused especially on the economic dimension among all the phenomena of life. It follows that economic conditions are the defining variables under all social conditions, and they constitute the ultimate impulses of all human action in the entire course of history.

Furthermore, it is changes in economic conditions alone that influence the life of the state and its policies, and the same holds true of science and religion. All cultural and cognitive production is thus a branch of economic life. And all of history, in fact, ought to be economic history.[18]

Such was the end result of the attempt to escape from the Church, its distorted religious concepts which had become intermeshed with human ideas, and its abuse of authority in the name of religion. Earlier it had led to the philosophy of Rationalist Idealism, with its many variations, including outright opposition to religion and the declaration of the supremacy of reason in the view of Fichte, and the advocacy of religion in the sense that according to Hegel, God Almighty is reason. Later, it led to the positivist philosophy as expounded by Comte, and ultimately to the dialectical materialism espoused by Karl Marx and his colleague Engels.

This prolonged path of deviance in European thought was a direct consequence of the distortion of religion arising from the formulations and concepts generated by Churches and successive councils as a means for them to exploit their authority.

A glance at the succession of stumbling paths followed by those who fled from God in order to disentangle themselves from the grasp of the Church shows that they failed to attain a sound result which might permit us to say, "this was their refuge from the riddles of metaphysics!"

For what sound knowledge was attained by rationalist idealist philosophy, for example? What is this "reason" which has been mustered to attain knowledge that is far removed from both God and nature?

---

[18] Taken from pages 283–317 of al-Bahi's book.

What does this philosophy know of the nature and characteristics of reason? And what does it know of its method of functioning, its influences? Where is this mind located? What is its nature, or its governing law? There are no adequate responses to these questions even in the twentieth century.

And what of the postulates presented by this philosophy as self-evident, on which it based all its assertions? Or the principle of contradiction on which Karl Marx came to rely? What is it? What is its real value? It is nothing but an abstract, intellectual proposition, not in any way consonant with reality.

Fichte utilized the principle of contradiction in the following manner.

"Every person begins with a concept of his own Self. The Self is sharply distinguished from the rest of the universe, the Not-Self, which it knows, but which is other than it. Thus the Self is also the Not-Self. But the existence of Not-Self is entirely dependent on the existence of Self and has no independent existence. Thus Self, which contains in itself Not-Self, is both Self and Not-Self.

"But the Not-Self has no reality. Whenever the human being looks into himself he is conscious of Self, and the things, which are outside the Self, i.e. the Not-Self, which are perceived by us as a separate reality, are but a product of mind.

"Hence, to start with, Self exists by itself and Not-Self does not exist. The Self (or mind) imposes its categories upon experience, and every object other than Self is a product of Self."

Now what determines with certainty that only "I" exists, and that "not I" does not exist to begin with, but is embedded in "I" and is its product?

What makes certain this postulate in reality? Nothing! It is simply a mental exercise on the part of Fichte undertaken in order to construct a school of thought. The whole basis of Rational Idealism has no connection at all with reality and no presence in human life. The Positivist school was justified in deriding this Idealism, which is unsupported by any real evidence and plays no role in human life, has no significance in reality, nor any efficacy in the life of people. However, the Positivists had nothing superior to offer themselves, for their own positions are still farther removed from the truth.

Although, as we have seen, the principle of contradiction has no correspondence to objective reality, Fichte considers it as the basis on which to establish that reason is the true existent, i.e., that the existence of which is not contingent on the existence of another reality.

The logic behind this principle, according to Fichte, is that reason is totally independent and exists for its own sake, its existence being its own, not the existence of another. The quiddity of reason then becomes evident through reason itself, and not through what is external to it, for if reason were contingent on what is external to it, then it would follow that "not I" is the point of departure.

That would involve a negation of reason itself, for the existence of "not I" would have no meaning other than the negation of the existence of "I," that is, of reason itself.[19].

What, however, determines in reality that the meaning of the existence of "not I" is the negation of the existence of "I"? And why such determinism? It is merely a proposition that is contradicted by the mind itself, when it disentangles itself from the restrictions imposed on it by this school of thought.

There is nothing, rationally speaking, that prevents "I" from existing while "not I" also exists, the existence of neither being contingent on the existence of the other.

What was at stake in all this was to create another god, other than the God of the church, a god without a clergy or cardinals, a pope or a church. "Reason" was made into a substitute god.

Likewise, Hegel utilized the principle of contradiction, but drawing on terms other than those used by Fichte.

While Fichte used the principle of dialectic in order to foster the supremacy of reason as a source of knowledge, as opposed to religion or nature, Hegel utilized the same principle to affirm the value of reason and simultaneously to advocate the idea of God anew; for he not only emphasized revelation as the ultimate source of truth but also made God coterminous with reason. Instead of the three terms used by Fichte in his dialectic to describe the three stages of thought, Hegel used his own threefold terminology of thesis, antithesis and synthesis.

"He conceived, in the ideational realm, that there is an absolute idea he termed absolute reason. This absolute reason has an eternal

---

[19] Ibid pp. 290–291.

and intrinsic existence that is prior to the creation of nature and prior to the creation of the finite mind. This absolute reason is God. Nature emanated from it while being distinct from it, given that it is remote and diffuse while absolute reason is one and unique and free of any restriction. With the existence of nature, the idea of absolute reason appeared, whilst its existence is contingent and finite.

Nature then is nothing other than the emergence of the "idea" from its first sphere. Therefore, it is both a necessity and an accident, and it does not entail freedom or choice. In this respect, it is the antithesis of the idea in absolute reason. And given that absolute reason is the thesis, then nature is the antithesis. Hence, the idea was changed from being absolute to being contingent, or from the antithesis to its opposite. The idea included its antithesis within itself. Nevertheless, the idea in nature strives anew to acquire its unity, after losing it because of the diffusion of beings contained within it. The realization thereof is abstract transcendent reason, which constitutes the final purpose of nature and combines within itself thesis and antithesis."[20]

This was one type of the Idealism which so distressed the Positivists of Europe. It dealt with abstract rational concepts in terms that do not correspond to objective reality and have no relation to real humans to real life.

However, the Positivists, when they denied first the God of the Church and then the god of reason, were no better guided themselves, for they created a god out of nature. But what is this nature? This nature, which supposedly created the mind and "imprints truth on the mind"? Is it a limited being or a universal essence? Or is it the totality of diffuse things such as bodies and forms and movements and appearances? Is it something with a reality independent from human perceptions? Or is it an image that is imprinted on the mind by means of the sensorily perceptible objects observable to man? Or is it something that has a truth in itself, so that what is impressed on the mind may or may not correspond to its reality?

And given that this nature is what created the human mind, is it a creator that creates from nothingness? And why then did it create mind or reason in man and not in other animals, or in plants? Does

---

[20] Al-Bahi, *al-fikr al-Islami al-hadith wa'ilaqatuhu bi'l-isti'mar al-gharbi*, pp. 293–295.

it possess a will capable of discrimination and choice, selecting one being from among all others to endow it with this unique gift?

Furthermore, if its reality is manifested only in human thought, is its appearance not contingent on the existence of the human mind? How then can nature be a creator of the mind, the mind on which it is dependent for its appearance?

In short, when referring to nature, these gentlemen are speaking of something amorphous and undefined.

What is nature? Is it the matter of the cosmos? If so, what is the essence of matter? It has become evident to them that what they used to term "matter" and regard as something stable in fact escapes definition. Matter dissolves and becomes rays. Are the rays identical with nature or with matter? Or is matter, or nature, simply the form embodying the rays? This god of nature is unquiet and unstable; it both moves and takes on different forms. In which one of its many states does it have the power to create the human mind? Is it also nature that creates its incessantly moving forms? From rays to atoms, from atoms to matter, and then from matter back to atoms, to rays! Life, living cells and the higher forms of life—how can this god create them and in which of its states? And who created the human whose mind nature created? Did it create it at the very outset or did it content itself with creating man's mind after finding him already existent?

If it is nature that imprints reality in the human mind, then why specifically the human mind? Does not nature speak and is it not heard by all living beings? Does it not imprint reality in the minds of mules, donkeys, parrots and monkeys? If so, are the facts which it imprints in the mind of the parrot or the monkey the same as those it imprints in the minds of Auguste Comte and Karl Marx?

And if it is nature that imprints reality in the human mind, then what actually counts as reality? Is it that the mind should decide that the earth is the center of the universe, or rather that the earth is simply a minor satellite of the sun? Is it the assertion that matter is solid and tangible or the assertion that matter is nothing but energy concentrated in ever-changing forms? Is it the conviction that nature is the product of the mind or the assertion that reason is nothing but an imprint left by matter?

Can all these rational conclusions be the reality which nature imprints upon the human mind? Is it subject to error in so doing, or does the mind itself distort the impression? And does the mind then possess an autonomous agency, an independent character, contrary to the assertion of the Positivists that it is nothing but what nature imprints?

We will address life, its origins and secrets, as depicted by the Islamic and other concepts, on a later occasion. Here we simply ask: what is this god offered us by the materialists? When we cannot perceive or apprehend any coherent sign of it in our minds or in external reality, why should we choose it or seek refuge in it? It is a void that escapes our touch, evades our vision, avoids the gaze of our intellect. [Unlike the Western thinkers] we—praise be to God—are not fleeing from the Church.

The transmutation to which Karl Marx and Engels subject human life, its essential impulses and the scope of its acivities, by confining it to the single arena of economics, becomes particularly repugnant when one ponders the greatness of the material universe itself, with all the remarkable provisions it makes for human life. This petty mode of thought cannot fail to arouse contempt and disgust, for it contradicts the feeling of awe which ought properly to be aroused by contemplating the sublimity of the universe and its consonance with the requirements of human life. Whoever adheres to this school of thought is in effect turning his back on all this awe-inspiring sublimity in order to imprison himself within the confines of economics and the means of production, conceived of not simply as the goal and motive of human activity but as the first cause, the creating deity, the ordering lord of creation.

We reiterate in conclusion that all these afflictions and problems, from start to finish, are due to the distortions inflicted by the Church and its councils on their concept of God, and the resulting endeavour of European thought to secede from the Church and its God. We praise God, therefore, that the Islamic concept has remained intact, that no Church was its custodian, and that no conflict occurred between its concept on the one hand and human reason and science on the other, a conflict which elsewhere has led man into a wilderness filled with debris.

We may mention here that the Islamic concept accords the human mind and knowledge broad scope of activity in all matters that lie beyond the basic concept and its fundamentals. It does not prevent reason from exploring the universe; on the contrary, it earnestly encourages such exploration. The Islamic concept in fact assigns vicegerency in the universe, within the context of the Divine paradigm, to the human mind and to human knowledge. From this we deduce the extent of God's benevolence and the mercy He has shown us first in bestowing on us this Divine concept, and then in preserving it as first revealed.

4

STABILITY

"And so, set thy face steadfastly towards the [one ever-true] faith,
turning away from all that is false, in accordance with the natural
disposition which God has instilled into man: [for,] not to allow any
change to corrupt what God has thus created—this is the [purpose
of the one] ever-true faith; but most people know it not."

(Ar-Rum: 30)

Divinity is the main characteristic of the Islamic concept from
which all other concepts originate. Since the Islamic concept is
divine and originates from God, it is the duty of all humanity to receive
it, respond to it, adapt to it and apply it in real life. It is not the product
of human thought, of a given environment, of a certain period or of
any other earthly factor, having been granted to man by his Creator as
a gift and a source of mercy. From this characteristic of the concept,
another property emerges, that of motion within a stable framework
around a stable pivot.

There is stability in the fundamentals and essential values of the
Islamic concept. The fundamentals do not change or evolve, as do the
external aspects of life and the forms of practical existence. Indeed,
the changes to which those aspects and forms are subject are the stable
fundamentals and values of the concept. This does not imply "freez-
ing" of the motion of thought or of life; indeed, it permits or even
encourages such motion to take place, albeit within a stable framework and around a stable pivot.

This combination of motion and stability marks the entirety of God's
handiwork in creation; it is not simply a trait of the Islamic concept.

The matter of this universe, whether it be the atom, the radiation that is released when the atom is destroyed, or any other matter, all has a stable essence that continues to move and assume constantly changing and evolving forms.

The atom has a fixed nucleus around which the electrons revolve in a fixed orbit. Each planet and star has its own orbit and axis around which it revolves in an orderly motion and is ruled by a certain law.

The humanity of man derives from the fact that he is a creature in whom God has inhaled His spirit, becoming distinguished thereby in his very nature from the rest of creation. The humanity of man is therefore stable and constant[21], although he passes through various biological phases from his beginning as a drop of sperm until he reaches old age. He also traverses various social phases that either elevate him or degrade him depending on his closeness to the source of his humanity. None of these phases or stages remove him from his fixed and stable nature as a human, nor from the impulses, capacities and potentialities proceeding from that nature.

This human desire for movement in order to change and develop terrestrial reality is likewise a stable and unchanging fact. It derives in the first place from the overall nature of the universe as manifested in the motion of primordial matter as well as the motion of the heavenly bodies. Second, it springs from the primordial nature of man himself, as necessitated by his function of divine vicegerent on earth. That function requires motion in order to develop and advance the terrestrial reality that surrounds man. human instinct, which is the required duty for succession on earth. The forms of this motion, however, are diverse, changing and constantly developing.[22]

"Motion within a stable framework and around a stable pivot" is therefore a hallmark of all of God's creation, and it follows that it should also be a prominent feature of the Islamic concept.

We will now set forth examples of the stable components and values of the Islamic concept; they represent the "stable pivot" around

---

21 Modern Darwinism is beginning to correct old Darwinism. It has been decided that the human being is a unique creature in his biological, intellectual and spiritual aspects, utterly separate from all other animals. There is still a step to be taken by the Darwinists: to recognize that man has had a fixed character from the very outset.

22 See Muhammad Qutb, Ma'rakat at-Taqalid.

which the Islamic approach rotates in its stable framework (they will be explained in depth in the second part of this research).

Everything that concerns the Divine reality, which is the basis for the Islamic concept, is a stable and immutable truth with a stable and immutable meaning.

The existence of God, His eternity and unity (in all of its different senses), His power, His sovereignty, His ordering of men's affairs, the absoluteness of His will, together with all the other attributes that relate to His governing the universe, life and mankind—these represent a stable and immutable truth.

It is similarly a stable and immutable truth that the whole universe with all its beings, animate and inanimate, is created by God. Thus God willed it, and so it was, and none had any share in His creation, nor in its ordering or administration, nor does any share in the attributes of divinity.

It is similarly a stable and immutable truth that worship belongs to God alone, the worship in which all of creation engages, including the prophets—peace be upon them.

It is similarly a stable and immutable truth that belief in God as He has described Himself to be, in His angels, books, and prophets (peace be upon them), the Last Day, and destiny, whether good or bad, is a condition for the validity and acceptability of people's actions and accepting them. Otherwise, they are fundamentally flawed, unredeemable, and rejected.

It is similarly a stable and immutable truth, a fact that God does not accept from men any religion He has not prescribed. The essential meaning of Islam is ascribing to God alone divinity and all of its properties; submitting to His will; and consenting to judging all things by His law and command. This and this only is the religion He approves.

It is similarly a stable and immutable truth that man as a species is a creature honored by God above all others; He has been entrusted as His vicegerent on earth and all things on earth have been subjugated to him. There is no material value on earth superior to this innate value of man or capable of diminishing it.

It is similarly a stable and immutable truth that all humans derive from a single origin, and accordingly they are all equal. The only value whereby they might attain precedence over each other is piety and good deeds, not any worldly value such as lineage, wealth, social position, class, or sex.

It is similarly a stable and immutable truth that the purpose of human existence is the worship of God, in the sense of absolute servitude to God alone with all that implies, such as obedience to His commands in all the affairs of life, large and small, in every intention, motion and deed.

It is similarly a stable and immutable truth that the principle of association among human beings is faith in the divine path rather than race, nation, colour, class, tribal affiliation, economic or political interests or any other worldly consideration.

It is similarly a stable and immutable truth that this world is the realm of labor and trial, and the next that of reckoning and requital. Man is being tried and tested in all that he does, in all the good or evil that befalls him, with every blessing and every misfortune, for all matters return ultimately to God.

These and similar truths and values are all stable and immutable, not liable to development; they are stable so that the phenomena of life and the forms of actuality may move within their framework while remaining linked to it, and their implications undergird all forms of human development, whether individual or collective.

The arena in which the meanings of these truths and values display themselves may expand just as the various aspects of human life and human knowledge expand. But their origin remains fixed and stable and all the meanings move within its framework.

For example, the truth that man acts as divine vicegerent on earth manifests itself in various ways. One form in which it shows itself is man cultivating the land, because the conditions of his life and the extent of his experiences make of agriculture a means sufficient for satisfying his needs at a certain stage, enabling him thereby to fulfil his function as vicegerent. Another form of its manifestation consists of man splitting the atom, or sending satellites into space to explore the nature of earth's atmosphere and the nature of the planets and their satellites. Both of these, as well as all that lies between them and beyond them, are forms assumed by man's vicegerent on earth, which is always capable of increase and expansion. However, the essence of man's vicegerent remains stable and fixed. Nothing on earth may elevate itself above man, for he is the master of the satellites and of all material production. of all productions.

The truth that the purpose of human existence is the worship of God is manifested in all the varied activities whereby man orients himself to God and which are necessitated by his expanding and constantly renewed function of vicegerent. Worship shows itself too in exclusive servitude to God by referring all matters to the criteria he has provided. The purpose itself never changes. If man does not orient himself to God in all his activities and he fails to refer all matters to the criteria God has provided, he will have violated this stable and immutable truth and transgressed against the purpose of his existence; his deeds will count as vain and unacceptable to the believer.

The value of having a stable concept of fundamentals and values is that it disciplines the progress and vital development of human life. It does not veer back and forth without guidance, as happened in the life of Europe when it cut loose from the moorings of belief and came to a miserable end, faintly disguised by a false glow and deceptive gleam that concealed misery, confusion, decadence, and degeneracy.

Its value also lies in providing man with a reliable scale in which to weigh the emotions, thoughts and concepts that occur to him, the various circumstances and relationships in which he finds himself involved. By weighing them in that scale, he sees how close he is to the right path or how distant from it. He thus remains at all times within the sphere of safety and does not wander into the wilderness where there are no fixed stars or waymarks to guide him.

Another value of the stable concept is that it tends to provide man's thought with a supportive or reinforcing element, preventing it from wavering under the impact of passions or extraneous influences. If there is no such supportive or reinforcing element, there can be no stability. Such an element is necessary to prevent human thought and life from giddily swaying with no direction.

It is an absolute need for the human soul and for human life that it should move within a stable framework and that it should rotate around a firm, unmoving pivot. This is the norm established and made manifest within the universe as a whole and which can be observed in all of the planets, which is that it moves within a fixed frame and around a fixed pivot. But this necessity is neglected today. Humanity has turned away from all fixed principles and let go of the reins that connected it to its pivot. It is like a planet tumbling from its sphere, disconnected from its orbit, liable to collide with another planet, thus destroying itself and ruining the whole universe.

> "But if the truth were in accord with their own likes and dislikes, the heavens and the earth would surely have fallen into ruin, and all that lives in them [would long ago have perished]!
>
> Nay, [in this divine writ] We have conveyed unto them all that they ought to bear in mind: and from this their reminder they [heedlessly] turn away!"   (Al-Mu'minun: 71)

Intelligent and alert is he who is not caught up in the dizziness of contemporary humanity. When he looks upon this luckless human race and sees the disastrous confusion pervading its concepts, its organizational forms, its traditions, its customs, it is as if he were watching some mentally confused person removing his clothes and ripping them apart, or someone deranged thrashing around in uncontrolled motion. Fashions change in thought and belief just as they do in dress, according to the dictates of the fashion houses. The observer of humanity sees before him a man howling in pain, running as if to escape, laughing like a madman, ranting like a drunkard, searching for some imaginary object, all the while throwing away his most precious possessions and embracing whatever filth his hands can scoop up!

A curse be upon such a state!

A curse like those related in myths!

The state that we have described kills the human being and transforms him into a tool in order to increase production. It does away with all the supports of his humanity, his appreciation of beauty, creativity, sublime meaning, in order to realize profits for a handful of usurers and traders in lust, film producers and fashion houses.

When you look at people's faces, their looks, their motions, their clothes, their thoughts, opinions and aspirations, it seems that they are fugitives or runaways who cannot settle on anything or pause to consider their state. Indeed they are fugitives, fleeing their own selves, their hungry, anxious, bewildered selves—selves that reject a stable axis and a stable framework. The human soul cannot, however, live in isolation from the order of the universe; it cannot attain happiness while in this state of constant flight, deprived of a guide and lacking all foundation!

Encircling this luckless humanity are those who benfit from the dominant confusion, this deadly bewilderment: a gang of usurers, film producers, makers of fashion, journalists and writers. Whenever humanity tires of its misery and begins to stumble, yearning for a return to a stable and fixed pivot, they call out for more lunacy, more bweilderment, more dizziness! The slogans they voice are "development," "freedom," "innovation," all this without any limit or regulating principle. It is in the name of these that they push humanity farther into the wilderness.

This is a crime, a repellent crime against all humanity, against this ill-fated generation.[23]

The idea of unfettered development, under all circumstances, with respect to all values and the fundamental concept from which those values derive, contradicts the clear principle of which both the universe and man's primordial nature are founded. It is from this contradiction that corruption inevitably arises, for the notion of unfettered development grants the right to exist, and justifies the existence of, every concept, every value, every state, every system, simply because it exists in historical time. Mere historical existence is a weak and superficial justification, one carrying no weight in the judging of concepts, values, or systems, for decisive is the actual content of those concepts, values and systems.

We know that European thought, in its flight from the Church and the desire, both hidden and apparent, to be free of its yoke, was inclined to negate in general any idea of stability and substituted for it the idea of comprehensive, unrestrained development, not sparing religious belief or law. On the contrary, it was precisely the concept of stability in the fundamental elements of belief and law that Europe wished to be rid of.

We can fully understand these tendencies in Western concept in light of our previous discussion; it can be explained, although not justified. However, our emphasis here is not on blaming Western thought in this respect, even though the position it asuumes is erroneous and defective, for after all, the religious belief it encountered had been

---

[23] For more detail, see my *al-Islam wa Mushkilat al-Hadara*.

distorted, perverted, and corrupted with pagan elements, and the Church was both tyrannical and corrupt, dominating intellectual and scientific life in the name of the superstitions that were its "fixed and stable belief."

Blaming Western thought is not, then, our emphasis. We insist rather on drawing attention to the real reasons for its tendency, or better to say its insistence, on vindicating the principle of absolute, unfettered development, not bound by any fixed principle, value or truth. What is at issue here is not "scientific truth" but a lustful obstinacy, an errant desire, fuelled by the desire to escape the grasp of the tyrannical Church.

While Darwin was laying down the principles of evolution, his researches embraced only a superficial and minute portion of the universe. They began after the beginning of life, and did not extend back to the source of life, or the will from which life emerged. Even if we assume the accuracy of this theory (and it is now under attack in its very core)[24], the very course of evolution itself proves that there is a firm will behind it, that it unfolds according to a fixed plan that does not allow for chance or coincidence. "Evolution" is part of motion, which is one of the laws of the universe, and motion, as we have said before, is not chaotic, for it takes place around a stable pivot and within a stable framework.

In any event, it was not the scientific method or scientific facts which compelled Darwin, when he could not discover the secret of life or account for it scientifically, to refrain from attributing it to God. The existence of life compels the admission that there is one who brings it into existence, and the orderliness of its progress and its harmony with the universe compels the further admission that the one who brought into existence must be possessed of will and choice, precise and complete knowledge, fully able to accomplish whatever he wills. Darwin, however, was fleeing from God, because he was fleeing from the Church and the god in whose name it was acting. He then attributed life to nature, which in his opinion has unlimited powers. He tried to propagate the illusion that there is no stability in absolutely anything at all, even though the entirety of his whole research revolved around the course of

---

[24] See Julian Huxley, *Man and Modern Science,* and Chrissy Morrison, *Man Cannot Stand Alone.*

life once it had come into being; he most certainly did not discuss abso-lutely "everything."[25]

The Marxist ideology is the most extreme of the "objective" ide-ologies that oppose the truth of movement within a fixed, stable frame-work and around a stable pivot. The acknowledgment of such an evident truth concerning the nature of the material universe would rob the ide-ology of its first pillar and nullify its claim to "progressiveness."

"Marx makes use of the dialectical logic of thesis and antithesis used by previous German philosophers such as Nietzsche and Hegel. However, Marx's approach differed from the "imaginative" approach of Nietzsche or the "ideal" one of Hegel; he applied it to economics in the history of human society.

"According to Marx, everything contains its opposite within itself, so that everything ultimately destroys itself: this is the general scheme of the antithesis. Marx used it to prove the inevitable ruin of societ-ies based on capitalism. Accodring to him, previous societies—monar-chical or feudal—were destroyed because they contained the element of contradiction within them, and capitalist society will be similarly destroyed by turning into its opposite—communist society with its single class of laborers.

"Now the principle of contradiction does more than transforming something into its opposite; the thing and its opposite are both trans-formed into something that embraces them both. Then that "some-thing" becomes in turn a thing which is transformed into opposite, and so on and so forth. Thus the logic underlying the principle is one of permanent transformation. However, Marxism restricts itself to the transformation of society, and it does not speak of, or anticipate the collapse and destruction of communist society or its transformation into its opposite, even though everything is supposed to contain its opposite which cause its ultimate demise.

"As a result of all this (the continuous transformation which Marx arbitrarily brings to an end with communism), anyone who affirms everlasting values believes in something that does not exist. Even those who believe that certain values pertaining to current times and situa-tions should be preserved are engaged in the affirmation of the unreal,

---

[25] See Muhammad Qutb, *al-Insan bayna al-Maddiyya wa 'l-Islam*, and *Ma'rakat al-Taqalid*.

for if one believes that everything changes it would be simple-minded to call for its preservation.

Similar to Hegel's formation of the antithetical principle, Marxism explains that everything contains within itself two opposing forces: the thesis and the antithesis, which destroy each other. From their ruins arises a new state, the synthesis which combines the thesis and the antithesis, which in turn becomes a new thesis, ripe for destruction by its antithesis. Thus the cycle begins anew, without any end in sight.[26]

"This is the formula that Marxism applies to society, giving rise to the concept of the class struggle on which Marxism insists as a distinctive part of its terminology, in place of the notion of antithesis espoused by Nietszche and Hegel. It is the principle of antithesis or contradiction applied to society that permits Marxism to claim that communism is more exalted in its values than any previous society. Societies with a monarchical system collapse and are transformed into their antitheses: societies with the king and his agents on the one hand and slaves and the poor on the other, from the struggle between these two elements arises a new synthesis: feudal society. Feudal society in turn collapses into its antithesis: the power of the landlords on the one hand and the peasants on the other. Their struggle results in the rise of capitalism. Marxism proclaims that capitalism will collapse into its antithesis: the power of the workers on one hand and that of the employers on the other, and from their struggle will arise Marxist society, socialist and classless.

"But does the antithetical principle stop with this new society? Or will it in turn also collapse into its antithesis, as the logic of the principle necessitates?"

"Marxism teaches that the evolution of society from one stage to the next is accompanied by an evolution of value. Therefore, feudalism is more advanced than monarchy; capitalism is more advanced than feudalism, and communism is more advanced than capitalist societies.

"The claim that each society is better than its predecessor is a great resource for communist propaganda; many people become fol-

---

[26] As we have seen, Marxism terminates its own law when it wishes, allowing it to operate only until the establishment of communism. This is meant to be a form of scientific thought!.

lowers of communism in the belief that they are working for a society better than any that ever existed."[27]

It is apparent from this presentation of Marxist fundamentals that Marxism is based not on reality but on the arbitrary desire to achieve certain results.

The principle of antithesis began as a purely imaginary and mental concept in the philosophy of Nietzsche and Hegel, and had nothing to do with reality, as we mentioned before. When Karl Marx applied it to the history of human society, he deliberately excluded all the components of human society that might undergo transformation with the exception of economics, a component which for all its importance clearly does not represent society as a whole.

Marx chooses, moreover, to focus on the history of a single society—European society—and selects certain points in that history. Now it is impossible for an individual, in whatever generation it might be, to discern all the factors and influences that play a decisive role in the history of a given society throughout its history, so he arbitrarily selects one type of human activity and neglects all the rest. Then, in a further piece of arbitrariness, he proclaims that every stage of human society is better in all respects than the preceding one, but stops the wheel of progress when it comes to communism; indeed, he wants to bring history itself to an end.

Despite the incoherence of Marxism and the arbitrariness on which it is based, its dismissal of fixed, stable values has come to contaminate not only its adherents but also its adversaries in Europe and America: whatever came before is discarded, and whatever newly occurs is embraced. The contamination lies, too, in dissolving all values that stand in the way of untrammelled satisfaction of the lusts, in mocking all fixed values, ethical or other. Behind this contamination stands a specific goal of Marxism; it is this that constitutes the essence of Marxism, for Marxism is not the logical result of some scientific study.

The idea of unfettered, limitless development is simply a justification for whatever one might wish to do. It is a justification for what the state wishes to do with the individual, for once there is no fixed principle or stable value where the individual might seek refuge when confronted with the state, he has no fixed rights or code to which he might

---

[27] Al-Bahi, *al-Fikr al-Islami al-Hadith*, pp. 311–315.

appeal. And just as the state is freed of any restrictions in dealing with the individual, the state frees the individual of all limits in the indulgence of his animal desires, by way of compensation for the values, liberties, and rights of which he has been deprived. This freedom of indulgence corresponds exactly to the tyrannical freedom state power grants itself. Instead of this deal remaining tacit between the parties, a matter of convention, it is placed on a "philosophical" or "scientific" basis, namely the principle of dialectical materialism.

This is the ideology that claims that religion is an opium and that stability of values in religion is intended to serve the ruling class.

The stability that characterizes the fundamentals and values of the Islamic concept, in addition to being an extension of the general order of the universe, guarantees for the life of Islam the principle of "motion within a fixed framework around a fixed pivot," thus bringing Islamic life and thought into harmony with the entire universe. It thereby protects Islam from the corruption that would befall the universe as a whole were it to be prey to the whims and passions of man, without any restraint or firm basis.

Stability is what preserves Islamic thought and society from the contamination that has afflicted Marxist thought and Communist societies; it is the same contamination that has befallen Western thought and societies in general.

Stability infuses the Muslim mind and Muslim society with tranquillity, the tranquillity that results from having a stable framework and a fixed pivot. The Muslim is thus aware that he is moving forward with firm steps along a continuous line stretching from yesterday through today to tomorrow, in constant growth and ascent, guided in all this by divine power.

Finally, this stability is what guarantees a Muslim fixed principles in his social life, principles to which both he and his rulers are subject. They are not left free to violate his freedoms and his rights in exchange for the masses, trampled beneath the boots of tyranny, having the freedom to indulge in their passions and animal desires.

The Islamic concept is based on the fact that there are two situations in human life in the evaluation of which time and place play no role; the value—or lack thereof—is intrinsic to the situation itself and weighed in God's unchanging scales.

Two situations alternating in human life at all times and in all places: guidance or misguidance, whatever form misguidance may assume; truth and falsehood, whatever form falsehood may assume; light and darkness, whatever form darkness may assume; divine law and human whim, whatever form whim may assume; Islam and Jahiliyya, whatever form Jahiliyya may assume; belief and unbelief, whatever form unbelief may assume. In short, either commitment to Islam as a religion, as a way of life and a social order, or unbelief, Jahiliyya, ignorant desires, darkness, falsehood, and misguidance.

> "Behold, the only [true] religion in the sight of God is [man's] self-surrender unto Him; and those who were vouchsafed revelation aforetime took, out of mutual jealousy, to divergent views [on this point] only after knowledge [thereof] had come unto them.
>
> But as for him who denies the truth of God's messages—behold—God is swift in reckoning!"   (Al-'Imran: 19)

> "For, if one goes in search of a religion other than self-surrender unto God, it will never be accepted from him, and in the life to come he shall be among the lost."   (Al-'Imran: 85)

> "Seeing that He is God, your Sustainer, the Ultimate Truth? For, after the truth [has been forsaken], what is there [left] but error? How, then, can you lose sight of the truth?"   (Yunus: 32)

> "And finally, [O Muhammad,] We have set thee on a way by which the purpose [of faith] may be fulfilled: so follow thou this [way], and follow not the likes and dislikes of those who do not know [the truth]."   (Al-Jathiyah: 18)

> "And [know] that this is the way leading straight unto Me: follow it, then, and follow not other ways, lest they cause you to deviate from His way.
>
> [All] this has He enjoined upon you, so that you might remain conscious of Him."   (Al-An'am: 153)

> "God is near unto those who have faith, taking them out of deep darkness into the light—whereas near unto those who are bent on denying the truth are the powers of evil that take them out of the

light into darkness deep: it is they who are destined for the fire,
therein to abide."   (Al-Baqarah: 257)

"Verily, it is We who bestowed from on high the Torah, wherein
there was guidance and light. On its strength did the prophets, who
had surrendered themselves unto God, deliver judgment unto those
who followed the Jewish faith; and so did the [early] men of God
and the rabbis, inasmuch as some of God's writ had been entrusted
to their care; and they [all] bore witness to its truth.

Therefore, [O children of Israel,] hold not men in awe, but
stand in awe of Me; and do not barter away My messages for a trifling gain: for they who do not judge in accordance with what God
has bestowed from on high are, indeed, deniers of the truth!"
                                                      (Al-Ma'idah: 44)

"Do they, perchance, desire [to be ruled by] the law of pagan ignorance? But for people who have inner certainty, who could be a better law-giver than God?"   (Al-Ma'idah: 50)

"O you who have attained to faith! Pay heed unto God, and pay heed
unto the Apostle and unto those from among you who have been
entrusted with authority: and if you are at variance over any matter,
refer it unto God and the Apostle, if you [truly] believe in God and
the Last Day. This is the best [for you], and best in the end."
                                                      (An-Nisa': 59)

Thus if the framework be stable, life—ideas, concepts, the social
order—can move within it freely and flexibly and respond to every
authentic development deriving from the general concept.

The greatest value of the characteristic of stability is making firm
the basis on which the concepts and consciousness of the Muslim rest;
Islamic life and society thus enjoy stability while being free to pursue the natural growth of ideas and conditions. They do not stagnate
within a dead, iron grasp, such as that exercised by the Church in the
Middle Ages, nor do they wander free of all restraint, like a doomed
star falling from its orbit, as happened in modern European history,
resulting in the deformed ideology that is Marxism.

It may well have been this characteristic that guaranteed the
Islamic society its cohesion and power for a thousand years despite all
the shoscks, blows and savage attacks upon it from the enemies surrounding it on every hand. It began to rupture and weaken only when

it excluded this characteristic from its worldview, and its enemies succeeded in replacing the commands of Islam with those of the West.[28]

There is no doubt that a society that is constantly pursuing ever-changing concepts has no stable basis on which to rely. The knowledge that is founded on human thought, which by nature can attain only cognition that is limited and suppositional, is bound to rest on supposition, speculation, and constantly changing hypotheses. This suppositional knowledge is then turned into a god, from which concepts, values and criteria are derived.

There is no doubt that such a society is always in danger of violent commotions and constant instability resulting in confused minds, anxious consciences, exhausted nerves, and pervasive corruption.

This is what befell European societies cut loose from any stable principle and now afflicts all of humanity as it strays into the wilderness in the wake of European society.

There is a need for a concept that has fixed fundamentals and values, deriving from a fixed source of knowledge and will. This source must see the whole picture, must be aware of the twists and turns; he cannot decree something today that will turn out to be wrong tomorrow; he cannot be subject to passion or desire, interfering in his estimations and decrees. Then there would be no harm in motion, change, development, growth and progress. On the contrary, they would be desirable and salubrious, in accord with human nature. Motion and change would then be correctly guided and conscious, aware of the fixed aim after which it strives, advancing towards it with measured steps.

We need take no precautions against stagnation in an iron grasp if we hold fast to the principle of "motion within a stable framework around a fixed pivot" that characterizes the Islamic concept. The danger of stagnation does not exist, because motion is the fundamental principle, just as it is in the universe, which after all is stagnant but is engaged in constant motion, change and development, being reconstituted each moment. All of this is combined, however, with the preservation of its essential nature.

When we examine Western schools of thought, we observe as their dominating characteristic the notion of absolute "development"

---

[28] See Muhammad Qutb, *Hal Nahnu Muslimun ?*.

without referring to any fixed origin. We must be aware of the historical factors that lie at the origin of this characteristic, namely a profound hostility towards religious modes of thought and the reasons for that hostility. We must be aware, too, that the paths followed by these schools of thought, with the hostility to religion that cannot be detached from them, are unsuitable for use in connection with our studies of Islam.

Some of us borrow from Western thought either its methods or the conclusions it reaches, like scraps of paper torn out of a book. Then we mix them into our discussions of Islam, thought, and society. The result is ignorance paraded as knowledge, with stupidity and malice sometimes added as extra ingredients.

In his book *Islam at the Crossroads*, Muhammad Asad, the former Leopold Weiss, writes as follows:

"History tells us that all human culture and civilizations are organic entities and resemble living beings. They experience all the phases through which organic life is bound to pass: they are born, they have youth, ripe age, and at the end comes decay, like plants that wither and fall to dust. Cultures die at the end of their time and give room to other, freshly born ones.

"Is this the case with Islam? It would appear so at a first superficial look. No doubt, Islamic culture has had its splendid rise and its blossoming age, and it had the power to inspire men to great deeds and sacrifice. It transformed nations and changed the face of the earth, and later it stood still and became stagnant. And then it became an empty word, so that at present we witness its utter debasement and decay. But is this all?

"If we believe that Islam is not a mere culture among many others, not a mere outcome of human thoughts and endeavours, but a Law decreed by God Almighty to be followed by humanity at all times and everywhere, then one's perspective changes totally. If Islamic culture is or was the result of our following a revealed law, we can never admit that, like other cultures, it is chained to the lapse of time and limited to a particular period. What appears to be the decay of Islam is in reality nothing but the death and emptiness of our hearts which are too idle and too lazy to hear the eternal voice. No sign is available that mankind, in its present stature, has outgrown Islam. It has not been able to produce a better system of ethics than that expressed in Islam. It has not been able to put the idea of human brotherhood on a practical footing, as Islam did in its supra-national concept of *ummah*. It has not been able to create a social structure in which the conflicts and frictions among its members are as efficiently reduced to a minimum as in the social plan of Islam. And it has not been able to enhance the dignity of man, his feeling of security, his spiritual hope, and last, but surely not least, his happiness.

"In all these things the present achievements of the human race fall considerably short of the Islamic program. Where, then is the justification for saying that Islam is "out of date?" Is it only because its foundations are purely religious, and religious orientation is out of fashion today? But if we see that a system based on religion in the Islamic sense of *din* has been able to evolve a practical program of life more complete, more concrete, and more congenial to man's constitution than any other thing the human mind has been able to produce by way of reforms and proposals, is not precisely this a very weighty argument in favour of the enlightened, religious outlook?

"Islam, we have every reason to believe, has been fully vindicated by the positive achievements of man and indeed pointed them out as desirable long before they were attained. Equally, it has been vindicated by the shortcomings, errors, and pitfalls of human development, because it loudly and clearly warned against them long before mankind recognized them as errors. Quite apart from one's religious beliefs, there is, from a purely intellectual view-point, every inducement to follow confidently the practical guidance of Islam.

"We need not 'reform' Islam, as some Muslims think, for it is already perfect in itself. What we must reform is our attitude toward religion, our laziness, our self-conceit, our shortsightedness, in one word, our defects, and not some supposed defects of Islam.

"Islam as a spiritual and social institution, cannot be 'improved.' In these circumstances, any change in its conceptions or its social organization caused by the intrusion of foreign cultural influences is in reality retrograde and destructive, and therefore to be deeply regretted. A change there must be, but a change from within ourselves, and it should go in the direction of Islam, and not away from it."[29]

---

[29] Muhammad Asad, *Islam at the Crossroads*, pp. 150–155.

We say that that loss affects not only us Muslims, but all mankind. It affects mankind by polluting and distorting the only source of God's guidance still left for mankind, by muddying or poisoning the only source from which pure divine guidance is to be had. It affects mankind by depriving it of a fixed, stable focus, on this trembling earth that sways with vain desires, on which corruption has appeared, on dry land and sea, thanks to the deeds of men.[30] The sole refuge left for mankind is the fixed and stable path that leads to God.

People who try to shake this refuge in the name of renewal, reform, or development, or becoming emancipated from the remnants of the Middle Ages or some similar slogan, are our real enemies. They are enemies of the entire human race. They are the ones we should pursue and ask the entire human race to pursue.

They talk in the name of "progress" and against "reaction," while they are still feeding off the intellectual output of the 18th or 19th centuries, (the European output, that is, not theirs). They have not caught up with the output of the 20th century, and are at least half a century behind in their ideas. They are unaware that an intellectual movement opposing Marxism has become a widespread phenomenon in European thought while they were worshipping the dialectical materialism of Marxism and its offshoots, not to mention Darwinism and its derivatives. In reality, they are reactionaries claiming to be progressives. True progressivism today requires a return to religion, where tranquillity, certainty and peace are to be found, after the confusion, anxiety and perplexity of the last three centuries.

God has protected us from the evil of all these historical circumstances that made the Western thought go astray in ignorant deviation. We would be the most foolish of the foolish if we were to go astray in similar fashion, but by choice, without the excuse of historical factors.

We would not only be squandering ourselves in the wilderness, but cause all mankind to lose the stable refuge to which it may one day turn in order to find security, assurance and stability, after so much bewilderment, anxiety and confusion.

Let us therefore, appreciate the weight of our responsibility, not only toward ourselves, but towards the whole of mankind.

---

30 The last part of this sentence is a paraphrase of *Qur'an*, 30 :41.

5

COMPREHENSIVENESS

"For of all things do We take account in a record clear."

(Ya Sin: 12)

The third characteristic of the Islamic concept is comprehensiveness. It derives from its first characteristic, namely divinity. It is created by God and not by humans, and comprehensiveness is a trait of whatever God creates.

By contrast, man's existence is limited in regard to time and place, for he is created at a given point in time, starting from nothing and ending once his created existence is exhausted. He is restricted to a given place, whether as an individual, a generation, or a race; he cannot be in more than one place at any given time, nor can he transcend place in general. He can exist only in a given time, and he cannot transcend time as such. Man is similarly limited with respect to knowledge, experience, and perception. His knowledge begins after he comes into existence, and the extent of it is determined by the temporal and spatial limitations to which he is subject. In addition to all this, he is subject to weakness, to desire, to wishes and passions, to deficiency and ignorance.

Whenever human beings, beset by these circumstances, think of establishing for themselves a creedal concept or a way of life for themselves, the result will inevitably bear the same marks as their own existence. Their thoughts are particular, in the sense that they are suitable for a certain time but not for another, for a certain place but not for another, for a certain situation but not for another, for a certain level but not for another. They do not treat a matter from all its angles and aspects, with all its connections and implications, all its components and causes, for all of these extend out in time and space, in relations of cause and effect, beyond the being of man and the scope of his perception. Add to this the fact that human thought is beset with weakness and arbitrariness.

It is therefore impossible that any idea or path for life elaborated by man should be truly comprehensive; it is bound to be partial, resulting in deficiency, or temporary, resulting in confusion and the ineluctable need for change. This, in fact, is the explanation for the theory of contradiction and dialectic which emerged in the history of European thought. When, however, it is God Almighty Who elaborates the creedal concept and the way of life that springs from it, they will be free from the weakness, deficiency, fallibility and mutability that accompany human strivings. It is for this reason that comprehensiveness is one of the characteristics of the Islamic concept.

This characteristic displays itself in various forms.

One of these most important is attributing the whole of existence—its first emergence, every motion thereafter, every emanation, every alternation, change and development—together with its sovereignty and control, its direction and coordination, to the will of the Divine Essence, the Perpetual, Immortal, Eternal, and Absolute. This essence is endowed with will and absolute power; He originates the universe and everything within it, every living being, every motion, every change, every development and transformation, in accordance with His decree and purely through the orientation to it of His will. It is God Who created this universe and Who through His will brings about every change.

This is the most important aspect of the doctrine of God's oneness, that on which the whole Islamic concept rests, and much of the Qur'an is taken up by its exposition; we cannot cite all the relevant verses here. Some will be cited later in this book in our chapters on "positivism" and the oneness of God as characteristics of the Islamic concept. Here we will content ourselves with an attempt to understand the value of this characteristic.

In the first place, it provides us with a comprehensible interpretation of the universe as a whole, its origin and its development. More particularly, it provides us with a comprehensible explanation for the origin of the phenomenon of life in solid matter, for life is without doubt something other than matter, and cannot be regarded as one of its dimensions.

From the outset of his own existence, man is confronted with the existence of the universe, and he seeks to understand and interpret it. He is confronted with its symmetry, and balance, the wondrous coordination of its parts with its whole, none of which could be explained as accidental, for accident itself is governed by laws that are incompatible with such coordination.

Man's own life confronts him with many questions that are at least as profound as those raised by the existence of the universe, if not more so. For example, how did life appear in a dead substance? How was it set in motion, and how does it continue to move in this wondrous fashion, surrounded by thousands of correspondences and precise calculations?

The Islamic concept alone is able to give a clear explanation of all these correspondences in the structure of the universe. It alone can answer our questions about the origins and development of the universe. It alone can explain the emergence of life from a dead substance, without demanding of us that we avoid asking a single question or that we assign the origins of life to some ill-defined entity like "nature."

This distance between existence and non-existence is one the human mind has difficulty in travelling. How did this world come into being? How did nature come into being, if by nature material existence is intended? How can the human mind travel this great distance unless it attributes the origin of existence to a creative will, a will which says to a thing, "be," and it is.[31] If one does not acknowledge this creative will, he will be completely incapable of explaining or interpreting anything and he will be reduced to speculation, just as the philosophers have been through the ages.

The distance between solid matter and the living cell is a corollary of the distance between existence and non-existence. It, too, is a great distance which the human mind cannot travel unless it attributes the emergence of the living cell to the same creative will that creates whatever it wishes, the divine will "that gives to all things their created form and then guides them" (Qur'an, 20:50).

The human mind and human existence find assurance in this answer, because it provides an escape from the notion life comes to

---

[31] An allusion to *Qur'an*, 36:82.

dead matter from another source that is dead and lacking in life, for something that lacks life itself cannot give it to others. We cannot say that life is a property of matter, hidden within it, for if that were so, why should it remain hidden for uncountable years to appear at a specific time, without one administering it and without any clear purpose?

Let this brief account of the matter suffice for our present purposes; we will speak of it in greater detail at a later point. We will now return to the characteristic of comprehensiveness which shows itself in the attributing of all things in the universe to God, His all-embracing will and sovereignty. Let us cite some of the Qur'anic verses which express this characteristic.

> "BEHOLD, everything have We created in due measure and proportion."   (Al-Qamar: 49)

> "He to whom the dominion over the heavens and the earth belongs, and who begets no offspring, and has no partner in His dominion: for it is He who creates every thing and determines its nature in accordance with [His own] design."   (Al-Furqan: 2)

> "God knows what any female bears [in her womb], and by how much the wombs may fall short [in gestation], and by how much they may increase [the average period]: for with Him everything is [created] in accordance with its scope and purpose."   (Ar-ra'd: 8)

> "He replied: "Our Sustainer is He who gives unto everything [that exists] its true nature and form, and thereupon guides it [towards its fulfilment]."   (Taha: 50)

> "Whenever We will anything to be, We but say unto it Our word "Be"—and it is."   (An-Nahl: 40)

> "VERILY, your Sustainer is God, who has created the heavens and the earth in six aeons, and is established on the throne of His almightiness. He covers the day with the night in swift pursuit, with the sun and the moon and the stars subservient to His command: oh, verily, His is all creation and all command. Hallowed is God, the Sustainer of all the worlds!"   (Al-A'raf: 54)

> "And [of Our sway over all the exists] they have a sign in the night: We withdraw from it the [light of] day—and lo! they are in darkness.

And [they have a sign in] the sun: it runs in an orbit of its own—[and] that is laid down by the will of the Almighty, the All-Knowing: and [in] the moon, for which We have determined phases [which it must traverse] till it becomes like an old date–stalk, dried-up and curved: [and] neither may the sun overtake the moon, nor can the night usurp the time of day, since all of them float through space [in accordance with Our laws]."   (Ya Sin: 37–40)

"And it is God who has created all animals out of water; and [He has willed that] among them are such as crawl on their bellies, and such as walk on two legs, and such as walk on four.

God creates what He wills: for, verily, God has the power to will anything."   (An-Nur: 45)

"ARE, THEN, they who are bent on denying the truth not aware that the heavens and the earth were [once] one single entity, which We then parted asunder?—and [that] We made out of water every living thing? Will they not, then, [begin to] believe?" (Al-Anbiya': 30)

"VERILY, God is the One who cleaves the grain and the fruit-kernel asunder, bringing forth the living out of that which is dead, and He is the One who brings forth the dead out of that which is alive. This, then, is God: and yet, how perverted are your minds!

[He is] the One who causes the dawn to break; and He has made the night to be [a source of] stillness, and the sun and the moon to run their appointed courses: [all] this is laid down by the will of the Almighty, the All-knowing.

And He it is who has set up for you the stars so that you might be guided by them in the midst of the deep darkness of land and sea: clearly, indeed, have We spelled out these messages unto people of [innate] knowledge!

And He it is who has brought you [all] into being out of one living entity, and [has appointed for each of you] a time-limit [on earth] and a resting-place [after death]: clearly, indeed, have we spelled out these messages unto people who can grasp the truth!

And He it is who has caused waters to come down from the sky; and by this means have We brought forth all living growth, and out of this have we brought forth verdure. Out of this do We bring forth close-growing grain; and out of the spathe of the palm tree, dates in thick clusters; and gardens of vines, and the olive tree, and the pomegranate: [all] so alike, and yet so different! Behold their fruit

when it comes to fruition and ripens! Verily, in all this there are messages indeed for people who will believe!"   (Al-An'am: 95–99)

Even with respect to events that have clear proximate causes, the
Qur'an refers their ultimate causation back to God's will:

"IT IS WE who have created you, [O men:] why, then do you not
accept the truth?

Have you ever considered that [seed] which you emit? Is it you
who create it—or are We the source of its creation?

We have [indeed] decreed that death shall be [ever-present]
among you: but there is nothing to prevent Us from changing the
nature of your existence and bringing you into being [anew] in a
manner [as yet] unknown to you.

And [since] you are indeed aware of the [miracle of your] coming into being in the first instance—why, then, do you not bethink
yourselves [of Us]?

Have you ever considered the seed which you cast upon the soil?
Is it you who cause it to grow—or are We the cause of its growth?
[For,] were it Our will, we could indeed turn it into chaff, and you
would be left to wonder [and to lament,] "Verily, we are ruined!
Nay, but we have been deprived [of our livelihood]!"

Have you ever considered the water which you drink? Is it you
who cause it to come down from the clouds—or are We the cause of
its coming down?

[It comes down sweet—but] were it Our will, We could make
it burningly salty and bitter: why, then, do you not give thanks
[unto Us]?

Have you ever considered the fire which you kindle? Is it you
who have brought into being the tree that serves as its fuel—or are
We the cause its coming into being?

It is We who have made it a means to remind [you of Us], and
a comfort for all who are lost and hungry in the wilderness [of their
lives].

Extol, then, the limitless glory of thy Sustainer's mighty name!"
                                              (Al-Waqi'ah: 57–74)

"And yet, [O believers,] it was not you who slew the enemy, but
it was God who slew them; and it was not thou who cast [terror into
them, O Prophet], when thou didst cast it, but it was God who cast
it: and [He did all this] in order that He might test the believers by

a goodly test of His Own or—daining. Verily, God is all-hearing,
all–knowing!" (Al-Anfal: 17)

We cannot extend here our discussion of the characteristic of comprehensiveness as it manifests itself in the oneness of God; we will address it further at a later point. Enough to say that it bestows tranquillity and assurance on the mind and the heart by depicting the unique and ultimate nature of the causes at work in the universe, and protects man from wandering guideless in the wilderness, from assigning the origins of life to unproven, often non-existent, entities, to nature, the intellect, to mythical beings as conceived by idolatrous creeds and adopted by philosophies throughout history.

In addition to the moral element which this concept creates and establishes in the heart and life of mankind, it gathers all the threads of the universe and places them in God's hand, His control and safekeeping.

Another form taken by the characteristic of comprehensiveness is that in just the same way that it treats of the essence, characteristics, effects and attributes of divinity, as the primary and supreme truth, it also discusses the nature of the servitude to God that permeates both the universe and human life. It expounds the nature of the universe, of life and of man; their origin, attributes, and conditions; the relations that exist among them; and finally the connection that links them all to the supreme divine reality.

It joins all this together in a single, logical concept, one appealing to man's essential nature, interacting with his mind and his conscience, with the totality of his being, easily and painlessly.

As a result of the comprehensiveness of the concept, there thus emerges a compendium of truths, precise, detailed, extensive, and complete, an all-embracing interpretation that neither needs anything added to it from another source nor can accept it. For it is more capacious and complete, more precise and profound, more coherent and harmonious, than any other source.

However, corruption has entered into the Islamic concept. Complexity and confusion arose when a group of people known as "Islamic philosophers" borrowed certain concepts from Greek philosophy and terms from Aristotle, Plotinus and the Christian theologians, and merged them with the Islamic concept.

This concept, with its comprehensiveness, extensiveness, precision, depth, authenticity and coherence, does not accept alien elements, even if the element in question be simply a technical term necessitated by the garb of alien thought. All technical terms and expressions have a certain history with implications and associations deriving from that history that cannot be shed by placing the expression in a new context separate from its historical one. The Islamic concept has its own special terms that conform to the nature of its linguistic derivation and its historical associations and implications. that have their own nature and suggestions. This is a subtle matter, requiring care both in understanding the concept and in expressing it.

The concept is based primarily on making God known to men in a way that is precise, complete, and comprehensive. It brings to their attention His essence, His attributes, and the unique characteristics of His divinity, all of which distinguish Him from His servants. It informs them too of the effects of that divinity in the universe and in mankind, in all living peoples and worlds. All of this is undertaken on a very large scale in the Qur'an, so that the divine existence becomes for the human soul a sure existence, clear, inspiring and effective. It takes hold of the soul and binds it to itself in such a way that it cannot break from it, forget or ignore it, because it constantly confronts the soul in its clarity and power and brings it under its dominion.

> "ALL PRAISE is due to God alone, the Sustainer of all the words, the Most Gracious, the Dispenser of Grace, Lord of the Day of Judgment!"
> (Al-Fatihah: 2–4)

> "GOD—there is no deity save Him, the Ever-Living, the Self-Subsistent Fount of All Being.
>
> Neither slumber overtakes Him, nor sleep. His is all that is in the heavens and all that is on earth. Who is there that could intercede with Him, unless it be by His leave?
>
> He knows all that lies open before men and all that is hidden from them, whereas they cannot attain to aught of His knowledge save that which He wills [them to attain].
>
> His eternal power overspreads the heavens and the earth, and their upholding wearies Him not. And he alone is truly exalted, tremendous."
> (Al-Baqarah: 255)

"GOD—there is no deity save Him, the Ever—Living, the Self-Subsistent Fount of All Being!

Step by step has He bestowed upon thee from on high this divine writ, setting forth the truth which confirms whatever there still remains [of earlier revelations]: for it is He who has bestowed from on high the Torah and the Gospel aforetime, as a guidance unto mankind, and it is He who has bestowed [upon man] the standard by which to discern the true from the false.

Behold, as for those who are bent on denying God's messages—grievous suffering awaits them: for God is almighty, an avenger of evil. Verily, nothing on earth or in the heavens is hidden from God. He it is who shapes you in the wombs as He wills. There is no deity save Him, the Almighty, the Truly Wise." (Al-'Imran: 2–6)

"SAY: "O God, Lord of all dominion! Thou grantest dominion unto whom Thou willest, and takest away dominion from who Thou willest; and Thou exaltest whom Thou willest, and abasest whom Thou willest. In Thy hand is all good. Verily, Thou hast the power to will anything.

Thou makest the night grow longer by shortening the day, and Thou makest the day grow longer by shortening the night. And Thou bringest forth the living out of that which is dead, and Thou bringest forth the dead out of that which is alive. And Thou grantest sustenance unto whom Thou willest, beyond all reckoning."

(Al-'Imran: 26–27)

"Say: "Unto whom belongs all that is in the heavens and on earth?" Say: "Unto God, who has willed upon Himself the law of grace and mercy."

He will assuredly gather you all together on the Day of Resurrection, [the coming of] which is beyond all doub: yet those who have squandered their own selves—it is they who refuse to believe [in Him], although His is all that dwells in the night and the day, and He alone is all-hearing, all-knowing.

Say: "Am I to take for my master anyone but God, the Originator of the heavens and the earth, when it is He who gives nourishment and Himself needs none?"

Say: "I am bidden to be foremost among those who surrender themselves unto God, and not to be among those who ascribe divinity to aught beside Him."

Say: "Behold, I would dread, were I [thus] to rebel against my Sustainer, the suffering [which would befall me] on that awesome Day [of Judgment]."

Upon him who shall be spared on that Day, He will indeed have bestowed His grace and this will be a manifest triumph.

And if God should touch thee with misfortune, there is none who could remove it but He; and if He should touch thee with good fortune—it is He who has the power to will anything: for He alone holds sway over His creatures, and He alone is truly wise, all-aware.

Say: "What could most weightily bear witness to the truth?" Say: "God is witness between me and you; and this Qur'an has been revealed unto me so that on the strength thereof I might warn you and all whom it may reach."

Could you in truth bear witness that there are other deities side by side with God? Say: "I bear no [such] witness!" Say: "He is the One God; and, behold, far be it from me to ascribe divinity, as you do, to aught beside Him!"   (Al-An'am: 12–19)

"God knows what any female bears [in her womb], and by how much the wombs may fall short [in gestation], and by how much they may increase [the average period]: for with Him everything is [created] in accordance with its scope and purpose." He knows all that is beyond the reach of a created being's perception as well as all that can be witnessed by a creature's senses or mind—the Great One, the One far above anything that is or ever could be! It is all alike [to Him] whether any of you conceals his thought or brings it into the open, and whether he seeks to hide [his evil deeds] under the cover of night or walks [boldly] in the light of day, [thinking that] he has hosts of helpers—both such as can be perceived by him and such as are hidden from him—that could preserve him from whatever God may have willed.

Verily, God does not change men's condition unless they change their inner selves; and when God wills people to suffer evil [in consequence of their own evil deeds], there is none who could avert it: for they have none who could protect them from Him.

HE IT IS who displays before you the lightning, to give rise to [both] fear and hope, and calls heavy clouds into being; and the thunder extols His limitless glory and praises Him, and [so do] the angels, in awe of Him; and He [it is who] lets loose the thunderbolts and strikes with them whom He wills.

Any yet, they stubbornly argue about God, not-withstanding [all evidence] that He alone has the power to contrive whatever His unfathomable wisdom wills!

Unto Him [alone] is due all prayer aiming at the Ultimate Truth, since those [other beings or powers] whom men invoke instead of God cannot respond to them in any way—[so that he who invokes them is] but like one who stretches his open hands towards water, [hoping] that it will reach his mouth, the while it never reaches him. Hence, the prayer of those who deny the truth amounts to no more than losing oneself in grievous error.

And before God prostrate themselves, willingly or unwillingly, all [things and beings] that are in the heavens and on earth, as do their shadows in the mornings and the evenings.

Say: "Who is the Sustainer of the heavens and the earth?"

Say: "[It is] God."

Say: "[Why,] then, do you take for your protectors, instead of Him, such as have it not within their power to bring benefit to, or avert harm from, themselves?"

Say: "Can the blind and the seeing be deemed equal?—or can the depths of darkness and the light be deemed equal?"

Or do they [really] believe that there are, side by side with God, other divine powers that have created the like of what He creates, so that this act of creation appears to them to be similar [to His]?

Say: "God is the Creator of all things; and He is the One who holds absolute sway over all that exists."   (Ar-Ra'd: 8–16)

"For unto Him belong all beings that are in the heavens and on earth; and those that are with Him are never too proud to worship Him and never grow weary [thereof]: they extol His limitless glory by night and by day, never flagging [therein].

And yet, some people choose to worship certain earthly things or beings as deities that [are supposed to] resurrect [the dead; and they fail to realize that], had there been in heaven or on earth any deities other than God, both [those realms] would surely have fallen into ruin!

But limitless in His glory is God, enthroned in His awesome almightiness far above anything that men may devise by way of definition!

He cannot be called to account for whatever He does, whereas they will be called to account."   (Al-Anbiya': 19–23)

"All that is in the heavens and on earth extols God's limitless glory: for He alone is almighty, truly wise!

His is the dominion over the heavens and the earth; He grants life and deals death; and He has the power to will anything.

He is the First and the Last, and the Outward as well as the Inward: and He has full knowledge of everything.

He it is who has created the heavens and the earth in six aeons, and is established on the throne of His almightiness.

He knows all that enters the earth, and all that comes out of it, as well as all that descends from the skies, and all that ascends to them.

And He is with you wherever you may be: and God sees all that you do.

His is the dominion over the heavens and the earth; and all things go back unto God [as their source].

He makes the night grow longer by shortening the day, and makes the day grow longer by shortening the night; and He has full knowledge of what is in the hearts [of men]."   (Al-Hadid: 1–6)

This concept makes known to mankind the universe in which they live, its characteristics, its connections with its Creator, the ways in which it points to its Creator, its preparedness for life and the living to arise within it, and the manner in which it has, by God's permission, been made subject to man. All this in a style comprehensible to man's innermost nature and intelligence, and conformable to the material reality he witnesses. The concept summons man to knowledge of the universe, its norms and its mysteries, and to interact with it as he should, based on the knowledge and perception he has acquired.

"Who has made the earth a resting-place for you and the sky a canopy, and has sent down water from the sky and thereby brought forth fruits for your sustenance: do not, then, claim that there is any power that could rival God, when you know [that He is One]."
(Al-Baqarah: 22)

"ALL PRAISE is due to God, who has created the heavens and the earth, and brought into being deep darkness as well as light: and yet, those who are bent on denying the truth regard other powers as their Sustainer's equals!"
(Al-An'am: 1)

"It is God who has raised the heavens without any supports that you could see, and is established on the throne of His almightiness: and He [it is who] has made the sun and the moon subservient [to His laws], each running its course for a term set [by Him]. He governs all that exists.

Clearly does He spell out these messages, so that you might be certain in your innermost that you are destined to meet your Sustainer [on Judgment Day].

And it is He who has spread the earth wide and placed on it firm mountains and running waters, and created thereon two sexes of every [kind of] plant; [and it is He who] causes the night to cover the day.

Verily, in all this there are messages indeed for people who think!

And there are on earth [many] tracts of land close by one another [and yet widely differing from one another]; and [there are on it] vineyards, and fields of grain, and date-palms growing in clusters from one root or standing alone, [all] watered with the same water: and yet, some of them have We favoured above others by way of the food [which they provide for man and beast].

Verily, in all this there are messages indeed for people who use their reason!"   (Ar-Ra'd: 2–4)

"It is He who sends down water from the skies; you drink thereof, and thereof [drink] the plants upon which you pasture your beasts; [and] by virtue thereof He causes crops to grow for you, and olive trees, and date-palms, and grapes, and all [other] kinds of fruit: in this, behold, there is a message indeed for people who think!

And He has made the night and the day and the sun and the moon subservient [to His laws, so that they be of use] to you; and all the stars are subservient to His command: in this, behold, there are messages indeed for people who use their reason!

And all the [beauty of] many hues which He has created for you on earth: in this, behold, there is a message for people who [are willing to] take it to heart!

And He it is who has made the sea subservient [to His laws], so that you might eat fresh meat from it, and take from it gems which you may wear.

And on that [very sea] one sees ships ploughing through the waves, so that you might [be able to] go forth in quest of some of His bounty, and thus have cause to be grateful [to Him].

And he has placed firm mountains on earth, lest it sway with you, and rivers and paths, so that you might find your way, as well as [various other] means of orientation: for [it is] by the stars that men find their way.

IS, THEN, HE who creates comparable to any [being] that cannot create?

Will you not, then, bethink yourselves?"   (An-Nahl: 10–17)

"ARE, THEN, they who are bent on denying the truth not aware that the heavens and the earth were [once] one single entity, which We then parted asunder?—and [that] We made out of water every living thing? Will they not, then, [begin to] believe?

And [are they not aware that] We have set up firm mountains on earth, lest it sway with them, and [that] We have appointed thereon broad paths, so that they might find their way, and [that] We have set up the sky as a canopy well-secured?

And yet, they stubbornly turn away from [all] the signs of this [creation], and [fail to see that] it is He who has created the night and the day and the sun and the moon—all of them floating through space!"   (Al-Anbiya': 30–33)

"Art thou not aware that it is God who has made subservient to you all that is on earth, and the ships that sail through the sea at His behest—and [that it is He who] holds the celestial bodies [in their orbits], so that they may not fall upon the earth otherwise than by His leave?

Verily, God is most compassionate towards men, a dispenser of grace."   (Al-Hajj: 65)

"And, indeed, We have created above you seven [celestial] orbits; and never are We unmindful of [any aspect of Our] creation.

And We send down water from the skies in accordance with a measure [set by Us], and then We cause it to lodge in the earth: but, behold, We are most certainly able to withdraw this [blessing]!

And by means of this [water] We bring forth for you gardens of date-palms and vines, wherein you have fruit abundant and whereof you eat."   (Al-Mu'minun: 17–19)

"Art thou not aware that it is God who causes the clouds to move onward, then joins them together, then piles them up in masses, until thou canst see rain come forth from their midst?

And He is who sends down from the skies, by degrees, mountain-
ous masses [of clouds] charged with hail, striking therewith whomever He wills and averting it from whomever He wills. [the while] the
flash of His lightning well-nigh deprives [men of their] sight!

It is God who causes night and day to alternate: in this [too],
behold, there is surely a lesson for all who have eyes to see!"

(An-Nur: 43–44)

"ART THOU NOT aware of thy Sustainer [through His works]?—
how He causes the shadow to lengthen [towards the night] when, had
He so willed, He could indeed have made it stand still: but then, We have
made the sun its guide; and then, [after having caused it to lengthen,]
We draw it in towards Ourselves with a gradual drawing-in.

And He it is who makes the night a garment for you, and [your]
sleep a rest, and causes every [new] day to be a resurrection.

And He it is who sends forth the winds as a glad tiding of His
coming grace; and [thus, too,] We cause pure water to descend from
the skies, so that We may bring dead land to life thereby, and give
to drink thereof to many [beings] of Our creation, beasts as well as
humans."   (Al-Furqan: 45–49)

"And [yet,] they have a sign [of Our power to create and to resur-
rect] in the lifeless earth which We make alive, and out of which
We bring forth grain, whereof they may eat; and [how] We make
gardens of date-palms and vines [grow] thereon, and cause springs
to gush [forth] within it, so that they may eat of the fruit thereof,
though it was not their hands that made it.

Will they not, then, be grateful?

Limitless in His glory is He who has created opposites in whatever the earth produces, and in men's own selves, and in that of
which [as yet] they have no knowledge.

And [of Our sway over all that exists] they have a sign in the
night: we withdraw from it the [light of] day—and lo! They are in
darkness.

And [they have a sign in] the sun: it runs in an orbit of its own—
[and] that is laid down by the will of the Almighty, the All-knowing;
and [in] the moon, for which we have determined phases [which it
must traverse] till it becomes like an old date-stalk, dried–up and
curved: [and] neither may the sun overtake the moon, nor can the
night usurp the time of day, since all of them float through space [in
accordance with Our laws]."   (Ya Sin: 33–40)

"SAY: "Would you indeed deny Him who has created the earth in two aeons? And do you claim that there is any power that could rival Him, the Sustainer of all the worlds?"

For He [it is who, after creating the earth,] placed firm mountains on it, [towering] above its surface, and bestowed [so many] blessings on it, and equitably apportioned its means of subsistence to all who would seek it: [and all this He created] in four aeons.

And He [it is who] applied His design to the skies, which were [yet but] smoke; and He [it is who] said to them and to the earth, "Come [into being], both of you, willingly or unwillingly!—to which both responded, "We do come in obedience."

And He [it is who] decreed that they become seven heavens in two aeons, and imparted unto each heaven its function. And we adorned the skies nearest to the earth with lights, and made them secure: such is the ordaining of the Almighty, the All-knowing."

(Fussilat: 9–12)

"Do they not look at the sky above them—how we have built it and made it beautiful and free of all faults?

And the earth—We have spread it wide, and set upon it mountains firm, and caused it to bring forth plants of all beauteous kinds, thus offering an insight and a reminder unto every human being who willingly turns unto God.

And We send down from the skies water rich in blessings, and cause thereby gardens to grow, and fields of grain, and tall palm-trees with their thickly-clustered dates, as sustenance apportioned to men; and by [all] this We bring dead land to life: [and] even so will be [man's] coming-forth from death."   (Qaf: 6–11)

In these verses, God informs man of life and the living, acquainting him with their source, as well as the properties and qualities of life, to the degree that man is able to comprehend. He links man with all living things, in that he and they alike are servants of God, submitted to His will, and created by Him. He reminds man of the blessings He has bestowed upon him by making many of these living things subject to him.

"ARE, THEN, they who are bent on denying the truth not aware that the heavens and the earth were [once] one single entity, which We then parted asunder?—and [that] We made out of water every living thing? Will they not, then, [begin to] believe?" (Al-Anbiya': 30)

"And it is God who has created all animals out of water; and [He has willed that] among them are such as crawl on their bellies, and such as walk on two legs, and such as walk on four.

God creates what He wills: for, verily, God has the power to will anything."   (An-Nur: 45)

"Although there is no beast that walks on earth and no bird that flies on its two wings which is not [God's] creature like yourselves: no single thing have We neglected in Our decree.

And once again: Unto their Sustainer shall they [all] be gathered."   (Al-An'am: 38)

"And there is no living creature on earth but depends for its sustenance on God; and He knows its time-limit [on earth] and its resting-place [after death]: all [this] is laid down in [His] clear decree."
                                                                  (Hud: 6)

"And how many a living creature is there that takes no thought of its own sustenance, [the while] God provides for it as [He provides] for you—since He alone is all-hearing, all-knowing."   (Al-Ankabut: 60)

"O MEN! If you are in doubt as to the [truth of] resurrection, [remember that] verily, We have created [every one of] you out of dust, then out of a drop of sperm, then out of a germ-cell, then out of an embryonic lump complete [in itself] and yet incomplete, so that We might make [your origin] clear unto you.

And whatever We will [to be born] We cause to rest in the [mothers'] wombs for a term set [by Us], and then We bring you forth as infants and [allow you to live] so that [some of] you might attain to maturity: for among you are such as are caused to die [in childhood], just as many a one of you is reduced in old age to a most abject state, ceasing to know anything of what he once knew so well.

And [if, O man, thou art still in doubt as to resurrection, consider this:] thou canst see the earth dry and lifeless—and [suddenly,] when We send down waters upon it, it stirs and swells and puts forth every kind of lovely plant!"   (Al-Hajj: 5)

"He [it is who] brings forth the living out of that which is dead, and brings forth the dead out of that which is alive, and gives life to the earth after it had been lifeless: and even thus will you be brought forth [from death to life]."   (Ar-Rum: 19)

"And [yet,] they have a sign [of Our power to create and to resurrect] in the lifeless earth which We make alive, and out of which we bring forth grain, whereof they may eat; and [how] we make gardens of date-palms and vines [grow] thereon, and cause springs to gush [forth] within it, so that they may eat of the fruit thereof, though it was not their hands that made it.

Will they not, then, be grateful?

Limitless in His glory is He who has created opposites in whatever the earth produces, and in men's own selves, and in that of which has [as yet] they have no knowledge."   (Ya Sin: 33–36)

"The Originator [is He] of the heavens and the earth. He has given you mates of your own kind—just as [He has willed that] among the beasts [there be] mates—to multiply you thereby: [but] there is nothing like unto Him, and He alone is all-hearing all-seeing."

(Ash-Shura: 11)

One should also take heed of his sustenance:

"And He it is who sends down, again and again, waters from the sky in due measure: and [as] We raise therewith dead land to life, even thus will you be brought forth [from the dead].

And He it is who has created all opposites. And He [it is who] has provided for you all those ships and animals whereon you ride. In order that you might gain mastery over them, and that, whenever you have mastered them, you might remember your Sustainer's blessings and say: "Limitless in His glory is He who has made [all] this subservient to our use—since [but for Him,] we would not have been able to attain to it."   (Zukhruf: 11–13)

"Let man, then, consider [the sources of] his food: [how it is] that We pour down water, pouring it down abundantly: and then We cleave the earth [with new growth], cleaving it asunder, and thereupon We cause grain to grow out of it, and vines and edible plants, and olive trees and date-palms, and gardens dense with foliage, and fruits and herbage, for you and for your animals to enjoy."   (Abasa: 24–32)

"EXTOL the limitless glory of thy Sustainer's name: [the glory of] the All-Highest,

Who creates [every thing], and thereupon forms it in accordance with what it is meant to be, and who determines the nature [of all that exists], and thereupon guides it [towards its fulfilment], and who brings forth herbage, and thereupon causes it to decay into rust-brown stubble!"   (Al-A'la: 1–5)

"For, before God prostrates itself all that is in the heavens and all that is on earth—every beast that moves, and the angels: [even] these do not bear themselves with false pride: they fear their Sustainer high above them, and do whatever they are bidden to do."

(An-Nahl: 49–50)

"ART THOU NOT aware that it is God whose limitless glory all [creatures] that are in the heavens and on earth extol, even the birds as they spread out their wings? Each [of them] knows indeed how to pray unto Him and to glorify Him: and God has full knowledge of all that they do."   (An-Nur: 41)

God informs man, comprehensively and in great detail, of his source and his origin, his nature and characteristics; his position with respect to being as a whole; the purpose of his existence; the ways in which he should worship his Lord; his strengths and his weaknesses, his duties and obligations—in short, everything, great and small, that touches on his life in this world and his destiny in the hereafter. All this is present in the following verses:

"AND, INDEED, We have created man out of sounding clay, out of dark slime transmuted—whereas the invisible beings We had created, [long] before that, out of the fire of scorching winds.

And lo! Thy Sustainer said unto the angels: "Behold, I am about to create mortal man out of sounding clay, out of dark slime transmuted; and when I have formed him fully and breathed into him of My spirit, fall down before him in prostration!"

Thereupon the angels prostrated themselves, all of them together, save Iblis: he refused to be among those who prostrated themselves."   (Al-Hijr: 26–31)

"NOW, INDEED, We create man out of the essence of clay, and then We cause him to remain as a drop of sperm in [the womb's] firm keeping, and then We create out of the drop of sperm a germ-cell, and then We create out of the germ-cell an embryonic lump, and then We create within the embryonic lump bones, and then We clothe the bones with flesh—and then We bring [all] this into being as a new creation: hallowed, therefore, is God, the best of artisans!

And then, behold! after all this, you are destined to die; and then, behold! You shall be raised from the dead on Resurrection Day."   (Al-Mu'minun: 12–16)

"And [tell them that] I have not created the invisible beings and men to any end other than that they may [know and] worship Me. [But withal,] no sustenance do I ever demand of them, nor do I demand that they feed Me: for, verily, God Himself is the Provider of all sustenance, the Lord of all might, the Eternal!"   (Adh-Dhariyat: 56–58)

"AND LO! Thy Sustainer said unto the angels: "Behold, I am about to establish upon earth one who shall inherit it."

They said: "Wilt Thou place on it such as will spread corruption thereon and shed blood—whereas it is we who extol Thy limitless glory, and praise Thee, and hallow Thy name?"

[God] answered: "Verily, I know that which you do not know."

(Al-Baqarah: 30)

"NOW, INDEED, We have conferred dignity on the children of Adam, and borne them over land and sea, and provided for them sustenance out of the good things of life, and favoured them far above most of our creation."   (Al-Isra': 70)

"[For although] We did say, "Down with you all from this [state]," there shall, none the less, most certainly come unto you guidance from Me: and those who follow My guidance need have no fear, and neither shall they grieve; but those who are bent on denying the truth and giving the lie to Our messages—they are destined for the fire, and therein shall they abide."   (Al-Baqarah: 38–39)

"CONSIDER the flight of time!

Verily, man is bound to lose himself unless he be of those who attain to faith, and do good works, and enjoin upon one another the keeping to truth and enjoin upon one another patience in adversity."

(Al-'Asr)

"NOW, VERILY, it is We who have created man, and we know what his innermost self whispers within him: for we are closer to him than his neck-vein."   (Qaf: 16)

"Verily, We have created man into [a life of] pain, toil and trial."

(Al-Balad: 4)

"IS MAN, then, not aware that it is We who create him out of a [mere] drop of sperm-whereupon, lo! He shows himself endowed with the power to think and to argue?"   (Ya Sin: 77)

"THUS, INDEED, have We given in this Qur'an many facets to every kind of lesson [designed] for [the benefit of] mankind.
    However, man is, above all else, always given to contention."
                                                        (Al-Kahf: 54)

"VERILY, man is born with a restless disposition.
    [As a rule,] whenever misfortune touches him, he is filled with self-pity, and whenever good fortune comes to him, he selfishly with-holds it [from others].
    Not so, however, those who consciously turn towards God in prayer."   (Al-Ma'arij: 19–22)

"God wants to lighten your burdens: for man has been created weak."   (An-Nisa': 28)

"For [thus it is:] when affliction befalls man, he cries out unto Us, whether he be lying on his side or sitting or standing; but as soon as We have freed him of his affliction, he goes on as though he had never invoked Us to save him from the affliction that befell him! Thus do their own doings seem goodly unto those who waste their own selves."   (Yunus: 12)

"And thus it is: if We let man taste some of Our grace, and then take it away from him—behold, he abandons all hope. Forgetting all gratitude [for Our past favours]. And thus it is: if We let him taste ease and plenty after hardship has visited him, he is sure to say, "Gone is all affliction from me!"—for, behold, he is given to vain exultation, and glories only in himself."   (Hud: 9–10)

"As it is, man [often] prays for things that are bad as if he were pray-ing for something that is good: for man is prone to be hasty [in his judgments]."   (Al-Isra': 11)

"Nay, verily, man becomes grossly overweening whenever he believes himself to be self–sufficient."   (Al-'Alaq: 6–7)

"Consider the human self, and how it is formed in accordance with what it is meant to be, and how it is imbued with moral failings as well as with consciousness of God! To a happy state shall indeed attain he who causes this [self] to grow in purity, and truly lost is he who buries it [in darkness]."   (Ash-Shams: 7–10)

"Verily, We create man in the best conformation, and thereafter We reduce him to the lowest of low—excepting only such as attain to faith and do good works: and theirs shall be a reward unending!"
                                                                    (At-Tin: 4–6)

In these and other verses of the Qur'an, the purpose is clearly to expound and elaborate the fundamental truths that serve as a complete and comprehensive basis for the Islamic concept as a whole. This concept derives from a firm divine source, unquestionable in its precise and detailed knowledge and free of all need from any source external to itself, such as the partial and suppositional knowledge of man which causes him to wander in the wilderness without a guide.

The third aspect of comprehensiveness in the Islamic concept consists of attributing everything in the universe—life and the living, humans and objects—to a single comprehensive will. For it deals with all the major truths: the truth of divinity, which is the primary, supreme, and most fundamental truth; the true nature of the universe, of life, and of man. It then addresses human existence in all its dimensions, aspirations, and needs, and connects them to a single point of orientation where man may seek whatever he needs, a point to which he directs his hopes and his fears, shunning its anger and seeking its pleasure, for it is the Creator, Possessor and Disposer of all things. Man is similarly directed to a single source from which to obtain his concepts, values, criteria, norms and laws and where he will find an answer to whatever question may confront him. His life thus becomes fully integrated in terms of consciousness and conduct, creed and way of life, need and its fulfilment, life and death, effort and motion, health and sustenance, this world and the hereafter. It is not sundered apart, drawn in different directions, or faced with the choice among diverging paths.

When human life is thus integrated, it attains the best of all possible states, for unity is a characteristic of the Creator and His stamp on creation, a unity from which a multiplicity of phenomena, species and forms arises. From the unity of man emerges likewise a multiplicity of individuals with their varying capacities, but that unity is also a unity of purpose, namely worship in all of its different aspects and forms.

When human life is brought into accord with its true nature, man's powers will attain their zenith and be fully coordinated with the universe as a whole, interacting with it as he should and attaining the greatest of accomplishments.

This was fully realized among that chosen group who were the first Muslims; the roles God thereby bestowed on them had profound effects on human life and history. When this realization occurs once more—as, God willing, it inevitably will—God will again cause much to be accomplished threby, whatever be the obstacles. For the truth to be realized is a power that brooks no resistance, a power that draws on that of the universe and its Creator.

One result of the integration of man's life is that the entirety of human activity becomes a single movement, directed toward realizing the purpose of human existence—worship of God alone, manifested in all the aspects of man's vicegerent. This dynamic integration of man's life is perhaps the supreme characteristic of Islam, for it it supplies an interpretation of all the realities that confront man and provides him with direction in all aspects of his activity. It is Islam, and Islam alone, that enables man to live both for this world and for the hereafter, to work for God and to work for his own livelihood, to realize the human perfection to which his religion is pointing him while engaged in the daily activities which his function as divine vicegerent imposes on him. Nothing is asked of him in return from him save one thing: that he devote all his worship to God alone, whether it be in acts of devotion or practical life. He must orient himself to that goal with every act and motion, with every deed and intention. He must not go beyond the broad sphere of the permitted, which includes all the wholesome plaesures of life. God created man with certain capacities in order that he employ and make use of them, for it is by means of them that man attains the purpose of his existence, with ease and facility, tranquillity and assurance, and the complete freedom that results from servitude to God.

This characteristic makes Islam suitable as a complete way of life, embracing individual belief and social order; not only do these two not contradict each other, they are interconnected with each other, indeed inseparable from each other. They are like a single indivisible package; to tear it apart would ruin the religion of Islam.

The division of human activity into "acts of worship" and "transactions" occurred relatively late when scholars began to write on jurisprudence. Although the original intention was simply to draw a technical distinction—this being a characteristic of scholarly exertion—it began to have regrettable effects first in the conceptual realm and then in the entirety of Islamic life. People started to imagine that the attribute of worship belonged only to the first category and did not apply to the second. There can be no doubt that this is a serious deviation from the Islamic concept and that it led to a general deviation in the life of Islamic society.

According to the Islamic concept, there is no activity in human life to which the concept of worship does not apply or in which its realization may not be sought. The entirety of the Islamic way of life has as its aim the attainment of this aim, first and last. Human activity does not attain its true purpose, as clearly defined by the Qur'an, unless and until it is in conformity with the divine plan in all its aspects. It is only then that God will truly be worshipped in exclusivity; otherwise, man will have deserted true worship and servitude to God and abandoned the purpose that God has willed for human existence. In a word, he will have abandoned religion.

When we examine the places in the Qur'an where the acts designated by the jurists as "acts of worship" are mentioned, an inescapable truth confronts us: they are never isolated from other types of activity, precisely those designated by the jurists as "transactions." They occur in one and the same context of Qur'anic guidance, each of them constituting one half of the path of worship that is the purpose of human existence.

The division between the two categories led some people to imagine that they could be Muslim simply if they performed the "acts of worship" in accordance with the ordinances of Islam, while they conduct their "transactions" in accordance with some other criterion, derived from other than God—a "god" who permits them to do what God has not permitted them.

This is a great illusion. Islam is an indivisible unity. Whoever separates it into halves in this way has abandoned the unity and abandoned religion. This must be borne in mind by every Muslim who seeks to make a reality of his Islam and at the same time the purpose of his existence. It is necessary to understand this not only in order to correct our concept of religion—important as that aim may be—but also in order to appreciate life as it is meant to be appreciated, in all its perfection and harmony. The value of human life as a whole is enhanced when it becomes synonymous with the worship of God and when every activity, great or small, becomes part of that worship; there is no degree higher than this to which man can become elevated, nor any loftier perfection. This is the state in which revelation is received, in which the ascension of the Prophet—upon whom be peace and blessings—occurred:

> "HALLOWED is He who from on high, step by step, has bestowed upon His servant the standard by which to discern the true from the false, so that to all the world it might be a warning."   (Al-Furqan: 1)

> "LIMITLESS in His glory is He who transported His servant by night from the Inviolable House of Worship [at Mecca] to the Remote House of Worship [at Jerusalem]—the environs of which We had blessed—so that We might show him some of Our symbols: for, verily, He alone is all-hearing, all-seeing."   (Al-Isra': 1)

In his book *Islam at the Crossroads*, Muhammad Asad (known as Leopold Weiss before embracing Islam) explains precisely the difference in this respect that exists between the Islamic concept and other concepts. It is the Islamic concept that enables man to realize the seriousness of life and the significance attached importance to every motion man makes.

In the chapter "The Open Road of Islam," he states:

"Thus, the conception of 'worship' in Islam is different from that in any other religion. Here it is not restricted to the purely devotional practices, for example prayers or fasting, but extends over the whole of man's practical life as well. If the object of our life as a whole is to be the worship of God, we necessarily must regard this life, in the totality of all its aspects, as one complex moral responsibility. Thus, all our actions, even the seemingly trivial ones, must be performed as acts of worship, that is, performed consciously as constituting a part of God's universal plan. Such a state of things is, for the man of average capability, a distant ideal; but is it not the purpose of religion to bring ideals into real existence?

"The position of Islam in this respect is unmistakable. It teaches us, firstly, that the permanent worship of God in all the manifold actions of human life is the very meaning of this life, and, secondly, that the achievement of this purpose remains impossible so long as we divide our life into two parts, the spiritual and the material. They must be bound together, in our consciousness and our action, into one harmonious entity. Our notion of God's Oneness must be reflected in our own striving towards a coordination and unification of the various aspects of our life.

"A logical consequence of this attitude is a further difference between Islam and all other known religious systems. It is to be found in the fact that Islam, as a teaching, undertakes to define not only the metaphysical relations between man and his Creator but also—and with scarcely less insistence—the earthly relations between the individual and his social surroundings. The worldly life is not regarded as a mere empty shell, as a meaningless shade of the hereafter that is to come, but as self-contained, positive entity. God himself is a Unity not only in essence but also in purpose; and, therefore, His creation is a Unity, possibly in essence, but certainly in purpose.

"Worship of God in the wide sense just explained constitutes, according to Islam, the meaning of human life. And it is this conception alone that shows us the possibility of man's reaching perfection within his individual, earthly life. Of all religious systems, Islam alone declares that individual perfection is possible in our earthly existence. Islam does not postpone this fulfilment until after a suppression of the so-called "bodily" desires, as the Christian teaching does; nor does Islam promise a continuous chain of rebirths on a progressively higher plane, as is the case with Hinduism; nor does Islam agree with Buddhism, according to which perfection and salvation can be obtained only through an annihilation of the individual Self and its emotional links with the world. No, Islam is emphatic in the assertion that man can reach perfection in his earthly, individual life and by making full use of all the worldly possibilities of his life."[32]

The comprehensiveness of the Islamic concept, in all its forms, is assuring to human nature because it treats it as a unified whole and imposes on it neither hardship nor dispersion. It protects it from orien-

---

[32] Muhammad Asad, *Islam at the Crossroads* pp. 17–20.

tation to other than God at any time and in any act, and from accepting domination by any power other than God, in any aspect of life. Command, sovereignty and power belong to God alone, whether in individual "acts of worship" or "transactions," whether in this world or the next, whether in the heavens or on eart, whether in the realm of the unseen or that of the manifest, whether in labor or prayer—in every breath and instant, in every motion, step and stillness.

> "For [then they will come to know that] it is He [alone] who is God in heaven and God on earth, and [that] He alone is truly wise, all-knowing."   (Zukhruf: 84)

6

BALANCE

"There are no imperfections in the creation of the All-Merciful"
(Al-Mulk: 3)

The fourth characteristic of this concept is balance, balance in its fundamentals, and balance in its implications and derivatives. It is connected to the previous characteristic, that of comprehensiveness, for the comprehensiveness is marked by balance.

This unique attribute has safeguarded it against extremes, contradictions and excesses, aflictions which no other concept has been able to avoid, whether it be a question of philosophical concepts or religious concepts distorted by what humans have added to them or subtracted from them, or the misinterpretations to which they have subjected them.

The characteristic of balance appears in several ways, of which we shall now mention the most important. To begin with, there is a balance between that which man receives simply to perceive and then to submit to it, his duty ending with submission; and that which he receives first to perceive, but then to search out its proofs and evidences, to seek to understand its purposes, to reflect on its practical implications, and to apply it in actual life.

Human nature is content with both these components of the concept, because both respond to an inherent aspect of human nature as fashioned by the the Maker. God knew that human perception could not accommodate all the secrets of being, and He therefore placed in man contentment with the unknown and contentment with the known—a balance between the two in man and in the entirety of being.

A faith from which the unseen and the unknown are absent, which offers no truth transcending human perception, is in reality not a faith at all, and man will not find in it an answer to his hidden yearnings for the realm of the unknown, concealed behind multiple veils. Similarly, a faith that contains nothing but incomprehensible riddles is also no faith at all, for the nature of man contains an element of awareness and his mind needs something comprehensible which he can practise and on which he can act. A comprehensive faith is one that answers both needs, reflecting the balance present in man's own nature and corresponding to the aspirations and capacities inherent within him.

The nature of the divine essence, the manner in which the divine will attaches to creation, the nature of the spirit—these are matters that cannot be fully comprehended. But as for the divine attributes—being, unity, power, will, creator-hood—these are matters that the human intellect can exert itself in understanding, for it can perceive their necessity as the corollaries of His essence, apart from which Islam presents convincing proofs concerning them. The nature of the universe, the source of its existence, its relationship to its Creator, its preparedness for the receipt of life, its relationship to man; the various forms, degrees and expressions of life; the nature of man and the purpose of his being—all these topics are dealt with in clear, logical, and satisfying fashion, supported by convincing and easily accepted proofs.

> "[Or do they deny the existence of God?] Have they themselves been created without anything [that might have caused their creation]?— or were they, perchance, their own creators? [And] have they created the heavens and the earth?
>
> Nay, but they have no certainty of anything!"   (At-Tur: 35–36)

"And yet, some people choose to worship certain earthly things or beings as deities that [are supposed to] resurrect [the dead; and they fail to realize that], had there been in heaven or on earth any deities other than God, both [those realms] would surely have fallen into ruin!

But limitless in His glory is God, enthroned in His awesome almightiness [far] above anything that men may devise by way of definition!

He cannot be called to account for whatever He does, whereas they will be called to account: and yet, they choose to worship [imaginary] deities instead of Him!

Say [O Prophet]: Produce an evidence for what you are claiming: this is a reminder [unceasingly voiced] by those who are with me, just as it was a reminder [voiced] by those who came before me.

But nay, most of them do not know the truth, and so they stubbornly turn away [from it]." (Al-Anbiya': 21–24)

"Is, then, He who has created the heavens and the earth not able to create [anew] the like of those [who have died]?

Yea, indeed—for He alone is the all-knowing Creator: His Being alone is such that when He wills a thing to be, He but says unto it, "Be"—and it is." (Ya Sin: 81–82)

"And [now] he [argues about Us, and] thinks of Us in terms of comparison, and is oblivious of how he himself was created! [And so] he says, "Who could give life to bones that have crumbled to dust?"

Say: "He who brought them into being in the first instance will give them life [once again], seeing that He has full knowledge of every act of creation." (Ya Sin: 78–79)

"Nay—who is it that has created the heavens and the earth, and sends down for you [life-giving] water from the skies? For it is by this means that We cause gardens of shining beauty to grow—[whereas] it is not in your power to cause [even one single of] its trees to grow!

Could there be any divine power besides God? Nay, they [who think so] are people who swerve [from the path of reason]!

Nay—who is it that has made the earth a fitting abode [for living things], and has caused running waters [to flow] in its midst, and has set upon it mountains firm, and has placed a barrier between the two great bodies of water?

Could there be any divine power besides God? Nay, most of those [who think so] do not know [what they are saying]!

Nay—who is it that responds to the distressed when he calls out to Him, and who removes the ill [that caused the distress], and has made you inherit the earth?

Could there be any divine power besides God? How seldom do you keep this in mind!

Nay—who is it that guides you in the midst of the deep darkness of land and sea, and sends forth the winds as a glad tiding of His coming grace?

Could there be any divine power besides God? Sublimely exalted is God above anything to which men may ascribe a share in His divinity!

Nay—who is it that creates [all life] in the first instance, and then brings it forth anew? And who is it that provides you with sustenance out of heaven and earth?

Could there be any divine power besides God?

Say: "[If you think so,] produce your evidence—if you truly believe in your claim!"   (An-Naml: 60–64)

"And among His wonders is this: He creates you out of dust—and then, lo! You become human beings ranging far and wide!

And among His wonders is this: He creates for you mate out of your own kind, so that you might incline towards them, and He engenders love and tenderness between you: in this, behold, there are messages indeed for people who think!

And among his wonders is the creation of the heavens and the earth, and the diversity of your tongues and colours: for in this, behold, there are messages indeed for all who are possessed of [innate] knowledge!

And among His wonders is your sleep, at night or in daytime, as well as your [ability to go about in] quest of some of His bounties: in this, behold, there are messages indeed for people who [are willing to] listen!

And among His wonders is this: He displays before you the lightning, giving rise to [both] fear and hope, and sends down water from the skies, giving life thereby to the earth after it had been lifeless: in this, behold, there are messages indeed for people who use their reason!

And among His wonders is this: the skies and the earth stand firm at His behest.

[Remember all this: for] in the end, when He will call you forth from the earth with a single call—lo! You will [all] emerge [for judgment]."   (Ar-Rum: 20–25)

These are some of the decisive proofs put forward in the verses concerning man's own person and the universe he inhabits, put forward for consideration and contemplation; human perception is invited to examine them and measure their adequacy as evidence.

Thus one finds in the Islamic concept everything that responds to the aspirations of human nature: the known and the unknown; the

realm of the unseen that can be comprehended neither by the mind
nor by the eye, and the realm of the manifest, where the mind and the
heart may find what they desire; a realm broader than man's perception that induces in him a sense of the majesty of the Creator, and
another in which his perception may freely operate, inducing in him a
sense of man's value in the cosmos and his nobility in the eyes of God.
Thus does man's being find balance.

Another form of balance is that between the absoluteness of the
divine will and the stability of the norms that govern human life. His
will is absolute and subject to no restraints; it creates all things simply
by orienting itself to them. There is no principle governing it, nor any
form imposed on it, whenever it wills to do what it wills:

"Whenever We will anything to be, We but say unto it Our word
"Be"—and it is."   (An-Nahl: 40)

"[Zachariah] exclaimed: "O my Sustainer! How can I have a son
when old age has already overtaken me, and my wife is barren?"
      Answered [the angel]: "Thus it is: God does what He wills.""
                                                    (Al-'Imran: 40)

"Said she: "O my Sustainer! How can I have a son when no man has
ever touched me?"
      [The angel] answered: "Thus it is: God creates what He wills:
when He wills a thing to be, He but says unto it, 'Be'—and it is.""
                                                    (Al-'Imran: 47)

"And his wife, standing [nearby], laughed [with happiness]; whereupon We gave her the glad tiding of [the birth of] Isaac and, after
Isaac, of [his son] Jacob.
      Said she: "Oh, woe is me! Shall I bear a child, now that I am
an old woman and this husband of mine is an old man? Verily, that
would be a strange thing indeed!"
      Answered [the messengers]: "Dost thou deem it strange that
God should decree what He wills? The grace of God and His blessing be upon you, O people of this house! Verily, ever to be praised
sublime is He!""   (Hud: 71–73)

"Verily, in the sight of God, the nature of Jesus is as the nature of
Adam, whom He created out of dust and then said unto him, "Be"—

and he is. [This is] the truth from thy Sustainer: be not, then, among
the doubters!"
(Al-'Imran: 59–60)

"And [will make him] an apostle unto the children of Israel."
"I HAVE COME unto you with a message from your Sustainer.
I shall create for you out of clay, as it were, the shape of [your]
destiny, and then breathe into it, so that it might become [your]
destiny by God's leave; and I shall heal the blind and the leper, and
bring the dead back to life by God's leave, and I shall let you know
what you may eat and what you should store up in your houses.
Behold, in all this there is indeed a message for you, if you are
[truly] believers."

(Al-'Imran: 49)

"Or [art thou, O man, of the same mind] as he who passed by a
town deserted by its people, with its roofs caved in, [and] said, "How
could God bring all this back to life after its death?"
Thereupon God caused him to be dead for a hundred years;
whereafter He brought him back to life [and] said: "How long hast
thou remained thus?"
He answered: "I have remained thus a day, or part of a day."
Said [God]: "Nay, but thou hast remained thus for a hundred
years! But look at thy food and thy drink-untouched is it by the passing of years—and look at thine ass! And [We did all this so that We
might make thee a symbol unto men. And look at the bones [of animals and men]—how We put them together and then clothe them
with flesh!"
And when [all this] became clear to him, he said: "I know [now]
that God has the power to will anything!"   (Al-Baqarah: 259)

"They exclaimed: "Burn him, and [thereby] succour your gods, if
you are going to do [anything]!"
[But] We said: "O fire! Be thou cool, and [a source of] inner
peace for Abraham!"—and whereas they sought to do evil unto him,
We caused them to suffer the greatest loss."   (Al-Anbiya': 68–70)

"And as soon as the two hosts came in sight of one another, the followers of Moses exclaimed: "Behold, we shall certainly be overtaken
[and defeated]!"
He replied: "Nay indeed! My Sustainer is with me, [and] He
will guide me!"

Thereupon We inspired Moses thus: "Strike the sea with thy staff!"—whereupon it parted, and each part appeared like a mountain vast."
                                                    (Ash-Shuára: 61–63)

"O PROPHET! When you [intend to] divorce women, divorce them with a view to the waiting—period appointed for them, and reckon the period [carefully], and be conscious of God, your Sustainer.

Do not expel them from their homes; and neither shall they [be made to] leave unless they become openly guilty of immoral conduct.

These, then, are the bounds set by God—and he who transgresses the bounds set by God does indeed sin against himself: [for, O man, although] thou knowest it not, after that [first breach] God may well cause something new to come about."   (Al-Talaq: 1)

Such are some of the verses that demonstrate the absoluteness of the divine will and its freedom from any law or determination that man might imagine.

At the same time, God wishes that His will should customarily appear to man in the form of consistent norms and regular patterns, which men can observe, perceive and and order their lives and interact with the universe accordingly. They must, however, remain aware that His will is absolute and that He does whatsoever He wishes, even if it contradicts the norms and patterns to which they are accustomed. It is, in fact, a norm of the divine will, transcending all other norms, that it is absolute, in whatever norm or pattern it may manifest itself. It is for this reason that God draws man's attention and consideration to the norms present in creation; to the understanding of them, insofar as man's mind is capable; and to benefit from them in his practical life.

"ART THOU NOT aware of that [king] who argued with Abraham about his Sustainer, [simply] because God had granted him kingship?

Lo! Abraham said: 'My Sustainer is He who grants life and deals death.'

[The king] replied: 'I [too] grant life and deal death!'

Said Abraham: 'Verily, God causes the sun to rise in the east: cause it, then, to rise in the west!'

Thereupon he who was bent on denying the truth remained dumbfounded: for God does not guide people who [deliberately] do wrong."   (Al-Baqarah: 258)

"[And] neither may the sun overtake the moon, nor can be night usurp the time of day, since all of them float through space [in accordance with Our laws]."   (Ya Sin: 40)

"Such has been God's way with those who [sinned in like manner and] passed away aforetime—and never wilt thou find any change in God's way!"   (Al-Ahzab: 62)

"[MANY] WAYS of life have passed away before your time. Go, then, about the earth and behold what happened in the end to those who gave the lie to the truth."   (Al-'Imran: 137)

"[But] can, then, they [who deny the truth] learn no lesson by recalling how many a generation We have destroyed before their time?— [people] in whose dwelling—places they [themselves now] walk about?

   In this, behold, there are messages indeed: will they not, then, listen."   (As-Sajdah: 26)

"And indeed, [O Muhammad, even] before thee did We send forth apostles—each one unto his own people—and they brought them all evidence of the truth: and then, [by causing the believers to triumph,] we inflicted Our retribution upon those who [deliberately] did evil: for We had willed it upon Ourselves to succour the believers."
                                                          (Ar-Rum: 47)

"And, indeed, We destroyed before your time [whole] generations when they [persistently] did evil although the apostles sent unto them brought them all evidence of the truth; for they refused to believe [them]. Thus do We requite people who are lost in sin."
                                                          (Yunus: 13)

"Yet if the people of those communities had but attained to faith and been conscious of Us, we would indeed have opened up for them blessings out of heaven and earth: but they gave the lie to the truth— and so we took them to task through what they [themselves] had been doing."   (Al-A'raf: 96)

   Made thus aware of the invariance of norms and the absoluteness of God's will, the human mind stands on firm ground; he knows its nature, the nature of the path, the aim to which he is tending, and the reward for his efforts. He learns the norms of the universe, the customs of life, the capacities of the earth, profiting from them and his own experiences to construct a sound scientific method. At one and the same time, his spirit is connected to God and his heart, to His will; he deems nothing to be beyond His will and never despairs when confronted by the pressures of life. He lives with a liberated mind, free of all iron restraints or imagining God to be similarly limited. Thus his senses remain sharp, his hope remains lively, and he is free of repetitious familiarity.

A Muslim pays due attention to causes as he is commanded to do, and he acts according to the norms he observes in the universe. He does this not because he believes that causes and means truly give rise to effects, for he refers everything back to the Creator of causes; all things are connected to Him behind the veil of causality. This comes after he has fulfilled his duty by striving, laboring and dealing with causes, in obedience to divine command.

For a Muslim, therefore, the stable pattern of norms he sees in the universe serves as the basis for his experience, theoretical and practical, and his dealings with the universe and its mysteries and hidden resources. None of the benefits of empirical science or practical activity escape him. At the same time, his heart is kept vital thanks to its connection with God, and his conscience is replete with ethical and behavioral awareness. As a result, his life becomes lofty, blessed, and pure, attaining the utmost perfection attainable on earth for man with all his limitations.

As for the balance between the limitless sphere of the divine will and the limited sphere of human will, this has been a familiar topic throughout the history of dialectics, of all beliefs, philosophies, and idolatrous cults. It is the topic of destiny, or free will vs. predestination.

Islam affirms the absoluteness of God's will and its unique and exclusive agency,but at the same time it affirms the positive nature of human will, awarding to man the primary role on earth as the divine vicegerent. This is a vast role, providing man with a central place in the universe as a whole and granting him broad scope for exercizing agency and effect. It is, however, perfectly balanced with the absoluteness of the divine will and its exclusive possession of true agency, beyond external causality, for human agency is itself part of that external causality. Man's very existence to begin with, his will and his deeds, his motion and activity, all are subsumed within the scope of God's absolute will which embraces the entirety of existence.

Thus we read in the Noble Qur'an:

"NO CALAMITY can ever befall the earth, and neither your own selves, unless it be [laid down] in Our decree before We bring it into being: verily, all this is easy for God."   (Al-Hadid: 22)

"Say: "Never can anything befall us save what God has decreed! He is our Lord Supreme; and in God let the believers place their trust!"   (Al-Tawbah: 51)

"Wherever you may be, death will overtake you—even though you be in towers raised high."

Yet, when a good thing happens to them, some [people] say, "This is from God," whereas when evil befalls them, they say, "This is from thee [O fellow-man]!"

Say: "All is from God."

What, then, is amiss with these people that they are in no wise near to grasping the truth of what they are told?"   (An-Nisa': 78)

"Then, after this woe, He sent down upon you a sense of security, an inner calm which enfolded some of you, whereas the others, who cared mainly for themselves, entertained wrong thoughts about God—thoughts of pagan ignorance—saying, "Did we, then, have any power of decision [in this matter]?"

Say: 'Verily, all power of decision does rest with God'—[but as for them,] they are trying to conceal within themselves that [weakness of faith] which they would not reveal unto thee, [O Prophet, by] saying, 'If we had any power of decision, we would not have left so many dead behind.'

Say [unto them]: "Even if you had remained in you homes, those [of you] whose death had been ordained would indeed have gone forth to the places where they were destined to lie down."

And [all this befell you] so that God might put to a test all that you harbour in your bosoms, and render you innermost hearts pure of all dross: for God is aware of what is in the hearts [of men]."   (Al-'Imran: 154)

On the other hand:

"[Thinking that] he has hosts of helpers—both such as can be perceived by him and such as are hidden from him—that could preserve him from whatever God may have willed.

Verily, God does not change men's condition unless they change their inner selves; and when God wills people to suffer evil [in consequence of their own evil deeds], there is none who could avert it: for they have none who could protect them from Him."   (Ar-Ra'd: 11)

"This, because God would never change the blessings with which He has graced a people unless they change their inner selves: and [know] that God is all-hearing, all-seeing."   (Al-Anfal: 53)

"Consider the human self, and how it is formed in accordance with what it is meant to be, and how it is imbued with moral failings as well as with consciousness of God!

To a happy state shall indeed attain he who causes this [self] to grow in purity, and truly lost is he who buries it [in darkness]."
                                                        (Ash-Shams: 7–10)

"For he who commits a sin, commits it only to his own hurt; and God is indeed all-knowing, wise."   (An-Nisa': 111)

Then we read:

"Nay, verily, this is an admonition, and whoever wills may take it to heart.

But they [who do not believe in the life to come] will not take it to heart unless God so wills, [for] He is the Fount of all God–consciousness, and the Fount of all forgiveness."
                                                        (Al-Muddaththir: 54–56)

"VERILY, all this is an admonition: whoever, then, so wills, may unto his Sustainer find a way.

But you cannot will it unless God wills [to show you that way]: for, behold, God is indeed all-seeing, wise."   (Al-Insan: 29–30)

"AND DO YOU, now that a calamity has befallen you after you had inflicted twice as much [on your foes], ask yourselves, "How has this come about?" Say: "It has come from your own selves."

Verily, God has the power to will anything: and all that befell you on the day when the two hosts met in battle happened by God's leave, so that He might mark out the [true] believers."
                                                        (Al-'Imran: 165–166)

Once one reads these different groups of verses, he realizes how extensive is the idea of "destiny" in the Islamic concept, for it depicts the broad area in which human will can operate within the limits of an all-encompassing destiny.

Deviant philosophies and faiths are at a loss to explain this matter; they are confused and bewildered. This includes those Muslim theologians who followed the method of Greek philosophy rather than that of Islam.

According to the Islamic concept, there is in fact no problem at all with respect to destiny and free will, once the matter be correctly addressed.

"Destiny," with respect to man, is that which originates and creates all originated and created events, things, and living beings; it is what adminsters and conditions human life.[33] Man in this respect is identical to the rest of creation: everything within it is created in accordance with a measure and all of its motions are undertaken in accordance with destiny. However, with respect to man, the destiny ordained by God is fulfilled through his own will and action and the changes that they effect in themselves.

> "[Thinking that] he has hosts of helpers—both such as can be perceived by him and such as are hidden from him—that could preserve him from whatever God may have willed.
>
> Verily, God does not change men's condition unless they change their inner selves; and when God wills people to suffer evil [in consequence of their own evil deeds], there is none who could avert it: for they have none who could protect them from Him."   (Ar-Ra'd: 11)

The referring of all matters back to God's absolute will does not invalidate or cancel out human will and endeavour. The two sometimes come together in one and the same Qura'nic text, as we see in the third group of verses quoted above.

When when we consider the matter from the viewpoint of our own experience we tend to assume that contradiction and opposition exist between the supreme will of God and the activity of man, exercized

---

[33] It will be helpful to the reader to note that "destiny" serves here as the translation of *qadar*, which has the sense of "measured amount"; "destiny" is, therefore the fixed amount of life and other qualities bestowed on created beings. (Ed.)

within the compass of that will. The correct method to follow, however, is not to derive our concepts from preconceived rational ideas,
but on the contrary to derive our rational ideas from the verses of the
Qur'an that inform us of matters subject to God's predestination which
we would have been unable to grasp in the absence of revelation.

The Qur'an states:

"Whosoever will, let him embark on a path to his Lord."

(Al-Insan: 29)

"They will not unless He wills."   (Al-Insan :30)

"Nay, but man will be evidence against himself, even though he were
to put up his excuses."   (Al-Qiyama : 14–15)

"And whomsoever God wills to guide, his bosom He opens wide
with willingness towards self-surrender [unto Him]; and whomsoever He wills to let go astray, his bosom He causes to be tight and
constricted, as if he were climbing unto the skies: it is thus that God
inflicts horror upon those who will not believe."   (Al-An'am: 125)

God also says:

"WHOEVER does what is just and right, does so for his own good;
and whoever does evil, does so to his own hurt: and never does God
do the least wrong to His creatures."   (Fussilat: 46)

It follows, then, according to a Muslim's concept of his God, of the
justice inherent in the requital for deeds, and of the comprehensiveness
of His will, that the respective weight carried by divine will and human
act, as indicated in these verses, should permit man a degree of agency in
his deeds that will serve as a basis for moral responsibility in this world
and reward or punishment in the next, without contradicting the absolute will of God that encompasses all men, all things, and all events.

How?

All the modalities of God's acts, including the manner in which His
will connects with the desires of His creation, are beyond the capacity
of human reason to comprehend. The Islamic concept advises that it
be left to the domain of God's absolute knowledge, while assuring man
of His justice, mercy, and generosity. Human thought, restricted as it
is by temporal and spatial limitations and an infinite variety of influ-

ences, is in position to comprehend these relationships and modalities, or to pass judgement on the connections existing between the will of God and the act of man. All of this is left to the all-encompassing and guiding will of God, His absolute and perfect knowledge. It is God Who knows the true nature of man and the composition of his being, his innate capacities and his actual deeds, the extent of his free will, and the degree to which his free will will result in requital in the hereafter. It is only thus that balance is achieved, conceptually and emotionally, together with the confidence required to act in accordance with God's path and attain the true goal.

Similar considerations apply to what is called "the problem of evil and suffering." From the Islamic point of view, there is no problem.

Islam pronounces this world to be the abode of travail and toil and the next to be that of trial and requital. Life on this earth is a limited stage on a long journey. What happens to a human on this earth is not the end of all things; it is merely a prelude, a test to determine the degree man shall acquire in the hereafter.

With this concept, Islam solves the emotional aspect of this problem, bestowing confidence and steadfastness on the mind. The suffering endured by a virtuous person on earth because of the existence of evil and deficiency does not represent the totality of what is allotted him; it is simply what is placed on one side of the scales. Both sides are subject to a single will, a judge whose knowledge is exhaustive and who weighs all things most precisely.

This concept also addresses a reality that man finds in the depths of his conscience: namely, that the virtuous believer who strives to follow God's path in his own life and implement it in that of mankind in general will indeed experience evil and suffering, but be compensated with a sense of satisfaction and happiness even in this world, in advance of the reward that awaits him in the hereafter. This sense derives from his awareness that he is pleasing God in what he does, and that God is pleased with his virtuous strivings. It is a testimony deriving from man's innermost self that God has created man in such a way that he gains immediate reward while in the midst of the struggle against evil, for this struggle is in itself pleasurable. The sense of reward is then inherent in man; he is assured of receiving it, in both this world and the next.

"Those who believe, and whose hearts find their rest in the remembrance of God—for, verily, in the remembrance of God [men's] hearts do find their rest."   (Ar-Ra'd: 28)

"Could, then, one whose bosom God has opened wide with willingness towards self—surrender unto Him, so that he is illumined by a light [that flows] from his Sustainer, [be likened to the blind and deaf of heart]?

Woe, then, unto those whose hearts are hardened against all remembrance of God! They are most obviously lost in error."

(Az-Zumar: 22)

"[But,] behold, as for those who say, 'Our Sustainer is God.' And then steadfastly pursue the right way—upon them do angels often descend, [saying:] Fear not and grieve not, but receive the glad tiding of that paradise which has been promised to you! We are close unto you in the life of this world and [will be so] in the life to come; and in that [life to come] you shall have all that your souls may desire, and in it you shall have all that you ever prayed for, as a ready welcome from Him who is much–forgiving, a dispenser of grace!"

(Fussilat: 30–32)

"Be not, then, faint of heart, and grieve not: for you are bound to rise high if you are [truly] believers."   (Al-'Imran: 139)

"Say: "Are you, perchance, hopefully waiting for something [bad] to happen to us—[the while nothing can happen to us] save one of the two best things? But as far as you are concerned, we are hopefully waiting for God to inflict chastisement upon you, [either] from Himself or by our hands! Wait, then, hopefully; behold, we shall hopefully wait with you!"   (At-Tawbah: 52)

As for the existence of evil as such, and all the suffering arising there from, why indeed does it exist, given that God is capable of not bringing it into existence to begin with; and, if He had wished, all people would have been rightly guided from the very moment of their creation? This is a question that does not even arise in the context of the Islamic concept.

God is certainly capable of altering human nature, by means of this religion or by any other means, or of creating him with a different nature. But He willed to create man with precisely this nature, and the universe in precisely the manner we see. None of His creatures is entitled to ask Him why He willed it that way, because none of His creatures is a god endowed with the knowledge or comprehension, or even the possibility thereof, needed to grasp the total scheme of the universe, the nature of His creatures, and the wisdom inherent in their being created precisely the way that they are.

God alone knows all of this, for He alone created this universe and all that it contains. He alone discerns what is good and creates and sustains it, and He alone bestows the best of forms on His creation:

> "And then we create within the embryonic lump bones, and then We clothe the bones with flesh—and then We bring [all] this into being as a new creation: hallowed, therefore, is God, the best of artisans!"
> (Al-Mu'Minun: 14)

> "He replied: "Our Sustainer is He who gives unto every thing [that exists] its true nature and form, and thereupon guides it [towards its fulfilment]."
> (Ta Ha: 50)

> "And unto thee [O prophet] have We vouchsafed this divine writ, setting forth the truth, confirming the truth of whatever there still remains of earlier revelations and determining what is true therein. Judge, then, between the followers of earlier revelation in accordance with what God has bestowed from on high, and do not follow their errant views, forsaking the truth that has come unto thee.
> Unto every one of you have We appointed a [different] law and way of life. And if God had so willed, He could surely have made you all one single community: but [He willed it otherwise] in order to test you by means of what He has vouchsafed unto you. Vie, then, with one another in doing good works! Unto God you all must return; and then He will make you truly understand all that on which you were wont to differ."
> (Al-Ma'idah: 48)

> "And thereupon, by God's leave, they routed them. And David slew Goliath; and God bestowed upon him dominion, and wisdom, and imparted to him the knowledge of whatever He willed.
> And if God had not enabled people to defend themselves against one another, corruption would surely overwhelm the earth: but God is limitless in His bounty unto all the worlds."
> (Al-Baqarah: 251)

"Every human being is bound to taste death; and We test you [all] through the bad and the good [things of life] by way of trial: and unto Us you all must return." (Al-Anbiya': 35)

"Why?" is a question no serious believer would pose in this context, nor even a serious atheist. The believer, because of his deference to God, Whose essence and attributes he has learned from the Islamic concept, and because he is aware that the limited extent of his human perception does not permit him to operate in this realm. The atheist, because he does not recognize the existence of God; were he to do so, he would recognize that such matters fall within the domain of God and that whatever He chooses and wills is absolute good.

It is a question asked only by self-important, obstinate or foolish people, and it is not advisable to try to prove the matter to them by means of rational, human criteria, for it is in its very nature beyond the level of human reason. To understand the matter presupposes that man himself should be a god. One must concede all of this as true and accept the implications

As for the impulses that drive men to evil, misguidance and sin, Islam declares them to be too weak to gain complete dominance over man. Their dominance is one of trial and testing, as expressed in the struggle between man and Satan. Faith, the awareness of God, and seeking refuge with Him—all these form a strong barrier to the victory of Satan.

"[Whereupon Iblis] said: "O my Sustainer! Since Thou has thwarted me, I shall indeed make [all that is evil] on earth seem goodly to them and shall most certainly beguile them into grievous error— [all] save such of them as are truly Thy servants!"

Said He: This is, with Me, a straight way: verily, thou shalt have no power over My creatures—unless it be such as are [already] lost in grievous error and follow thee [of their own will]." (Al-Hijr: 39–42)

"Saying: "Down with you all from this [state of innocence, and be henceforth] enemies unto one another! None the less, there shall most certainly come unto you guidance from Me: and he who follows My guidance will not go astray, and neither will he be unhappy.

But as for him who shall turn away from remembering Me—his shall be a life of narrow scope; and on the Day of Resurrection We shall raise him up blind."

[And so, on Resurrection Day, the sinner] will ask: "O my Sustainer! Why hast Thou raised me up blind, whereas [on earth] I was endowed with sight?"

[God] will reply: "Thus it is: there came unto thee Our messages, but thou wert oblivious of them; and thus shalt thou be today consigned to oblivion!"   (Ta Ha: 123–126)

"And when everything will have been decided, Satan will say: "Behold, God promised you something that was bound to come true! I, too, held out [all manner of] promises to you—but I deceived you. Yet I had no power at all over you: I but called you—and you responded unto me. Hence, blame not me, but blame yourselves. It is not for me to respond to your cries, nor for you to respond to mine: for, behold I have [always] refused to admit that there was any truth in your erstwhile belief that I had a share in God's divinity."

Verily, for all evildoers there is grievous suffering in store."   (Ibrahim: 22)

"NOW whenever thou happen to read this Qur'an, seek refuge with God from Satan, the accursed.

Behold, he has no power over those who have attained to faith and in their Sustainer place their trust: he has power only over those who are willing to follow him, and who [thus] ascribe to him a share in God's divinity."   (An-Nahl: 98–100)

"Those who have attained to faith fight in the cause of God, whereas those who are bent on denying the truth fight in the cause of the powers of evil. Fight, then, against those friends of Satan: verily, Satan's guile is weak indeed!"   (An-Nisa': 76)

But there remains the following question: if God, may He be glorified, is the one who creates every human with specific capacities and predispositions which incline him either to good or to evil and misguidance, how can God inflict punishment on the evildoer and bestow reward on the doer of good, whether in this world or the hereafter?

The question is deceptive if posed in this form, and it is refuted by what the Qur'an tells us. God created man originally in the best of forms; he loses that high rank only by being heedless of God; he is to be tested with good and evil; and he has the capacity to choose and prefer, while seeking the aid of God, Who assists all who strive to attain His satisfaction.

"Verily, We create man in the best conformation, and thereafter We reduce him to the lowest of low—excepting only such as attain to faith and do good works: and theirs shall be a reward unending!"

(At-Tin: 4–6)

"Consider the human self, and how it is formed in accordance with what it is meant to be, and how it is imbued with moral failings as well as with consciousness of God! To a happy state shall indeed attain he who causes this [self] to grow in purity, and truly lost is he who buries it [in darkness]."   (Ash-Shams: 7–10)

"Verily, it is We who have created man out of a drop of sperm intermingled, so that We might try him [in his later life]: and therefore We made him a being endowed with hearing and sight.

Verily, We have shown him the way: [and it rests with him to prove himself] either grateful or ungrateful.

[Now,] behold, for those who deny the truth We have readied chains and shackles, and a blazing flame."   (Al-Insan: 2–4)

"Verily, [O men,] you aim at most divergent ends!

Thus, as for him who gives [to others] and is conscious of God, and believes in the truth of the ultimate good—for him shall We make easy the path towards [ultimate] ease.

But as for him who is niggardly, and thinks that he is self-sufficient, and calls the ultimate good a lie—for him shall We make easy the path towards hardship."   (Al-Layl: 4–10)

"But as for those who strive hard in Our cause—We shall most certainly guide them onto paths that lead into Us: for, behold, God is indeed with the doers of good."   (Al-'Ankabut: 69)

The question is also refuted by our previous explanation of how God's destiny for humans is fulfilled in them by means of the way in which they exercize their own will, with respect both to themselves and to their surroundings.

In addition, the Islamic concept teaches the Muslim that God has imposed on him clear-cut duties and mandated clear-cut prohibitions. Both are set out unequivocally, and disclosed to human understanding without concealment or doubt. These are the things for which he shall be held accountable.

As for the unseen and destiny, and what lies beyond his perception, these are matters which a Muslim is not required to explore, and he has not been asked to do anything pertaining to them, except to believe in God's destiny, the good and the ill.

Therefore, the path of the Muslim is straightforward and defined. His path is to fulfill his clear-cut obligations, to the degree that he is able, and to avoid all that has been clearly prohibited. Further, he must learn what has been commanded or prohibited, and refrain from searching out whatever lies beyond the realm of his limited perception. For God, may He be glorified, would not impose on man anything lying beyond his capacities or a duty impossible for him to fulfill. Similarly, he would not forbid man anything from which he could not possibly abstain, or to doing which he would be irresistibly driven.

"God does not burden any human being with more than he is well able to bear: in his favour shall be whatever good he does, and against him whatever evil he does.

"O our Sustainer! Take us not to task if we forget or unwittingly do wrong!

"O our Sustainer! Lay not upon us a burden such as Thou didst lay upon those who lived before us! O Our Sustainer! Make us not bear burdens which we have no strength to bear!

"And efface Thou our sins, and grant us forgiveness, and bestow Thy mercy upon us! Thou art our Lord Supreme: succour us, then, against people who deny the truth!"   (Al-Baqarah: 286)

"And [so,] whenever they commit a shameful deed, they are wont to say, "We found our forefathers doing it," and, "God has enjoined it upon us."

Say: "Behold, never does God enjoin deeds of abomination, Would you attribute unto God something of which you have no knowledge?"

Say: "My Sustainer has [but] enjoined the doing of what is right; and [He desires you to] put your whole being into every act of worship, and to call unto Him, sincere in your faith in Him alone. As it was He who brought you into being in the first instance, so also [unto Him] you will return."   (Al-A'raf: 28–29)

Anyone who thinks that God would impose duties on humans that lie beyond their capacity, or prohibit them matters from which they cannot abstain cannot be a true believer.

Thus, a balance is achieved in faith and feeling, as balance is achieved in activity and movement. The Islamic concept stirs in the conscience the desire to do good and be steadfast, dynamic and effective, while at the same time seeking God's assistance in Whose hands rest all things.

The concept annuls and invalidates all kinds of negativism and procrastination, of paralysis and immobility, and the attribution of wrongdoing to God's will. The Muslim knows that God does not accept unbelief from His servants, and does not like sin to spread among the believers. He is not content that evil should remain uncontested, that truth should remain unchampioned, that the earth should remain without a vicegerent. The Muslim knows that man is in this world for the purpose of testing and trial; that he is being tested in all of his deeds and his states; that he will be requited for all the good and evil he does; that he has been placed on this earth as God's vicegerent; and that he either fulfills that role and is rewarded, or neglects it and is punished, even if that neglect is the result of fear.

Another form of balance is that existing between man's absolute servitude before God, and the position of honor he enjoys in the universe. It is this balance which has protected the Islamic concept from all the upheavals which have afflicted other religious concepts and beliefs, ranging from the deification of man in various ways to the belittling and even degradation of man.

From the outset, Islam makes a clear and total separation between the nature of divinity and the nature of man's servitude and the characteristics and attributes of each state; there is no doubt or confusion whatsoever in the matter.

"There is nothing like unto Him;" so none shares in His essence or nature.

"He is the first and the last, the apparent and the hidden;" so no one shares existence with Him.

"All that are upon the earth shall vanish; the face of thy Lord alone shall remain, the possessor of splendor and generosity;" so none shares in His eternity.

"He cannot be asked concerning what He does, but they can be asked concerning what they do;" so none shares in His sovereignty.

"He is the creator of all things;" so no one shares with Him creation.

"He spreads out sustenance for whomsoever He wills in due proportion;" so no one shares with Him the granting of sustenance.

"He knows and you do not know;" so no one shares with Him knowledge.

"There is none like unto Him;" so no one shares His status.

"Do they have partners who have legislated for them a religion that God has not permitted?;" so no one shares in His legislation for mankind.

As for man, he is a servant of God, as is every other creature in existence, a servant who does not share with God either essence or attribute, by contrast with what the Church says concerning Jesus, upon whom be peace, that he had a purely divine nature, or a nature that was both divine and human, depending on the interpretations put forward by different sects.

"[As for Jesus,] he was nothing but [a human being—] a servant [of Ours] whom We had graced [with prophethood], and whom We made an example for the children of Israel."   (Zukhruf: 59)

"Never did the Christ feel too proud to be God's servant, nor do the angels who are near unto Him. And those who feel too proud to serve Him and glory in their arrogance [should know that on Judgment Day] He will gather them all unto Himself."   (An-Nisa': 172)

"Not one of all [the beings] that are in the heavens or on earth appears before the Most Gracious other than as a servant."
(Maryam: 93)

But man, precisely by virtue of this servitude to God, is noble in the sight of God. He has infused His spirit into him, and ennobled him in the universe to such a degree that the angels—the closest of all of God's servants to Him—prostrate before man in acknowledgement of his nobility.

"And lo! thy Sustainer said unto the angels: "Behold, I am about to create mortal man out of sounding clay, out of dark slime trans-

muted; and when I have formed him fully and breathed into him of
My spirit, fall down before him in prostration!"

Thereupon the angels prostrated themselves, all of them
together."   (Al-Hijr: 28–30)

He is a vicegerent on this earth, given dominion over all it contains, for it has been made subservient to him even before he himself
existed:

"AND LO! Thy Sustainer said unto the angels: "Behold, I am about
to establish upon earth one who shall inherit it."

They said: "Wilt Thou place on it such as will spread corruption thereon and shed blood—whereas it is we who extol Thy limitless glory, and praise Thee, and hallow Thy name?"

[God] answered: "Verily, I know that which you do not know."

And He imparted unto Adam the names of all things; then He
brought them within the ken of the angels and said: "Declare unto
Me the names of these [things], if what you say is true."

They replied: "Limitless art Thou in Thy glory! No knowledge
have we save that which Thou hast imparted unto us. Verily, Thou
alone art all-knowing, truly wise.

Said He: "O Adam, convey unto them the names of these
[things]."

And as soon as [Adam] had conveyed unto them their names,
[God] said: "Did I not say unto you, 'Verily, I alone know the hidden
reality of the heavens and the earth, and know all that you bring into
the open and all that you would conceal'?"   (Al-Baqarah: 30–33)

"And He has made subservient to you, [as a gift] from Himself, all
that is in the heavens and on earth: in this, behold, there are messages indeed for people who think!"   (Al-Jathiyah: 13)

"And he has placed firm mountains on earth, lest it sway with you,
and rivers and paths, so that you might find your way."

(An-Nahl: 15)

"Art thou not aware that it is God who has made subservient to you all
that is on earth, and the ships that sail through the sea at His behest—
and [that it is He who] holds the celestial bodies [in their orbits], so
that they may not fall upon the earth otherwise than by His leave?

Verily, God is most compassionate towards men, a dispenser of
grace."   (Al-Hajj: 65)

Man attains his most elevated rank and highest position when he has attained servitude to God, for he is then in fullest conformity to his innate nature.

The rank of servitude to God is that with which the Messenger of God was characterized (peace be upon him) when he received revelation and when he undertook his nocturnal journey to Jerusalem and ascent to heaven.

This rank or status of man is what safeguards him against servitude to those who are themselves slaves—the servility of slaves to slaves; it is what preserves man's dignity, regardless of worldly position. It is what makes him bow his head to no one but God. It protects man from engaging in tyranny and self-aggrandizement, in arrogance and corruption, and mobilizes in his heart piety, reverential fear of the sole Lord before whom all servants are equal. It rejects all claims by His servants to any of the attributes of divinity, such as legislating for men's lives without permission from God, regarding one's own person as the source of legitimacy and his will as a law to rule over men's lives.

Therefore, there is no contradiction in the Islamic concept between man's elevated status, his dignity and worth, on the one hand, and his servitude to God Almighty, and belief in God's exclusive possession of divinity of God and all its attributes.

There is no need, therefore, when it is intended to elevate and honor man, to eliminate his servitude to God or to add to his human nature a divinity that does not belong to him, as did the heads of churches and synods, in order to glorify Jesus (peace be upon him).

> "Indeed, the truth deny they who say, "Behold, God is the Christ, son of Mary"—seeing that the Christ [himself] said, "O children of Israel! Worship God [alone], who is my Sustainer as well as your Sustainer." Behold, whoever ascribes divinity to any being beside God, unto him will God deny paradise, and his goal shall be the fire; and such evildoers will have none to succour them!
>
> "Indeed, the truth deny they who say, "Behold, God is the third of a trinity"—seeing that there is no deity whatever save the One God. And unless they desist from this their assertion, grievous suffering is bound to befall such of them as are bent on denying the truth. Will they not, then, turn towards God in repentance, and ask His forgiveness? For God is much-forgiving, a dispenser of grace.

The Christ, son of Mary, was but an apostle: all [other] apostles had passed away before him: and his mother was one who never deviated from the truth; and they both ate food [like other mortals].

Behold how clear We make these messages unto them: and then behold how perverted are their minds!"   (Al-Ma'idah: 72–75)

"AND LO! God said: "O Jesus, son of Mary! Didst thou say unto men, 'Worship me and my mother as deities beside God'?"

[Jesus] answered: "Limitless art Thou in Thy glory!

It would not have been possible for me to say what I had no right to [say]! Had I said this, Thou wouldst indeed have known it! Thou knowest all that is within myself, whereas I know not what is in Thy Self. Verily, it is Thou alone who fully knowest all the things that are beyond the reach of a created being's perception.

Nothing did I tell them beyond what Thou didst bid me [to say]: 'Worship God, [who is] my Sustainer as well as your Sustainer.' And I bore witness to what they did as long as I dwelt in their midst: but since Thou hast caused me to die, Thou alone hast been their keeper: for Thou art witness unto everything.

If thou cause them to suffer—verily, they are Thy servants: and if Thou forgive them—verily, Thou alone art almighty, truly wise!"   (Al-Ma'idah: 116–118)

"Never did the Christ feel too proud to be God's servant, nor do the angels who are near unto Him. And those who feel too proud to serve Him and glory in their arrogance [should know that on Judgment Day] He will gather them all unto Himself."   (An-Nisa': 172)

Likewise, there is no need to diminish God whenever it is desired to elevate man and his status on earth, by proclaiming his dominion and control whenever God enables him to make some new discovery in the world of matter or whenever He makes subservient to him some energy present in the universe.

God and man are not equal; they are not adversaries or competitors, where one must triumph in order for the other to be defeated.

Ancient Greek and Hebrew mythology have implanted in the minds of the Europeans an ugly and foolish notion to this effect, and there it has remained even after their conversion to Christianity.

The Greek myth depicts the great god Zeus as angry with the god Prometheus, because he had stolen the sacred fire (the secret of knowledge) and given it to man behind the back of the grand god, for Zeus did not wish man to have knowledge, lest man's status be elevated and that of Zeus reduced, and with him that of all the gods. He therefore delivered him over to the most brutal and savage reprisal.

The Hebrew myth depicts God as fearful lest man eat from the tree of life, after eating from the tree of knowledge, thus becoming one of the gods. Man was therefore expelled from paradise, and kept back from the tree of life by stout guards and flaming swords.

Then there is the myth launched by Nietzsche, writhing like an epileptic, in *Thus Spake Zarathustra*: the death of God and the birth of superman.

> "A monstrous word it is, issuing out of their mouths. They say nothing but a lie."   (Al-Kahf: 4)

In Islam, man always takes up his true place in quiet dignity and tranquillity. He is a servant of God, but by virtue of his servitude, also the most honored of God's creation. This is the most exalted, fitting and blessed station.

We therefore deduce from the foregoing that the European concepts, in which these various mythical visions were entrenched, becoming part and parcel of their thought processes and methodologies, together with the different schools that arose on their bases—all are in conflict, apparent or hidden, with the Islamic concept and Islamic methods of thought. Any borrowing from those concepts or the schools of thought arising from them carries within itself a natural enmity to Islam and Islamic thought; no such borrowing will therefore be fitting. It would, indeed, be like imbibing a poison that destroys the tissues of the body, damages its organs, and ultimately results in death, in case of a high dose.

A further type of balance in man's relations with his Lord is that existing between that which inspires fear, apprehension and awe, on the one hand, and that which inspires security, tranquillity and intimacy on the other. For God's attributes as they manifest in the universe, in the life of man and living beings in general, combine these two types of inspiration in perfect balance.

A Muslim reads in God's glorious book descriptions of God's characteristics which wrench his heart and shake him to his roots:

"O you who have attained to faith! Respond to the call of God and the Apostle whenever he calls you unto that which will give you life; and know that God intervenes between man and [the desires of] his heart, and that unto Him you shall be gathered."   (Al-Anfal: 24)

"[For] He is aware of the [most] stealthy glance, and of all that the hearts would conceal."   (Ghafir: 19)

"NOW, VERILY, it is We who have created man, and we know what his innermost self whispers within him: for we are closer to him than his neck-vein."   (Qaf: 16)

"But you will incur no sin if you give a hint of [an intended] marriage-offer to [any of] these women, or if you conceive such an intention without making it obvious: [for] God knows that you intend to ask them in marriage. Do not, however, plight your troth with them in secret, but speak only in a decent manner; and do not proceed with tying the marriage–knot ere the ordained [term of waiting] has come to its end. And know that God knows what is in your minds, and therefore remain conscious of Him; and know, too that God is much-forgiving, forbearing."   (Al-Baqarah: 235)

"AND PERFORM the pilgrimage and the pious visit [to Mecca] in honour of God; and if you are held back, give instead whatever offering you can easily afford. And do not shave your heads until the offering has been sacrificed; but he from among you who is ill or suffers from an ailment of the head shall redeem himself by fasting, or alms, or [any other] act of worship. And if you are hale and secure, then he who takes advantage of a pious visit before the [time of] pilgrimage shall give whatever offering he can easily afford; whereas he who cannot afford it shall fast for three days during the pilgrimage and for seven days after your return: that is, ten full [days]. All this relates to him who does not live near the Inviolable House of Worship.

And remain conscious of God, and know that God is severe in retribution."   (Al-Baqarah: 196)

"Hence, leave Me alone with such as give the lie to this tiding. We shall bring them low, step by step, without their perceiving how it has come about: for, behold, though I may give them rein for a while My subtle scheme is exceedingly firm!"   (Al-Qalam: 44–45)

"VERILY, thy Sustainer's grip is exceedingly strong!"   (Al-Buruj: 12)

"Aforetime, as a guidance unto mankind, and it is He who has bestowed [upon man] the standard by which to discern the true from the false.

Behold, as for those who are bent on denying God's messages—grievous suffering awaits them: for God is almighty, an avenger of evil."
(Al-'Imran: 4)

"And such is thy Sustainer's punishing grasp whenever He takes to task any community that is given to evildoing: verily, His punishing grasp is grievous, severe!"
(Hud: 102)

"And leave Me alone [to deal] with those who give the lie to the truth—those who enjoy the blessings of life [without any thought of God]—and bear thou with them for a little while: for, behold, heavy fetters [await them] with Us, and a blazing fire, and food that chokes, and grievous suffering on the Day when the earth and the mountains will be convulsed, and the mountains will [crumble and] become like a sand-dune on the move!"
(Al-Muzzamil: 11–14)

These descriptions of torment on the Day of Judgment are indeed terrifying.[34]

But at the same time, a Muslim reads of characteristics of his God that fill his heart with comfort and a sense of security, his spirit with a sense of intimacy and closeness, his soul with hope and confidence.

"AND IF MY servants ask thee about Me—behold, I am near; I respond to the call of him who calls, whenever he calls unto Me: let them, then, respond unto Me, and believe in Me, so that they might follow the right way."
(Al-Baqarah: 186)

"Nay—who is it that responds to the distressed when he calls out to Him, and who removes the ill [that caused the distress], and has made you inherit the earth?

Could there be any divine power besides God? How seldom do you keep this in mind!"
(Al-Naml: 62)

"Satan threatens you with the prospect of poverty and bids you to be niggardly, whereas God promises you His forgiveness and bounty; and God is infinite, all-knowing."
(Al-Baqarah: 268)

---

34 See my *Mashahid al-Qiyama fi 'l-Qur'an.*

"And thus have We willed you to be a community of the middle way, so that [with your lives] you might bear witness to the truth before all mankind, and that the Apostle might bear witness to it before you.

And it is only to the end that We might make a clear distinction between those who follow the Apostle and those who turn about on their heels that We have appointed [for this community] the direction of prayer which thou [O Prophet] hast formerly observed: for this was indeed a hard test for all but those whom God has guided aright. But God will surely not lose sight of your faith—for, behold, God is most compassionate towards man, a dispenser of grace."   (Al-Baqarah: 143)

"God wants to lighten your burdens: for man has been created weak."   (An-Nisa': 28)

"Why would God cause you to suffer [for your past sins] if you are grateful and attain to belief—seeing that God is always responsive to gratitude, all-knowing?"   (An-Nisa': 147)

"VERILY, those who attain to faith and do righteous deeds will the Most Gracious endow with love."   (Maryam: 96)

"And He alone is truly-forgiving, all-embracing in His love."
                                                          (Al-Buruj: 14)

"But there is [also] a kind of man who would willingly sell his own self in order to please God: and God is most compassionate towards His servants."   (Al-Baqarah: 207)

"[A divine writ] unerringly straight, meant to warn [the godless] of a severe punishment from Him, and to give unto the believers who do good works the glad tiding that theirs shall be a goodly reward—[a state of bliss] in which they shall dwell beyond the count of time."
                                                          (Al-Kahf: 2–3)

The images of bliss in the scenes of the Day of Resurrection convey inordinate comfort!

Thus a balance is achieved in the human conscience between fear and expectation, awe and intimacy, terror and tranquillity. Men proceed with their lives, moving forward on the path to God, with firm steps, open eyes, and a vigorous heart, replete with hope. Avoiding all slippery slopes, he ascends toward the bright horizon. He is neither frivolous nor negligent, neither oblivious nor forgetful. At the same time he is cognizant of God's care and assistance, His mercy and munificence, and aware that God does not wish him ill or hardship, nor does He cause him to trespass so that He might find satisfaction in wreaking vengeance on him. God far transcends that.

Compare this concept of God with the Greek concept of their god—harsh, envious, lustful, and resentful; the aberrant concept of the Israelites of their God—jealous and fanatical, tyrannical and reckless; Aristotle's concept of God—transcendent, uninvolved in the affairs of creation, and thinking only of himself, because he is the noblest of beings, and it behoves God to think only of the noblest of beings; or the materialists' concept of their god, "nature," who is deaf, blind and dumb. Such a comparison makes plain the great value of the balance to be found in the Islamic concept and its practical effect on human life and morality.

Furthermore, there is a balance between the sources of knowledge: knowledge derived from the hidden realm of the unseen, and knowledge derived from the perceptible universe; in other words: from revelation and sacred text, and from the universe and life.

At the beginning of the present book, we saw how concepts were transformed in Europe, from taking revelation alone as the source of knowledge, to taking reason alone as the source, and then taking nature alone as the source. Each group went to extremes in deifying a particular source of knowledge and negating other sources.

Islam, on the other hand, is characterized by comprehensiveness, balance, and the recognition of all actual truths, without going to extremes, without ulterior purpose, without ignorance, and without deficiency.

In its comfortable recognition of truth—complete and all-embracing—Islam has not overlooked a single source of knowledge, ranking all the sources as they deserve to be, with precision and balance.

Islam indeed attributes all matters in principle to God, His Will and contrivance, and likewise attributes all of creation to the will of the One God—the universe and all it comprises, including man, his reason and his faculties. There is therefore no contradiction in the universe—or "nature," as the Westerners call it—including economics, the god of Karl Marx, playing a role in assisting man to gain knowledge by means of his reason and other faculties placed within him. For all is from God—the universe and reason—just like revelation.

It is true that Islam considers revelation to be the ultimately veracious source of knowledge, unassailable by falsehood and immune to error; it is therefore the highest source. At the same time, however, it does not invalidate reason or the knowledge that man acquires from the universe in which he lives. The universe itself is God's open book and knowledge gushes forth from it. There is, however, a difference: the knowledge that man acquires of the universe by means of his own perception is fallible, whereas what man receives by way of revelation is absolutely veracious.

God created man's nature in harmony with the universe and all living beings, for all are His creation, all receive from Him, and all benefit from His guidance.

> "He replied: "Our Sustainer is He who gives unto every thing [that exists] its true nature and form, and thereupon guides it [towards its fulfilment]."   (Ta Ha: 50)

> "EXTOL the limitless glory of thy Sustainer's name: [the glory of] the All-Highest, Who creates [every thing], and thereupon forms it in accordance with what it is meant to be, and who determines the nature [of all that exists], and thereupon guides it [towards its fulfilment]."   (Al-A'la: 1–3)

> "And in everything have We created opposites, so that you might hear in mind [that God alone is One]."   (Adh-Dhariyat: 49)

> "Although there is no beast that walks on earth and no bird that flies on its two wings which is not [God's] creature like yourselves: no single thing have We neglected in Our decree.
> And once again: Unto their Sustainer shall they [all] be gathered."   (Al-An'am: 38)

> "HE IT IS who has made the earth a cradle for you, and has traced out for you ways [of livelihood] thereon, and [who] sends down waters from the sky: and by this means We bring forth various kinds of plants."   (Ta Ha: 53)

> "Out of this [earth] have We created you, and into it shall We return you, and out of it shall We bring you forth once again."   (Ta Ha: 55)

"Limitless in His glory is He who has created opposites in whatever the earth produces, and in men's own selves, and in that of which [as yet] they have no knowledge."   (Ya Sin: 36)

"The Originator [is He] of the heavens and the earth. He has given you mates of your own kind—just as [He has willed that] among the beasts [there be] mates—to multiply you thereby: [but] there is nothing like unto Him, and He alone is all-hearing all-seeing."
                                                        (Ash-Shura: 11)

There are numerous Qur'anic verses which speak of harmony and cooperation among all of God's creation, including man, which powerfully suggest that unity and solidarity characterize the very nature of creation:

"HAVE WE NOT made the earth a resting-place [for you], and the mountains [its] pegs?

And We have created you in pairs, and We have made your sleep [a symbol of] death and made the night [its] cloak and made the day [a symbol of] life.

And We have built above you seven firmaments, and have placed [therein the sun,] a lamp full of blazing splendour.

And from the wind-driven clouds We send down waters pouring in abundance, so that We might bring forth thereby grain, and herbs, and gardens dense with foliage."   (An-Naba': 6–16)

"[O MEN] Are you more difficult to create than the heaven which He has built?

High has He reared its vault and formed it in accordance with what it was meant to be; and He has made dark its night and brought forth its light of day.

And after that, the earth: wide has He spread its expanse, and has caused its waters to come out of it, and its pastures, and has made the mountains firm: [all this] as a means of livelihood for you and your animals."   (An-Nazi'at: 27–33)

"Let man, then, consider [the sources of] his food: [how it is] that We pour down water, pouring it down abundantly; and then We cleave the earth [with new growth], cleaving it asunder, and thereupon We cause grain to grow out of it, and vines and edible plants, and olive trees and date-palms, and gardens dense with foliage and fruits and herbage, for you and for your animals to enjoy."   ('Abasa: 24–32)

"AND GOD sends down water from the skies, giving life thereby to the earth after it had been lifeless: in this, behold, there is a message indeed for people who [are willing to] listen.

And, behold, in the cattle [too] there is indeed a lesson for you: We give you to drink of that [fluid] which is [secreted from] within their bellies between that which is to be eliminated [from the animal's body] and [its] life-blood: milk pure and pleasant to those who drink it.

And [We grant you nourishment] from the fruit of date-palms and vines: from it you derive intoxicants as well as wholesome sustenance—in this, behold, there is a message indeed for people who use their reason!

And [consider how] thy Sustainer has inspired the bee: "Prepare for thyself dwellings in mountains and in trees, and in what [men] may build [for thee by way of hives]; and then eat of all manner of fruit, and follow humbly the paths ordained for thee by thy Sustainer."

[And lo!] there issues from within these [bees] a fluid of many hues, wherein there is health for man.

In all this, behold, there is a message indeed for people who think!"   (An-Nahl: 65–69)

"And God has given you [the ability to build] your houses as places of rest, and has endowed you with [the skill to make] dwellings out of the skins of animals—easy for you to handle when you travel and when you camp—and [to make] furnishings and goods for temporary use of their [rough] wool and their soft, furry wool and their hair.

And among the many objects of His creation, God has appointed for you [various] means of protection: thus, He has given you in the mountains places of shelter, and has endowed you with [the ability to make] garments to protect you from heat [and cold], as well as such garments as might protect you from your [mutual] violence.

In this way does He bestow the full measure of His blessings on you, so that you might surrender yourselves unto Him."
                                                        (An-Nahl: 80–81)

There are many similar such verses, which we will cite later. What concerns us now is that basing itself on the harmony and concord that exist between the universe and man, Islam has made of nature, the universe and life a source of knowledge for man, derived either from the open book of nature or from man's own being. He is, in short, a source of his own knowledge.

Verses such as the following are to be found in the primary, most veracious source, that which presides over all other sources:

"VERILY, this Qur'an shows the way to all that is most upright, and gives the believers who do good deeds the glad tiding that theirs will be a great reward."   (Al-Isra': 9)

"And finally, [O Muhammad,] We have set thee on a way by which the purpose [of faith] may be fulfilled: so follow thou this [way], and follow not the likes and dislikes of those who do not know [the truth]."
                                                                  (Al-Jathiyah: 18)

"Behold, we have bestowed it from on high as a discourse in the Arabic tongue, so that you might encompass it with your reason.

In the measure that We reveal this Qur'an unto thee, [O Prophet,] We explain it to thee in the best possible way, seeing that ere this thou wert indeed among those who are unaware [of what revelation is]."   (Yusuf: 2–3)

"[For although] We did say, "Down with you all from this [state]," there shall, none the less, most certainly come unto you guidance from Me: and those who follow My guidance need have no fear, and neither shall they grieve; but those who are bent on denying the truth and giving the lie to Our messages—they are destined for the fire, and therein shall they abide."   (Al-Baqarah: 38–39)

"And, lo, We accepted your solemn pledge, raising Mount Sinai high above you, [saying,] "Hold fast with [all your] strength unto what We have vouchsafed you, and hearken unto it!"

[But] they say, "We have heard, but we disobey"—for their hearts are filled to overflowing with love of the [golden] calf because of their refusal to acknowledge the truth.

Say: "Vile is what this [false] belief of yours enjoins upon you—if indeed you are believers!"   (Al-Baqarah: 93)

We also find many verses that enjoin on man the acquisition of knowledge from the open book of the universe and the hidden book of the self:

"AND ON EARTH there are signs [of God's existence, visible] to all who are endowed with inner certainty, just as [there are signs thereof] within your own selves: can you not, then, see?"
(Adh-Dhariyat: 20–21)

"In time We shall make them fully understand Our messages [through what they perceive] in the utmost horizons [of the universe] and within themselves, so that it will become clear unto them that this [revelation] is indeed the truth. [Still,] is it not enough [for them to know] that thy Sustainer is witness unto everything?"   (Fussilat: 53)

"DO, THEN, they [who deny resurrection] never gaze at the clouds pregnant with water, [and observe] how they are created?
    And at the sky, how it is raised aloft?
    And at the mountains, how firmly they are reared?
    And at the earth, how it is spread out?
    And so, [O Prophet,] exhort them; thy task is only to exhort."
(Al-Ghashiyah: 17–21)

"Have, then they [who deny the truth] never considered the birds, enabled [by God] to fly in mid-air, with none but God holding them aloft? In this, behold, there are messages indeed for people who will believe!"
(An-Nahl: 79)

"Verily, in the creation of the heavens and of the earth, and the succession of night and day: and in the ships that speed through the sea with what is useful to man: and in the waters which God sends down from the sky. Giving life thereby to the earth after it had been lifeless, and causing all manner of living creatures to multiply thereon: and in the change of the winds, and the clouds that run their appointed courses between sky and earth: [in all this] there are messages indeed for people who use their reason."   (Al-Baqarah: 164)

Then there are many verses relating to the use of the intellect for attaining knowledge, either by reflecting on the tokens of God in creation or by contemplating the truths of revelation and life:

"Say: "I counsel you one thing only: Be [ever-conscious of] standing before God, whether you are in the company of others or alone; and then bethink yourselves [that] there is no madness in [this prophet,] your fellow-man; he is only a warner to you of suffering severe to come."
(Saba': 46)

"Will they not, then, try to understand this Qur'an? Had it issued from any but God, they would surely have found in it many an inner contradiction!"   (An-Nisa': 82)

"Have they, then, never journeyed about the earth, letting their hearts gain wisdom, and causing their ears to hear? Yet, verily, it is not their eyes that have become blind—but blind have become the hearts that are in their breasts!"   (Al-Hajj: 46)

"Verily, in the creation of the heavens and the earth, and in the succession of night and day, there are indeed messages for all who are endowed with insight, [and] who remember God when they stand, and when they sit, and when they lie down to sleep, and [thus] reflect on the creation of the heavens and the earth.

"O our Sustainer! Thou hast not created [aught of] this without meaning and purpose. Limitless art Thou in Thy glory! Keep us safe, then, from suffering through fire!"   (Al-'Imran: 190–191)

"And God has brought you forth from your mothers' wombs knowing nothing—but He has endowed you with hearing, and sight, and minds, so that you might have cause to be grateful."   (An-Nahl: 78)

These sources are thus in balance with each other, each in its proper place, working together to bestow knowledge on man. Such is the balanced concept of Islam; there is no confusion or clash among the sources of knowledge, and that which is not God is not deified.

The pedagogical method of the Qur'an repeatedly directs man's attention to the signs and indications found in the cosmos and in man's own being, to discovering the marks of His creativity in their own selves and on the horizons. It draws his attention to recognizing the Creator from His creation, to glorifying Him by perceiving the splendor manifest in His works, to loving Him by realizing the extent of His bounties. Man's perception itself bears the signs of God's work, marked as it is by precision, harmony, balance, and freedom from contradiction. It is not, for example, a small thing that man should deduce from his observation of the continuous change that pervades the universe and his own being, that permanence and immutability belong to God alone, and that all things pass away other than the Eternally Living Who never dies, the immutable goal to which all things tend. Nor is it a small thing that man deduces from his observation of the stable norms that regulate change, that matters do not proceed without purpose, that life is not in vain, and that man has not been left to his own devices. There is a process of governance and planning at work, of trial and reward, of precise and trenchant justice.

Man's attention is thus drawn repeatedly to the sources of knowledge, those manifest in the universe and those hidden in his own being, in order to draw knowledge both from God's open book and from His book of words, in harmony and balance, all drawn together, without contradiction, and unmarred by the petty hostilities that we see in the history of Western thought. Revelation, as the fundamental source of knowledge, does not necessitate the annulling of human perception; nor does the existence of the universe necessitate the annulling of reason or of God, Who is exalted above the feeble, auspicious concepts worshipped by the Westerners and their slaves.

Finally, there is a balance between the agency of man and that of the universe, between the station of man and that of the universe. The Islamic concept is free, in this respect as in others, from all the fluctuations and reversals that have accompanied human thought whenever it deviates from God's path.

The clarity and unambiguity of the Islamic concept with respect to the universe and man becomes fully manifest when one compares it to the myriad philosophies, concepts and beliefs that have accumulated throughout history.

Plato, for instance, ascribed to matter the lowest degree of value and importance. "For Plato, existence consists of two opposing planes: that of absolute reason, and that of pure matter. Power is the attribute of absolute reason, and impotence, the attribute of pure matter. Beings exist along a spectrum: the more they partake of reason, the higher they are, and the more they partake of matter, the lower they are. Pure matter is in opposition to absolute reason, and it can create nothing by its own will."[35]

Plotinus (or the Neo-Platonic school) likewise assigns matter the lowest of all degrees. The one and unique principle creates reason, reason creates the spirit, and spirit creates beings inferior to itself in descending degrees until they ultimately reach the world of pure matter, the world of generation and corruption."[36]

[35] Al-Aqqad, *Allah*, p.137.
[36] Ibid, p.188.

Christianity, as manufactured by the Church, considered evil in its entirety to be embodied in the corporeal world—that is, the world of matter—and good in its entirety to be present in the world of the spirit. It hence became necessary to denigrate all that is material, and to escape it in order to be saved from evil and corruption. This is also the path previously taken by Hinduism.

While the material realm had been effectively discarded by certain creeds and philosophies, there arose in the nineteenth century those who wished to make a god out of nature and man's reason a creation of that god. This was the wish of Comte and Nietzsche. Others wished to deify a single aspect of the material world; economics, in the face of which man's role is entirely passive, this, of course, is the view of Marx.

Over against these fluctuating views and exaggerations of various types stands the Islamic concept, resting on a firm and stable foundation. God is the Creator, the Originator, the Sovereign. Man and the universe are His creation, and they cooperate harmoniously with each other, each having a role in the life of the other. Man is the noblest of creation, most active and productive; matter is subservient to him, for he creates from it, changes and develops it, brings forth from it secrets God has placed within it, and learns from them.

The ennobling of man—which does not lead to a belittling of the material universe—guarantees man a lofty standing and bestows on his life such dignity that he does not stand in need of ennoblement by any material factor. But none of this leads either to a belittling of the material universe or to a neglect of material values.

There are but some examples of the balance that pervades the Islamic concept; here, we cannot go into further detail concerning them. Our purpose is to set them before the reader so that he may follow them as he advances on the path.[37]

---

[37] See Muhammad Qutb, *Manhaj al-Tarbiyat al-Islamiyya*.

7

POSITIVE ORIENTATION

"And say [unto them, O Prophet]: "Act! And God will behold your deeds, and [so will] His Apostle and the believers."

(At-Tawbah: 105)

The fifth outstanding characteristic of the Islamic concept is positivism, by which we mean that God's relationship with the universe, life and man is a positive one and that man is similarly endowed with a positive and active role within his own sphere.

According to the Islamic concept, the attributes of God are not negative attributes. Divine perfection does not have the negative sense that Aristotle supposed. Moreover, it is not confined to certain aspects of creation or dominion as the Persians imagined with respect to Ahuramazda, the god of light and good, ranged against Ahriman, the god of darkness and evil, each with his own domain. Nor is it limited to a single degree of creation as Plotinus imagined, or to a single people as the Israelites claim. Nor is it intermingled with the will of another form of being, as some Christian sects believe. Nor is it absolute nothingness, as is postulated by the materialists, who deny the very existence of the living God who has the attribute of will.

It will perhaps be appropriate, before expounding the clear and explicit Islamic concept, to review summarily the various concepts to which we have referred, the "debris," as we called it at the beginning of this book.

"The view of Aristotle in respect of God is that He is an everlasting, infinite being, without beginning or end, without action or will, for action implies desire for a thing and God is free of all desire. As for will, this implies a choice between two things, and God has the best and most suitable of all things to the degree of perfection, and so He has no need to choose between what is good and what is not, nor between what is good and what is better. It does not behove God, in Aristotle's view, that His action begin at a certain time, for He is eternal and everlasting, and nothing affects Him that might call for an action. Nothing is either new or old for His absolute being which has neither first nor last. The only thing befitting Him is the felicity of permanence, beyond which no wish is conceivable nor bounty imaginable.

"Given His absolute perfection, God is not concerned with creating the world, or even its primordial matter. Rather, this primordial matter is receptive to existence, and it is precisely its yearning for existence that brings it forth from potentiality into actuality, the existence being an effusion from God. Yearning first propels it in the direction of existence and then causes it advance from deficiency to perfection within the limits of its capacity. It cannot be said that it has been createed except in the sense just outlined."[38]

The Persians subscribed to dualism, believing that there is god of good, Ahuramazda, whose powers and concerns are restricted to the realm of light and good, and a god of evil, Ahriman, whose powers and concerns are restricted to the realm of darkness and evil, both of them being the offspring of an ancient god by the name of Zurvan.

"They claimed that the realm of light and the realm of darkness were separate before creation and that Ahuramazda set about creating the elements of virtue and compassion in his realm at a time when Ahriman was preoccupied with his own affairs in his distant realm. When one day he decided to inform himself of his brother's affairs, he saw a gleam of light coming from his realm and was stricken with fear. For he knew that the light would soon spread out and disseminate and leave him with neither refuge nor realm. So together with all the creatures of darkness—the demons of evil and corruption—he rose up in rebellion and brought to naught all the efforts of Ahuramazda, so that the universe was filled with vice and misery. A battle flared up which continues to this day.[39]

---

[38] See al-'Aqqad, *Haqa'iq al-Islam wa Abatil Khusumih*, pp. 33–34.
[39] Aqqad, *Allah* p.33–34.

As for Plotinus, who lived in the first years of the third century C.E. he goes to extremes in making his god transcendental, to a degree that goes beyond all reason. Aristotle had believed that divine perfection means that God perceives and contemplates only His own essence, the most noble of all existents, and is unaware of other beings since they are too lowly to warrant His noticing them. Plotinus went a step further and claimed that divine perfection excludes even God's awareness of His own essence, because He is transcendent above even that awareness.

"And it is self-evident that this view of the matter necessitates numerous intermediaries to connect this unique, solitary, utterly pure god first with supernal realities and then with lowly creatures, particularly compound, corporeal beings. Plotinus was thus obliged to say that the One created the intellect, that the intellect created the spirit, and that the spirit created beings inferior to itself, by a gradual process of descent, leading to the world of matter, or generation and corruption.[40]

Thus, for Plotinus, God's role is confined to the creation of the intellect, and that is where His task ends.

As for Jehovah, the god of the Children of Israel, as depicted by their deviant concepts, he is the private god of Israel, jealous, wrathful, destructive and vengeful when they worship other gods. When, however, they return to him, he is content; he regains his composure and desists from further acts of vengeance and destruction, even coming to regret what he has inflicted on his chosen people.

We have already referred to the concepts of the Church concerning Jesus and his will and their intermingling with divinity; they make the divine will coterminous with Jesus or embodied in him. We have also discussed in sufficient detail the concepts of the materialists.

We now turn from this accumulation of debris to the clear, straightforward, and fully convincing concept of Islam.

In the Islamic concept, man deals with an existing God, a Creator possessed of will, sovereignty and power, one Who acts as He wills, to Whom all things revert. The creation of the universe and its further unfolding, and every motion, change and development that take place within it—all are dependent on Him. Nothing happens in the

[40] Ibid, p.188.

universe except by His will and His knowledge, His power and His wise disposition of affairs. He is directly involved, by means of all of these attributes, with all of His servants and with all of their states and conditions.

The Noble Qur'ân pays great attention to this fundamental truth in all of its shapes and forms, presenting its various, inexhaustible and constantly renewed manifestations in every aspect of existence.

> "VERILY, your Sustainer is God, who has created the heavens and the earth in six aeons, and is established on the throne of His almightiness. He covers the day with the night in swift pursuit, with the sun and the moon and the stars subservient to His command: oh, verily. His is all creation and all command. Hallowed is God, the Sustainer of all the worlds!"   (Al-A'raf: 54)

> "Have they never journeyed about the earth and beheld what happened in the end to those [deniers of the truth] who lived before their time and were [so much] greater than they in power? And [do they not see that the will of] God can never be foiled by anything whatever in the heavens or on earth, since, verily, He is all-knowing infinite in His power?"   (Al-Fatir: 44)

> "SAY: "O God, Lord of all dominion! Thou grantest dominion unto whom Thou willest, and takest away dominion from who Thou willest; and Thou exaltest whom Thou willest, and abasest whom Thou willest. In Thy hand is all good. Verily, Thou hast the power to will anything."
>
> "Thou makest the night grow longer by shortening the day, and Thou makest the day grow longer by shortening the night. And Thou bringest forth the living out of that which is dead, and Thou bringest forth the dead out of that which is alive. And Thou grantest sustenance unto whom Thou willest, beyond all reckoning."
>   (Al-'Imran: 26–27)

> "For He alone holds sway over His creatures, and He alone is truly wise, all-aware."   (Al-An'am: 18)

> "God knows what any female bears [in her womb], and by how much the wombs may fall short [in gestation], and by how much they may increase [the average period]: for with Him everything is [created] in accordance with its scope and purpose.

He knows all that is beyond the reach of a created being's perception as well as all that can be witnessed by a creature's senses or mind—the Great One, the One far above anything that is or could ever be!

It is all alike [to Him] whether any of you conceals his thought or brings it into the open, and whether he seeks to hide [his evil deeds] under the cover of night or walks [boldly] in the light of day, [thinking that] he has hosts of helpers—both such as can be perceived by him and such as are hidden from him—that could preserve him from whatever God may have willed.

Verily, God does not change men's condition unless they change their inner selves; and when God wills people to suffer evil [in consequence of their own evil deeds], there is none who could avert it: for they have none who could protect them from Him.

HE IT IS who displays before you the lightning, to give rise to [both] fear and hope, and calls heavy clouds into being; and the thunder extols His limitless glory and praises Him, and [so do] the angels, in awe of Him; and He [it is who] lets loose the thunderbolts and strikes with them whom He wills.

Any yet, they stubbornly argue about God, not-withstanding [all evidence] that He alone has the power to contrive whatever His unfathomable wisdom wills!"   (Ar-Ra'd: 8–13)

"God annuls or confirms whatever He wills [of His earlier messages]—for with Him is the source of all revelation."   (Ar-Ra'd: 39)

"And if God should touch thee with misfortune, there is none who could remove it but He; and if He should touch thee with good fortune—it is He who has the power to will anything."   (Al-An'am: 17)

God's alone in the dominion over the heavens and the earth. He creates whatever He wills: He bestows the gift of female offspring on whoever He wills, and the gift of male offspring on whomever he wills: or He gives both male and female [to whomever He wills], and causes to be barren whomever He wills: for, verily, He is all-knowing, infinite in His power."   (Ash-Shura: 49–50)

"It is God [alone that has this power—He] who causes all human beings to die at the time of their [bodily] death, and [causes to be as dead], during their sleep, those that have not yet died: thus, He withholds [from life] those upon whom He has decreed death, and lets the others go free for a term set [by Him].

In [all] this, behold, there are messages indeed for people who
think!"   (Az-Zumar: 42)

"ART THOU NOT aware that God knows all that is in the heavens
and all that is on earth?
    Never can there be a secret confabulation between three per-
sons without His being the fourth of them, nor between five without
His being the sixth of them: and neither between less than that, or
more, without His being with them wherever they may be. But in
the end, on Resurrection Day, He will make them truly understand
what they did: for, verily, God has full knowledge of everything."
                                                     (Al-Mujadalah: 7)

It is on the rootedness of this truth in the mind and the life of man
that everything depends in the realm of belief. It is also this truth that
provides man with a moral awareness and a balance in which to weigh
his actions.

This positive nature of God's relationship with all of His creatures
is what distinguishes a serious and effective belief from one that is formal and negative. It is also what distinguishes a coherent human society within which the individual may act in a truly human fashion, and
one that is torn apart, abandoning man to a purely biological existence.
There is a great difference between someone who imagines that his
God is not concerned with him, does not sense his existence, or is not
even aware of his existence, as some philosophers would have it, and
someone who feels and knows that God is his Creator and Sustainer,
his Lord in this world and the hereafter. Likewise, there is a difference
between someone who has to deal with two quarrelling gods—as the
ancient Persians believed—or even with disparate gods—as idolatrous
creeds would proclaim—and someone who deals with a single God
with a single will and a single pattern of conduct, Who teaches His servants precisely what He wants of them to gain His pleasure and what
He abhors in them and will lead to His wrath.

There are those who find themselves dealing with a voluptuous,
arrogant, tyrannical, impetuous, and fickle god, like the god of the
Greeks, Zeus or Jupiter, whom they imagined to be envious, spiteful,
and obstinate, preoccupied with gluttony and lust, and concerned only
with whatever might secure his dominion and perpetuate his tyranny.
He would become angry with Aesculapius, the god of medicine, because

by curing the sick he would deprive him of the tax to be collected from the spirits of the dead as they were ferried across into Hades. He was similarly angry with Prometheus, the god of knowledge and crafts-manship, because he taught man how to use fire in his crafts and to make use of this knowledge to struggle against the gods. For this crime he was condemned to eternal punishment. It was not enough for Zeus to put him to death or to banish him from the pantheon; instead, he invented various forms of torment for him, such as chaining him to the side of a distant mountain where vultures would gnaw at his liver all day long. Then his liver would be restored at night, only to have it torn away again the following day by the vultures. Thus he remained in eternal torment; none could intercede for him, and none of his prayers for relief would be heard.[41] Zeus was also in the habit of deceiving his wife, and he would therefore dispatch the god of the clouds to obscure the sun as it rose in case his wife should discover him cavorting at day-break with his mistresses on the Olympian throne.[42]

There is a vast difference between those who imagine themselves to be dealing with such a god and who derive their moral concepts from him and those who deal with God, the Just, the Generous, the Merciful, Who dislikes all forms of abomination, hidden and open, Who forbids evil, and Who accepts repentance and loves those who purify themselves.

Finally, there are those who think that their god is nature, a deaf and dumb entity, which does not demand of him any rite or belief, any pattern or system of life, any morality or refinement of conduct; above all, it is not even aware of his existence, for it has no perception or awareness, no sense of good and evil. There is a vast difference between them and those who know that God is Eternal and Everlasting, the One to Whom all turn with their needs, the Vigilant Whom nothing escapes, the One Who calls to account, the Just Who wrongs none, the Merciful Who answers the distressed when they call on Him and relieves their distress. the Merciful Who answers to the plea of one seeking help.

There are, then, very great differences. Hence the supreme value of this characteristic of the Islamic concept, and the attention that

---

[41] 'Aqqad, *Haqa'iq al-Islam wa Abatil Khusumih*, pp.40–41.
[42] Ibid.

Islam has paid to anchoring it in the consciousness of the Muslims. The life of the first Islamic community was lived in the shade of continuous revelation, a revelation that connected directly with their lives and simultaneously took root in their consciousness. We clearly see the hand of God at work, and His eye observing, and His hearing witnessing, their daily affairs, their pesonal dealings, and their individual and collective lives.

We see the divine care intervening openly in the affair of a poor, small, unknown family, adjudicating the dispute of a husband and wife, when the Messenger of God had been unable to find a ruling on the dispute:

"God has indeed heard the words of her who pleads with thee concerning her husband, and complains unto God.

And God does hear what you both have to say: verily, God is all-hearing, all-seeing."   (Al-Mujadalah: 1)

We also see the case of Ibn Maktum, the poor, blind man, and his encounter with the Prophet depicted as follows:

"HE FROWNED and turned away because the blind man approached him!

Yet for all thou didst know, [O Muhammad,] he might perhaps have grown in purity, or have been reminded [of the truth], and helped by this reminder.

Now as for him who believes himself to be self-sufficient—to him didst thou give thy whole attention, although thou art not accountable for his failure to attain to purity; but as for him who came unto thee full of eagerness and in awe [of God]—him didst thou disregard!

NAY, VERILY, these [messages] are but a reminder: and so, whoever is willing may remember Him."   ('Abasa: 1–12)

We see too how God intervened in one great event after the other, as for example the Hijra:

"If you do not succour the Apostle, then [know that God will do so—just as] God succoured him at the time when those who were bent on denying the truth drove him away, [and he was but] one of two, when these two were [hiding] in the cave, [and] the Apostle said to his companion, "Grieve not: verily, God is with us. And thereupon

God bestowed upon him from on high His [gift of] inner peace, and aided him with forces which you could not see, and brought utterly low the cause of those who were bent of denying the truth, whereas God's cause remained supreme: for God is almighty, wise."

(At-Tawbah: 40)

Another example is the battle of Badr:

"EVEN AS thy Sustainer brought thee forth from thy home [to fight] in the cause of the truth, although some of the believers were averse to it, [so, too,] they would argue with thee about the truth [itself] after it had become manifest—just as if they were being driven towards death and beheld it with their very eyes.

And, lo, God gave you the promise that one of the two [enemy] hosts would fall to you: and you would have liked to seize the less powerful one, whereas it was God's will to prove the truth to be true in accordance with His words, and to wipe out the last remnant of those who denied the truth—so that He might prove the truth to be true and the false to be false, however hateful this might be to those who were lost in sin.

Lo! You were praying unto your Sustainer for aid, whereupon He thus responded to you: "I shall, verily, aid you with a thousand angels following one upon another!"

And God ordained this only as a glad tiding, and that your hearts should thereby be set at rest—since no succour can come from any save God: verily, God is almighty, wise!

[Remember how it was] when He caused inner calm to enfold you, as an assurance from Him, and sent down upon you water from the skies, so that He might purify you thereby and free you from Satan's unclean whisperings and strengthen your hearts and thus make firm your steps.

Lo! Thy Sustainer inspired the angels [to convey this His message to the believers]: "I am with you!"

[And He commanded the angels:] "And give firmness unto those who have attained to faith [with these words from Me]: I shall cast terror into the hearts of those who are bent on denying the truth: strike, then, their necks, [O believers,] and strike off every one of their finger-tips!"

(Al-Anfal: 5–12)

Or in the contrasting case of the Battle of Uhud:

"AND, INDEED, God made good His promise unto you when, by His leave, you were about to destroy your foes—until the moment when you lost heart and acted contrary to the [Prophet's] command, and disobeyed after He had brought you within view of that [victory] for this world [alone], just as there were among you such as cared for which you were longing. There were among you such as cared for this world [alone], just as there were among you such as cared for the life to come: whereupon, in order that He might put you to a test, He prevented you from defeating your foes.

But now he has effaced your sin: for God is limitless in His bounty unto the believers.

[Remember the time] when you fled, paying no heed to anyone, while at your rear the Apostle was calling out to you—wherefore He requited you with woe in return for [the Apostle's] woe, so that you should not grieve [merely] over what had escaped you, nor over what had escaped you, nor over what had befallen you: for God is aware of all that you do.

Then, after this woe, He sent down upon you a sense of security, an inner calm which enfolded some of you, whereas the others, who cared mainly for themselves, entertained wrong thoughts about God—thoughts of pagan ignorance—saying, "Did we, then, have any power of decision [in this matter]?"

Say: "Verily, all power of decision does rest with God"—[but as for them,] they are trying to conceal within themselves that [weakness of faith] which they would not reveal unto thee, [O Prophet, by] saying, "If we had any power of decision, we would not have left so many dead behind."

Say [unto them]: "Even if you had remained in your homes, those [of you] whose death had been ordained would indeed have gone forth to the places where they were destined to lie down."

And [all this befell you] so that God might put to a test all that you harbour in your bosoms, and render your innermost hearts pure of all dross: for God is aware of what is in the hearts [of men]."

(Al-'Imran: 152–154)

Similar divine intervention can be seen to have taken place in all the encounters of the first Muslims. Nor was such intervention restricted to them; it was God's custom in every state and situation, the norm He observed with respect to all other messengers—peace and blessings be upon them—as we can deduce from the narratives in the Qur'an.

Thus God intervened directly and unmistakably in the struggle of Moses—upon whom be peace—against the Pharaoh and his people:

"THESE ARE MESSAGES of a divine writ clear in itself and clearly showing the truth.

We [now] convey unto thee some of the story of Moses and Pharaoh, setting forth the truth for [the benefit of] people who will believe.

Behold, Pharaoh exalted himself in the land and divided its people into castes. One group of them he deemed utterly low: he would slaughter their sons and spare [only] their women; for, behold, he was one of those who spread corruption [on earth].

But is was Our will to bestow Our favour upon those [very people] who were deemed [so] utterly low in the land, and to make them forerunners in faith and to make them heirs [to Pharaoh's glory], and to establish them securely on earth, and to let Pharaoh and Haman and their hosts experience through those [children of Israel] the very thing against which they sought to protect themselves.

And so, [when he was born] We inspired [thus] the mother of Moses: "Suckle him [for a time], and then, when thou hast cause to fear for him, cast him into the river, and have no fear and do not grieve—for We shall restore him to thee, and shall make him one of Our message—bearers!"

And [some of] Pharaoh's household found [and spared] him: for [We had willed] that he become an enemy unto them and [a source of] grief, seeing that Pharaoh and Haman and their hosts were sinners indeed!

Now the wife of Pharaoh said: "A joy to the eye [could this child be] for me and thee! Slay him not: he may well be of use to us, or we may adopt him as a son!" And they had no presentiment [of what he was to become].

On the morrow, however, an aching void grew up in the heart of the mother of Moses, and she would indeed have disclosed all about him had We not endowed her heart with enough strength to keep alive her faith [in Our promise]. And so she said to his sister. "Follow him"—and [the girl] watched him from afar, while they [who had taken him in] were not aware of it.

Now from the very beginning We caused him to refuse the breast of [Egyptian] nurses: and [when his sister came to know this,] she said: "Shall I guide you to a family that might rear him for you, and look after him with good will?"

And thus We restored him to his mother, so that her eye might be gladdened, and that she might grieve no longer, and that she might know that God's promise always comes true—even though most of them know it not!"   (Al-Qasas: 2–13)

Similar was the case of Noah, upon whom be peace:

"[LONG] BEFORE those [who now deny resurrection] did Noah's people call it a lie; and they gave the lie to Our servant and said, "Mad is he!"—and he was repulsed.

Thereupon he called out to his Sustainer, "Verily. I am defeated; come Thou, then, to my succour!"

And so We caused the gates of heaven to open with water pouring down in torrents, and caused the earth to burst forth with springs, so that the waters met for a purpose pre-ordained: but him We bore on that [vessel] made of [mere] planks and nails, and it floated under Our eyes: a recompense for him who had been rejected with ingratitude."   (Al-Qamar: 9–14)

And with Abraham:

"They exclaimed: "Burn him, and [thereby] succour your gods, if you are going to do [anything]!"

[But] We said: "O fire! Be thou cool, and [a source of] inner peace for Abraham!"—and whereas they sought to do evil unto him, We caused them to suffer the greatest loss: for We saved him and Lot, [his brother's son, by guiding them] to the land which We have blessed for all times to come.

And We bestowed upon him Isaac and [Isaac's son] Jacob as an additional gift, and caused all of them to be righteous men, and made them leaders who would guide [others] in accordance with Our behest: for We inspired them [with a will] to do good works, and to be constant in prayer, and to dispense charity: and Us [alone] did they worship."   (Al-Anbiya': 68–73)

The direct involvement of God in the affairs of all living beings and the entire universe is likewise made manifest in the Qur'an:

"Verily, it is God [alone] who upholds the celestial bodies and the earth, lest they deviate [from their orbits]—for if they should ever deviate, there is none that could uphold them after He will have ceased to do so.

[But,] verily, He is ever-forbearing, much—forgiving!"

(Al-Fatir: 41)

"Have, then they [who deny the truth] never considered the birds, enabled [by God] to fly in mid-air, with none but God holding them aloft? In this, behold, there are messages indeed for people who will believe!"   (An-Nahl: 79)

"And how many a living creature is there that takes no thought of its own sustenance, [the while] God provides for it as [He provides] for you—since He alone is all-hearing, all-knowing."   (Al-Ankabut: 60)

"Have you ever considered the seed which you cast upon the soil? Is it you who cause it to grow—or are We the cause of its growth? [For,] were it Our will, we could indeed turn it into chaff, and you would be left to wonder [and to lament,] "Verily, we are ruined! Nay, but we have been deprived [of our livelihood]!"

Have you ever considered the water which you drink? Is it you who cause it to come down from the clouds—or are We the cause of its coming down?

[It comes down sweet—but] were it Our will, We could make it burningly salty and bitter: why, then, do you not give thanks [unto Us]?

Have you ever considered the fire which you kindle? Is it you who have brought into being the tree that serves as its fuel—or are We the cause its coming into being?

It is We who have made it a means to remind [you of Us], and a comfort for all who are lost and hungry in the wilderness [of their lives]."   (Al-Waqi'ah: 63–73)

"Have, then, they [who deny the truth] never yet seen how We visit the earth [with Our punishment], gradually depriving it of all that is best thereon?

For, [when] God judges, there is no power that could repel His judgment: and swift in reckoning is He!"   (Ar-Ra'd: 41)

In its entirety, the Qur'ân represents indeed a vast unfolding of this positivism of the Islamic concept, a characteristic second in importance only to the divine unity, for the monotheism of Islam is a positive and active one, not negative like that of Aristotle or Plotinus. The rooting of this truth in the consciousness of the early Muslim community is what gave rise to a society utterly unique in the entire history of mankind. They lived that truth as a living reality within their own selves, day and night, morning and evening, in every aspect of their daily lives. They lived with God, aware of His existence within themselves and their lives more vividly than anything their physical senses could perceive. They lived in God's protection and care, under His eye and watched over by Him. They felt His hand intervening directly in all their affairs, great and small, guiding their steps, and scrutinizing all that they did. It was this that enabled them to combine sensitivity with confidence; alertness with tranquillity; trust in God with activity; fear with hope; humility before God with dignity deriving from God; submission to God with triumph over the enemies of God. It was thus that God accomplished on earth the great work of redemption, elevation and purity, in a way unprecedented and unequalled in the history of man.

The other, complementary aspect of positivism in the Islamic concept is the positive role of man, and especially the believer, in the universe and the totality of life. As soon as this concept becomes lodged in man's consciousness, he begins to actualize its meaning in practical life, to translate it into reality. The believer understands that he is an active and effective force, with respect both to himself and the universe surrounding him. The Islamic concept is not a negative one, existing purely in the mind as an ideal or theory, a type of Sufi spirituality. It is, as it were, a design for establishing a desirable state of affairs, a design that has no value except as the motive force for a relentless quest to attain its goal.

This is what the Islamic concept stirs up in the mind of the Muslim. He is constantly aware of an insistent summons from within the depths of his being demanding of him that he establish the concept in the real world; he devotes himself and all the energy his faith infuses in him to positive and constructive effort for erecting a reality in which the concept shall be fully realized in men's lives.

Wherever belief or the believers are mentioned in the Qur'an, it is always in conjunction with work and action, these being the practical expression of belief. For belief is not a mere question of sentiment, but of sentiment that spills over into action for the sake of realizing the Islamic concept.

"[Know that true] believers are only those who have attained to faith in God and His Apostle and have left all doubt behind, and who strive hard in God's cause with their possessions and their lives: it is they, they who are true to their word!"   (Al-Hujurat: 15)

"God has promised those of you who have attained to faith and do righteous deeds that, of a certainty, He will cause them to accede to power on earth, even as He caused [some of] those who lived before them to accede to it; and that, of a certainty, He will firmly establish for them the religion which He has been pleased to bestow on them; and that, of a certainty, He will cause their erstwhile state of fear to be replaced by a sense of security—[seeing that] they worship Me [alone], not ascribing powers to aught beside Me.

But all who, after [having understood] this, choose to deny the truth—it is they, they who are truly iniquitous!"   (An-Nur: 55)

"YOU ARE indeed the best community that has ever been brought forth for [the good of] mankind: you enjoin the doing of what is right and forbid the doing of what is wrong, and you believe in God.

Now if the followers of earlier revelation had attained to [this kind of] faith, it would have been for their own good; [but only few] among them are believers, while most of them are iniquitous."

(Al-'Imran: 110)

"And thus does their Sustainer answer their prayer: "I shall not lose sight of the labour of any of you who labours [in My way], be it man or woman: each of you is an issue of the other. Hence, as for those who forsake the domain of evil, and are driven from their home-lands, and suffer hurt in My cause, and fight [for it], and are slain—I shall most certainly efface their bad deeds, and shall most certainly bring them into gardens through which running waters flow, as a reward from God: for with God is the most beauteous of rewards."

(Al-'Imran: 195)

"CONSIDER the flight of time!

Verily, man is bound to lose himself unless he be of those who attain to faith, and do good works.

And enjoin upon one another the keeping to truth, and enjoin upon one another patience in adversity."   (Al-'Asr: 1–3)

There is no faith or belief if it be purely a question of sentiments held in the heart or concepts in the mind without external expression in life. Faith is not a mere collection of devotional rituals unaccompanied by actions designed to make life in its entirety subject to God's law.

By virtue of the Islamic concept, the individual Muslim feels that he is personally required to bear witness to religion. His conscience will not rest, nor will his mind be at ease, nor will he feel that he has adequately fulfilled God's claims of gratitude upon him for the blessings of Islam, nor will he permit himself to hope for deliverance from punishment in this world and the hereafter—unless he bears full witness to his religion, through effort and struggle with his own person and property.[43]

> "And thus have We willed you to be a community of the middle way, so that [with your lives] you might bear witness to the truth before all mankind, and that the Apostle might bear witness to it before you.
>
> And it is only to the end that We might make a clear distinction between those who follow the Apostle and those who turn about on their heels that We have appointed [for this community] the direction of prayer which thou [O Prophet] hast formerly observed: for this was indeed a hard test for all but those whom God has guided aright. But God will surely not lose sight of your faith—for, behold, God is most compassionate towards man, a dispenser of grace."
>
> (Al-Baqarah: 143)

> "Do you claim that Abraham and Ishmael and Isaac and Jacob and their descendants were 'Jews' or 'Christians'?" Say: "Do you know more than God does? And who could be more wicked than he who suppresses a testimony given to him by God? Yet God is not unmindful of what you do."   (Al-Baqarah: 140)

He fulfils this obligation by beginning with his inner self. He brings every aspect of his personal life, every detail of his activity, into conformity with the requirements of the concept on which his faith is based. He is required to bear practical witness to this religion—not witness of the tongue or even witness of the heart—with every act he

---

43 See *Shahadat al-Haqq*, by al-Sayyid Abu al-A'laMawdoodi, amir of the Jama'at-i Islami of Pakistan.

undertakes. It is practical witness of this type that confirms the existence of real, visible and palpable faith.

Next he bears witness by summoning others to this way of life and expounding it to them. In so doing, he will be motivated by several factors. The first is the knowledge that he is paying his debt to God for the blessing of Islam. The second is that he is expressing love for others, in that he wishes to guide them to the good that he has been granted and does not wish to guard jealously for himself or for his family, tribe, nation, or race, for he has learned from the Islamic concept that all men are brothers. The third is his awareness that he will bear on his shoulders the responsibility for their going astray unless he has conveyed the message to them. This is a heavy responsibility to bear, once borne by the prophets—upon whom be peace and blessings—and now by him in succession to them: be it to his family or clan, or people or race. This is because the Islamic concept teaches him that all mankind are brethren.

> "[We sent all these] apostles as heralds of glad tidings and as warners, so that men might have no excuse before God after [the coming of] these apostles: and God is indeed almighty, wise."   (An-Nisa': 165)

> "Whoever chooses to follow the right path, follows it but for his own good; and whoever goes astray, goes but astray to his own hurt: and no bearer of burdens shall be made to bear another's burden.
>
> Moreover, We would never chastise [any community for the wrong they may do] ere We have sent an apostle [to them]."
>
> (Al-Isra': 15)

Finally, he undertakes this task by striving to realize God's purpose in the life of mankind by establishing that the social order deriving from the Islamic concept flourishes. This is because the Islamic concept is a design for a real world, intended for implementation. Only then will Islam have real existence on earth, for Islam has no existence unless there be a society living in accordance with its order, recognizing God and His exclusive possession of divinity and deriving its basic mode of life from Him alone. Then only will Muslims deserve the aid and support that God has promised them, laying down conditions that are utterly clear:

"Those who have been driven from their homelands against all right
for no other reason than their saying, "Our Sustainer is God!"

For, if God had not enabled people to defend themselves against
one another, [all] monasteries and churches and synagogues and
mosques—in [all of] which God's name is abundantly extolled—
would surely have been destroyed [ere now].

And God will most certainly succour him who succours His
cause: for, verily, God is most powerful, almighty, [well aware of]
those who, [even] if We firmly establish them on earth, remain constant in prayer, and give in charity, and enjoin the doing of what is
right and forbid the doing of what is wrong; but with God rests the
final outcome of all events."   (Al-Hajj: 40–41)

The very nature of the Islamic concept motivates man to live a
positive and active life, in order to achieve its purposes in real and
practical terms. A Muslim knows from his Islamic concept that man
is a positive and effective force on this earth, not a passive element.
He has been created as a vicegerent in order to realize God's purposes
on earth, to build, restore, change, develop and achieve growth. He is
assisted in this vicegerent by God by the divinely established norms of
the universe in which he lives:

"It is He who sends down water from the skies; you drink thereof,
and thereof [drink] the plants upon which you pasture your beasts;
[and] by virtue thereof He causes crops to grow for you, and olive
trees, and date-palms, and grapes, and all [other] kinds of fruit: in
this, behold, there is a message indeed for people who think!

And He has made the night and the day and the sun and the
moon subservient [to His laws, so that they be of use] to you; and all
the stars are subservient to His command: in this, behold, there are
messages indeed for people who use their reason!

And all the [beauty of] many hues which He has created for you
on earth: in this, behold, there is a message for people who [are willing to] take it to heart!

And He it is who has made the sea subservient [to His laws], so
that you might eat fresh meat from it, and take from it gems which
you may wear.

And on that [very sea] one sees ships ploughing through the
waves, so that you might [be able to] go forth in quest of some of His
bounty, and thus have cause to be grateful [to Him].

And he has placed firm mountains on earth, lest it sway with you, and rivers and paths, so that you might find your way, as well as [various other] means of orientation: for [it is] by the stars that men find their way."   (An-Nahl: 10–16)

Man is also assisted by the faculties and capacities that God has placed within him for the sake of fulfilling the task of vicegerent:

"And God has brought you forth from your mothers' wombs knowing nothing—but He has endowed you with hearing, and sight, and minds, so that you might have cause to be grateful."   (An-Nahl: 78)

The condition of his vicegerent is well-known to the Muslim:

"[For although] We did say, "Down with you all from this [state]," there shall, none the less, most certainly come unto you guidance from Me: and those who follow My guidance need have no fear, and neither shall they grieve; but those who are bent on denying the truth and giving the lie to Our messages—they are destined for the fire, and therein shall they abide."   (Al-Baqarah: 38–39)

Man's awareness that he is enjoined to act and to work, and that he will enjoy assistance in so doing, banishes from him all sense of passivity vis-à-vis the universe, whether it be a question of natural forces or of what God has destined for him. For he has the innate capacities that have been bestowed on him, and the forces of the universe have been made subject to him in order to assist him. As we have pointed out, there is a balance between God's absolute will and the positive activity of man. that he is assigned the responsibility to work, and that he shall be assisted in doing so, relieves him of feelings of negativism, in the order of this universe—whether in relation to universal forces, or in relation to the Providence of God, the Exalted; in fact, he is endowed with the capabilities, while the forces of the universe have been subjected to assist him. In effect, there is balance between the absolute Will of God and the positive actions and movements of humans. This, we have previously discussed.

The banishing of all passivity and negativism enables the Muslim to act dynamically and effectively. However, Islam does not restrict itself to negating passivity; it provides the Muslim with motivation for positive action by teaching him that it is precisely through him and his works that God's will is implemented on earth:

"[Thinking that] he has hosts of helpers—both such as can be perceived by him and such as are hidden from him—that could preserve him from whatever God may have willed.

Verily, God does not change men's condition unless they change their inner selves; and when God wills people to suffer evil [in consequence of their own evil deeds], there is none who could avert it: for they have none who could protect them from Him."   (Ar-Ra'd: 11)

"Fight against them! God will chastise them by your hands, and will bring disgrace upon them, and will succour you against them: and He will soothe the bosoms of those who believe, and will remove the wrath that is in their hearts.

And God will turn in His mercy unto whom He wills: for, God is all–knowing, wise."   (At-Tawbah: 14–15)

"THUS IT IS: if the hypocrites, and they in whose hearts is disease, and they who, by spreading false rumours, would cause disturbances in the City [of the Prophet] desist not [from their hostile doings], We shall indeed give thee mastery over them, [O Muhammad]—and then they will not remain thy neighbours in this [city] for more than a little while."   (Al-Ahzab: 60)

"And thereupon, by God's leave, they routed them. And David slew Goliath; and God bestowed upon him dominion, and wisdom, and imparted to him the knowledge of whatever He willed.

And if God had not enabled people to defend themselves against one another, corruption would surely overwhelm the earth: but God is limitless in His bounty unto all the worlds."   (Al-Baqarah: 251)

"[Since they have become oblivious of God,] corruption has appeared on land and in the sea as an outcome of what men's hands have wrought: and so He will let them taste [the evil of] some of their doings, so that they might return [to the right path]."   (Ar-Rum: 41)

Islam also teaches him that mere sentiment in the heart or a word on the tongue are not sufficient; he is required to translate everything into practical terms in his life and will be held accountable for all that he does and be requited accordingly. Even guidance from God may be attained as a result of appropriate striving:

"But as for those who strive hard in Our cause—We shall most certainly guide them onto paths that lead unto Us: for, behold, God is indeed with the doers of good."   (Al-'Ankabut: 69)

"Do you think that you could enter paradise unless God takes cognizance of your having striven hard [in His cause], and takes cognizance of your having been patient in adversity?"   (Al-'Imran: 142)

"And say [unto them, O Prophet]: "Act! And God will behold your deeds, and [so will] His Apostle, and the believers: and [in the end] you will be brought before Him who knows all that is beyond the reach of a created being's perception as well as all that can be witnessed by a creature's senses or mind—and then He will make you understand what you have been doing."   (At-Tawbah: 105)

Based on all the foregoing, a Muslim senses that his existence on earth is neither haphazard nor a fleeting coincidence. Rather, it is predetermined; his path, direction and the aim of his life are all laid out for him. His presence on earth requires of him movement and positive action, directed to himself, to others around him, to the earth of which he has been made a vicegerent, and to the universe to which he belongs. Man cannot sufficiently thank God for His bestowal on him of the blessings of life and faith, nor can he aspire to escape God's reckoning and punishment unless he performs a positive role as His vicegerent on earth, in accordance with the conditions and path laid down by by God. He must implement this path in his own life and that of others and strive to remove corruption from this earth on which he is a steward. In fact, corruption arises from not applying the religion of God in actual life, in the world of mankind. The onus of such corruption, whenever it occurs, is for man to bear on himself, unless he bears witness to God in his own person, in society, and in the entire world that surrounds him.

This is how the Muslim sees matters. It elevates his worth in his own view just as it elevates his responsibilities once he realizes the burden of responsibility that lies on his shoulders. He struggles and exerts himmself so that when he meets God he will have fulfilled the trust and borne true witness. He may then count as having fulfilled his debt toward God, as far as is possible, and hope for salvation from God's torment and hellfire.

8

REALISM

Say: "Glory be to my Lord! Am I anything more than a mortal messenger?"
(Al-Isra':93)

The sixth characteristic of the Islamic concept is realism.[44] It is a concept that deals with objective truths, possessed of real and verifiable existence and a real and positive impact. It does not deal with abstract mental concepts, nor with ideal forms that have no analogues or existence in the real world. The design that Islam proposes for human life is also characterized by realism, because it is capable of being realized in the actualities of human life.

The realism in question is, however, an idealistic realism, or, if you prefer, a realistic idealism, because it aims at the highest levels and the most perfect forms to which humanity is capable of ascending.

We will now attempt to explain these two aspects of realism in the Islamic concept.

To begin with, the Islamic concept deals with objective truths, possessed of real and verifiable existence and a real and positive impact. It deals, too, with the reality of Divinity, as exemplified in its positive impact and real effectiveness. It deals with the cosmic reality, as exemplified in its concrete phenomena, whether impacting or being impacted upon. Finally, it deals with the human reality, as exemplified in people, in real life.

---

[44] We use this expression in the connotation of its Arabic name, devoid of all other historic associations in other environments. It specifically means: to realize something in the real world. By reviewing the whole chapter, the meaning of this term becomes clearer.

The god with whom this concept deals is God, the sole possessor of divinity and all of its attributes. All of these attributes, however, pertain to the real world; their real and actual effects can be perceived there. The human intellect is not left to wander in the wilderness trying to define those attributes at will, through a series of abstract, logical propositions, by means of metaphysics, for the effects of His attributes are real and present in the universe. Human perception needs only to turn to those real effects in order to observe the attributes of divinity manifested in God's handiwork:

"EXTOL, then, God's limitless glory when you enter upon the evening hours, and when you rise at morn; and [seeing that] unto Him is due all praise in the heavens and on earth, [glorify Him] in the afternoon as well, and when you enter upon the hour of noon.

He [it is who] brings forth the living out of that which is dead, and brings forth the dead out of that which is alive, and gives life to the earth after it had been lifeless: and even thus will you be brought forth [from death to life].

And among His wonders is this: He creates you out of dust— and then, lo! You become human beings ranging far and wide!

And among His wonders is this: He creates for you mates out of your own kind, so that you might incline towards them, and He engenders love and tenderness between you: in this, behold, there are messages indeed for people who think!

And among His wonders is the creation of the heavens and the earth, and the diversity of your tongues and colours: for in this, behold, there are messages indeed for all who are possessed of [innate] knowledge!

And among His wonders is your sleep, at night or in daytime, as well as your [ability to go about in] quest of some of His bounties: in this, behold, there are messages indeed for people who [are willing to] listen!

And among His wonders is this: He displays before you the lightning, giving rise to [both] fear and hope, and sends down water from the skies, giving life thereby to the earth after it had been lifeless: in this, behold, there are messages indeed for people who use their reason!

And among His wonders is this: the skies and the earth stand firm at His behest.

[Remember all this: for] in the end, when He will call you forth from the earth with a single call—lo! you will [all] emerge [for judgment].

For, unto Him belongs every being that is in the heavens and on earth; all things devoutly obey His will.

And He it is who creates [all life] in the first instance, and then brings it forth anew: and most easy is this for Him, since His is the essence of all that is most sublime in the heavens and on earth, and He alone is almighty, truly wise." (Ar-Rum: 17–27)

"VERILY, God is the One who cleaves the grain and the fruit-kernel asunder, bringing forth the living out of that which is dead, and He is the One who brings forth the dead out of that which is alive. This, then, is God: and yet, how perverted are your minds!

[He is] the One who causes the dawn to break; and He has made the night to be [a source of] stillness, and the sun and the moon to run their appointed courses: [all] this is laid down by the will of the Almighty, the All-Knowing.

And He it is who has set up for you the stars so that you might be guided by them in the midst of the deep darkness of land and sea: clearly, indeed, have We spelled out these messages unto people of [innate] knowledge!

And He it is who has brought you [all] into being out of one living entity, and [has appointed for each of you] a time-limit [on earth] and a resting-place [after death]: clearly, indeed, have we spelled out these messages unto people who can grasp the truth!

And He it is who has caused waters to come down from the sky; and by this means have We brought forth all living growth, and out of this have we brought forth verdure. Out of this do We bring forth close-growing grain; and out of the spathe of the palm tree, dates in thick clusters; and gardens of vines, and the olive tree, and the pomegranate: [all] so alike, and yet so different! Behold their fruit when it comes to fruition and ripens! Verily, in all this there are messages indeed for people who will believe!

And yet, some [people] have come to attribute to all manner of invisible beings a place side by side with God—although it is He who has created them [all]; and in their ignorance they have invented for Him sons and daughters!

Limitless is He is His glory, and sublimely exalted above anything that men may devise by way of definition: the Originator of the heavens and the earth! How could it be that He should have a child without there ever having been a mate for Him—since it is He who has created everything, and He alone knows everything?

Such is God, your Sustainer: there is no deity save Him, the Creator of everything: worship, then, Him alone—for it is He who has everything in His care. No human vision can encompass Him, whereas He encompasses all human vision: for He alone is unfathomable, all–aware." (Al-An'am: 95–103)

"Say: "All praise is due to God, and peace be upon those servants of His whom He chose [to be His message-bearers]!""

Is not God far better than anything to which men [falsely] ascribe a share in His divinity?

Nay—who is it that has created the heavens and the earth, and sends down for you [life-giving] water from the skies? For it is by this means that We cause gardens of shining beauty to grow—[whereas] it is not in your power to cause [even one single of] its trees to grow!

Could there be any divine power besides God? Nay, they [who think so] are people who swerve [from the path of reason]!

Nay—who is it that has made the earth a fitting abode [for living things], and has caused running waters [to flow] in its midst, and has set upon it mountains firm, and has placed a barrier between the two great bodies of water?

Could there be any divine power besides God? Nay, most of those [who think so] do not know [what they are saying]!

Nay—who is it that responds to the distressed when he calls out to Him, and who removes the ill [that caused the distress], and has made you inherit the earth?

Could there be any divine power besides God? How seldom do you keep this in mind!

Nay—who is it that guides you in the midst of the deep darkness of land and sea, and sends forth the winds as a glad tiding of His coming grace?

Could there be any divine power besides God? Sublimely exalted is God above anything to which men may ascribe a share in His divinity!

Nay—who is it that creates [all life] in the first instance, and then brings it forth anew? And who is it that provides you with sustenance out of heaven and earth?

Could there be any divine power besides God?

Say: "[If you think so,] produce your evidence—if you truly believe in your claim!" (An-Naml: 59–64)

"The Originator [is He] of the heavens and the earth. He has given you mates of your own kind—just as [He has willed that] among the beasts [there be] mates—to multiply you thereby: [but] there is nothing like unto Him, and He alone is all-hearing all-seeing.

His are the keys of the heavens and the earth: He grants abundant sustenance, or gives it in scant measure, unto whomever He wills: for, behold, He has full knowledge of everything." (Ash-Shura: 11–12)

"Verily, it is God [alone] who upholds the celestial bodies and the earth, lest they deviate [from their orbits]—for if they should ever deviate, there is none that could uphold them after He will have ceased to do so.

[But,] verily, He is ever-forbearing, much-forgiving!" (Al-Fatir: 41)

Thus, the Islamic concept deals with a God Whose existence is indicated by His creation, Who possesses will and implements His will; indeed, the entire movement of this universe and all that happens within it demonstrate His will and His power.

The concept of God in Islam is fundamentally at variance with the concepts of Plato, Aristotle and Plotinus in this regard. Their concept of God deals with an "ideal," archetypal god, on whom they impose an ideal nature of their own imagining and conceiving, a god without will and without the power to act. Such deficiencies are, indeed, necessitated by his perfection and ideal nature, and they cause the philosophers to hypothesize the existence of various intermediaries between God and creatures, these being so many idolatrous and mythical figures in the paganism of the Greeks.

"Existence in Plato's school of thought consists of two levels: the level of absolute reason and the level of primordial matter, known as *hylé*. All capabilities derive from absolute reason, and all failure and deficiency from primordial matter; and between these two stand beings varying in degree: they rise to the extent that they derive from absolute reason, and descend in proportion to what they obtain from primordial matter.

Some of these median beings are gods or minor gods, and others are human souls; Plato accepted their existence as a means of explaining the evil, pain and shortcomings to be found in this world. Absolute mind is perfection not bound by space and time, and nothing emanates from it except goodness and virtue. These intermediate gods were the ones who undertook creation, because of their placing between the all-powerful god and the utterly impotent primordial matter, evil, pain and shortcomings being the work of these intermediaries.

"All material phenomena are vain and deceptive, for they are mutable and appear to the senses in shapes and forms deprived of all stability. Permanence and immutability belong only to pure reason. Within pure reason reside the real forms or ideals (amthâl), as they are described in Arabic texts. Like pure reason, they are permanent and eternal, and are not amenable to diminution or corruption. Knowledge is possible through ideas, through generalized images and forms.

"These forms are the archetypes for every being that are then clothed in matter, in hylé. Every tree, for example, has one or more attributes missing from the ideal form. Where is the tree that has no elements missing from it? It is in God's mind and has been there since eternity. Every attachment of primordial matter to a tree is an imitation of the ideal form.

"For Aristotle, God is the first principle, or the first mover. He is pure thought, the rational soul contemplating itself in the eternal forms that constitute at once the essence of the world and of God.

"There must be behind all movements a mover, and a mover must have a mover preceding it. And so on, until the mind reaches a first mover, one who moves of itself, or who moves and is not moved, for reason rejects indefinite projection into the past.

"This mover is necessarily eternal, with no beginning and no end. It must be perfect. God, the prime mover, unmoved, moves and orders all things according to the eternal laws and forms, the perfect and changeless ideas which constitute the divine wisdom, or mind of God. These ideas are not objective to the senses, but they are real to thought, for they remain and are unchanged and immutable, even when all the sense objects to which they correspond are destroyed. They are perfect and everlasting. The highest of the ideas is the good.

"This mover ontologically precedes the world, a precedence of cause but not of time, as predicates precede consequences in the mind but not in time, because time is the movement of the world, or as has been said, 'the world is not created in time'. Aristotle believes in the timelessness of the world to be likely, but in his 'Dialogues' he asserts that the eternity of the world is a notion that cannot be proven or demonstrated by evidence.

"Just as the soul is the form of the body, God is the form of the world—its inherent nature, functions and purposes. All causes, ultimately, go back to the first cause uncaused, all motions to the prime mover unmoved; we must assume some origin for the motion and power in the world, and this source is God. As God is the sum and the source of all motion, so He is the totality and goal of all purposes in nature; He is the final, as well as the first cause. God is not the Creator of the material world, but its animating form; God, to Aristotle, is pure thought, rational soul contemplating itself in the eternal forms that constitute the essence of the world and God.

"If God's will is eternal and unchanging, then the existence of the world must also be eternal, along with God, because the will of God is the cause of the world's existence. Man may wish something today but there is a delay in his performance, for lack of means, or an unexpected event, or, a change of will, and all these are alien to God (i.e. God transcends such limitations).

"Aristotle went so far in this analogy as to say that God the Exalted does not know of the existence of things because they are below His perception and that He knows only their perfect or archetypal forms. He perceives with his reason only the most excellent of the intelligible, and there is nothing more excellent than his own essence; it is therefore that alone which he perceives.

"Plotinus went to the farthest extent in placing God above all. For him, God is above all things and all characterizations, and He therefore transcends existence itself. This does not mean that he does not exist or is non-existent, given that non-existence is below and not above existence. It means that the reality of his existence is not measurable by the existing forms. He is absolutely one, and nothing is similar to him in existence or attribute. Plotinus even suggested that God is unaware of his own essence, for he is exalted even above discernment of any kind."[45]

---

[45] 'Aqqad, *Allah*, pp. 187–188.

These concepts represent the highest point that human thought can attain in depicting the perfection and transcendence of God. But the God they portray is the product of human thought, a god without existence in the actual world of reality. All his attributes and characteristics are derived from abstract, rational speculation, not from an awareness of the real world and the indications it gives of the characteristics of the Creator, or from the revelation in which God describes Himself as He is actually is.

As a result, these concepts go to extremes in a form of idealism that has no grounding in reality, for they were derived not from reality, but from abstract rational processes and assumptions. Precisely this idealism injects impotence and deficiency into the concept of God, as can be deduced from the extracts just cited, although the aim is precisely the opposite—to emphasize the perfection of God.

When these attempts are measured against the Islamic concept, what "realism" means becomes discernible. The divine reality is a positive and effective reality in our actual existence, and its characteristics and attributes are reflected in its real impact on our actual existence. This is spelled out in detail by the Glorious Qur'an as it describes the divine reality in simple but profound and clear terms. It draws its illustrations from the reality of the universe and the reality of human life, with a natural, simple and beautiful realism.

It is with this kind of realism that the Islamic concept deals with the universe, the actual universe comprising bodies and dimensions, forms and conditions, motions, effects, favulties and capacities. It does not deal with a universe that is a pure "idea" without shape or form; a shapeless, primordial matter; a form or an idea existing in absolute reason; a nature that acts as creator and imprints its forms on the human reason; or a realm that barely exists, if at all.

The universe to which the Qur'ân directs man's heart and his mind is none other than this present creation with its obvious and perceptible existence; it is the heavens and the earth, the stars and the planets, animate and inanimate beings, life and death, night and day, light and darkness, rain, lightning and thunder, shade and heat—conditions and circumstances with real existence and real effects.

When Islam directs human perception to this universe as a proof of the existence and Oneness of the Creator, His Power and His Will, His

Sovereignty and Knowledge, it is to a universe that has a real existence and real effects, not to a latent "idea," or animating will; to a form in the Divine mind; not to a formless heap of matter which is in contradistinction to that form, or distorts it when it acquires it; or to a universe which is the creation of the mind or conversely the creator of the mind.

In the Islamic concept, the universe consists of all of God's creations, those whom He addressed with the command, "be!," which they instantly obeyed, creations existing in harmony in their common subservience to God, serving Him, subject to His will, and fulfilling the purpose for which they have been created:

> "ALL PRAISE is due to God, who has created the heavens and the earth, and brought into being deep darkness as well as light: and yet, those who are bent on denying the truth regard other powers as their Sustainer's equals!"
> (Al-An'am: 1)

> "VERILY, your Sustainer is God, who has created the heavens and the earth in six aeons and is established on the throne of His almightiness, governing all that exists. There is none that could intercede with Him unless He grants leave therefor.
>
> Thus is God, your Sustainer: worship, therefore, Him [alone]: will you not, then, keep this in mind?
>
> Unto Him you all must return: this is, in truth, God's promise—for, behold, He creates [man] in the first instance, and then brings him forth anew to the end that He may reward with equity all who attain to faith and do righteous deeds; whereas for those who are bent on denying the truth there is in store a draught of burning despair and grievous suffering because of their persistent refusal to acknowledge the truth.
>
> He it is who has made the sun a [source of] radiant light and the moon a light [reflected], and has determined for it phases so that you might know how to compute the years and to measure [time]. None of this has God created without [an inner] truth.
>
> Clearly does He spell out these messages unto people of [innate] knowledge: for, verily, in the alternating of night and day, and in all that God has created in the heavens and on earth there are messages indeed for people who are conscious of Him!"
> (Yunus: 3–6)

> "It is God who has raised the heavens without any supports that you could see, and is established on the throne of His almightiness: and He [it is who] has made the sun and the moon subservient [to His

laws], each running its course for a term set [by Him]. He governs all that exists.

Clearly does He spell out these messages, so that you might be certain in your innermost that you are destined to meet your Sustainer [on Judgment Day].

And it is He who has spread the earth wide and placed on it firm mountains and running waters, and created thereon two sexes of every [kind of] plant; [and it is He who] causes the night to cover the day.

Verily, in all this there are messages indeed for people who think!

And there are on earth [many] tracts of land close by one another [and yet widely differing from one another]; and [there are on it] vineyards, and fields of grain, and date-palms growing in clusters from one root or standing alone, [all] watered with the same water: and yet, some of them have We favoured above others by way of the food [which they provide for man and beast].

Verily, in all this there are messages indeed for people who use their reason!"   (Ar-Ra'd: 2–4)

"AND, INDEED, We have set up in the heavens great constellations, and endowed them with beauty for all to behold; and we have made them secure against every satanic force accursed—so that anyone who seeks to learn [the unknowable] by stealth is pursued by a flame clear to see.

And the earth—We have spread it out wide, and placed on it mountains firm, and caused [life] of every kind to grow on it in a balanced manner, and provided thereon means of livelihood for you [O men] as well as for all [living beings] whose sustenance does not depend on you.

For, no single thing exists that does not have its source with Us; and nought do We bestow from on high unless it be in accordance with a measure well–defined.

And we let loose the winds to fertilize [plants], and We send down water from the skies and let you drink thereof: and it is not you who dispose of its source—for, behold, it is We—We alone—who grant life and deal death, and it is We alone who shall remain after all else will have passed away!"   (Al-Hijr: 16–23)

"And among the many objects of His creation, God has appointed for you [various] means of protection: thus, He has given you in the mountains places of shelter, and has endowed you with [the ability to make] garments to protect you from heat [and cold], as well as such garments as might protect you from your [mutual] violence.

In this way does He bestow the full measure of His blessings on you, so that you might surrender yourselves unto Him."

(An-Nahl: 81)

"ARE, THEN, they who are bent on denying the truth not aware that the heavens and the earth were [once] one single entity, which We then parted asunder?—and [that] We made out of water every living thing? Will they not, then, [begin to] believe?

And [are they not aware that] We have set up firm mountains on earth, lest it sway with them, and [that] We have appointed thereon broad paths, so that they might find their way, and [that] We have set up the sky as a canopy well-secured?

And yet, they stubbornly turn away from [all] the signs of this [creation], and [fail to see that] it is He who has created the night and the day and the sun and the moon—all of them floating through space!"

(Al-Anbiya': 30–33)

"O MEN! If you are in doubt as to the [truth of] resurrection, [remember that] verily, We have created [every one of] you out of dust, then out of a drop of sperm, then out of a germ-cell, then out of an embryonic lump complete [in itself] and yet incomplete, so that We might make [your origin] clear unto you.

And whatever We will [to be born] We cause to rest in the [mothers'] wombs for a term set [by Us], and then We bring you forth as infants and [allow you to live] so that [some of] you might attain to maturity: for among you are such as are caused to die [in childhood], just as many a one of you is reduced in old age to a most abject state, ceasing to know anything of what he once knew so well.

And [if, O man, thou art still in doubt as to resurrection, consider this:] thou canst see the earth dry and lifeless—and [suddenly,] when We send down waters upon it, it stirs and swells and puts forth every kind of lovely plant!

All this [happens] because God alone is the Ultimate Truth, and because He alone brings the dead to life, and because He has the power to will anything.

And [know, O man] that the Last Hour is bound to come, beyond any doubt, and that God will [indeed] resurrect all who are in their graves."

(Al-Hajj: 5–7)

"Art thou not aware that it is God who has made subservient to you all that is on earth, and the ships that sail through the sea at His behest—and [that it is He who] holds the celestial bodies [in their orbits], so that they may not fall upon the earth otherwise than by His leave?

Verily, God is most compassionate towards men, a dispenser of grace—seeing that it is He who gave you life, and then will cause you to die, and then will bring you back to life: [but,] verily, bereft of all gratitude is man!"   (Al-Hajj: 65–66)

"And, indeed, We have created above you seven [celestial] orbits; and never are We unmindful of [any aspect of Our] creation.

And We send down water from the skies in accordance with a measure [set by Us], and then We cause it to lodge in the earth: but, behold, We are most certainly able to withdraw this [blessing]!

And by means of this [water] We bring forth for you gardens of date-palms and vines, wherein you have fruit abundant and whereof you eat."   (Al-Mu'minun: 17–19)

"ART THOU NOT aware that God sends down water from the skies, whereby We bring forth fruits of many hues—just as in the mountains there are streaks of white and red of various shades, as well as [others] raven-black, and [as] there are in men, and in crawling beasts, and in cattle, too, many hues?

Of all His servants, only such as are endowed with [innate] knowledge stand [truly] in awe of God: [for they alone comprehend that,] verily, God is almighty, much-forgiving."   (Al-Fatir: 27–28)

"Do they not look at the sky above them—how We have built it and made it beautiful and free of all faults?

And the earth—We have spread it wide, and set upon it mountains firm, and caused it to bring forth plants of all beauteous kinds, thus offering an insight and a reminder unto every human being who willingly turns unto God.

And We send down from the skies water rich in blessings, and cause thereby gardens to grow, and fields of grain, and tall palm-trees with their thickly-clustered dates, as sustenance apportioned to men: and by [all] this We bring dead land to life: [and] even so will be [man's] coming-forth from death."   (Qaf: 6–11)

"HALLOWED be He in whose hand all dominion rests, since He has the power to will anything: He who has created death as well as life, so that He might put you to a test [and thus show] which of you is best in conduct, and [make you realize that] He alone is almighty, truly forgiving.

[Hallowed be] He who has created seven heavens in full harmony with one another: no fault wilt thou see in the creation of the Most Gracious. And turn thy vision [upon it] once more: canst thou see any flaw?

Yea turn thy vision [upon it] again and yet again: [and every time] thy vision will fall back upon thee, dazzled and truly defeated...

And, indeed, We have adorned the skies nearest to the earth with lights, and have made them the object of futile guesses for the evil ones [from among men]: and for them have We readied suffering though a blazing flame." (Al-Mulk: 1–5)

"ART THOU NOT aware of thy Sustainer [through His works]?—how He causes the shadow to lengthen [towards the night] when, had He so willed, He could indeed have made it stand still: but then, We have made the sun its guide; and then, [after having caused it to lengthen,] We draw it in towards Ourselves with a gradual drawing-in.

And He it is who makes the night a garment for you, and [your] sleep a rest, and causes every [new] day to be a resurrection.

And He it is who sends forth the winds as a glad tiding of His coming grace; and [thus, too,] We cause pure water to descend from the skies, so that We may bring dead land to life thereby, and give to drink thereof to many [beings] of Our creation, beasts as well as humans." (Al-Furqan: 45–49)

The Islamic concept thus deals with a universe that has a real existence, an existence different, it is true, from the existence of God, but nonetheless a real existence with attributes perceptible in the real world, not derived from purely abstract mental concepts or fanciful claims lacking all evidence. The reality of the universe in the Islamic concept becomes fully clear when we measure it against the concept of Brahmanism, which posits being exclusively for Brahma, the supreme deity, and regards the material universe as absolute non-being; being, however, has become dissolved in non-being, resulting in the presence of evil in the world. For being is absolute good and absolute perfection, while non-being is absolute evil and absolute deficiency. Man can extricate himself from evil—i.e., everything that has bodily form—only by abandoning the body so that the being present in it can return to its absolute state and be freed from imprisonment in the evil matter in which it has been dissolved.

Likewise, the realism of the universe in the Islamic concept is shown clearly when we examine Plato's concept of material existence. According to him, it is a mere shadow of the ideal form. The tree that you see is a shadow of the idea of "tree" that is latent within the absolute intellect. It is deficient and does not represent the the perfect idea or archetype that is present in the divine intellect. The "universal soul" is the link between "ideal" entities and things endowed with form in the palpable and visible material world, these being mere shadows and therefore unreal.

For Plotinus, as we have seen, the One is God; the intellect emanated from Him, the spirit or the "universal soul" emanated from the intellect, and it is the "universal soul" that created the sensible world on behalf of the intellect. The sensible world is derived from matter, the lowest of all things, darkness, corruption, and evil.

When you compare these concepts which derive from nothing but the fantasies and forced interpretations of the human intellect and have no connection whatsoever with the objective realities of the universe—when you compare them with the Islamic concept as presented in the Qur'anic verse we have cited, then the meaning of the "realism" we discern in the Islamic concept becomes fully clear.

Likewise, the Islamic concept deals with real and actual man as represented in the human race as it actually exists, man with his specific composition, with flesh, blood and nerves, with an intelligence, a soul and a spirit, with inclinations and desires, with likes and necessities, man who eats food and walks in the markets. He lives and he dies, he begins and he ends, he exerts effects and is subject to effects. He loves and he hates; he hungers and despairs; he rises and falls; he believes and denies; he is guided and misguided. He makes the earth flourish or works corruption upon it.

> "O MANKIND! Be conscious of your Sustainer, who has created you out of one living entity, and out of it created its mate, and out of the two spread abroad a multitude of men and women. And remain conscious of God, in whose name you demand [your rights] from one another, and of these ties of kinship. Verily God is ever watchful over you!"   (An-Nisa': 1)

"O men! Behold, We have created you all out of a male and a female, and have made you into nations and tribes, so that you might come to know one another. Verily, the noblest of you in the sight of God is the one who is most deeply conscious of Him. Behold God is all-knowing, all-aware." (Al-Hujurat: 13)

"Limitless in His glory is He who has created opposites in whatever the earth produces, and in men's own selves, and in that of which has [as yet] they have no knowledge." (Ya Sin: 36)

"NOW, INDEED, We create man out of the essence of clay, and then We cause him to remain as a drop of sperm in [the womb's] firm keeping, and then We create out of the drop of sperm a germ-cell, and then We create out of the germ-cell an embryonic lump, and then We create within the embryonic lump bones, and then We clothe the bones with flesh—and then We bring [all] this into being as a new creation: hallowed, therefore, is God, the best of artisans." (Al-Mu'minun: 12–14)

"HAS THERE [not] been an endless span of time before man [appeared—a time] when he was not yet a thing to be thought of?

Verily, it is We who have created man out of a drop of sperm intermingled, so that We might try him [in his later life]: and therefore We made him a being endowed with hearing and sight.

Verily, We have shown him the way: [and it rests with him to prove himself] either grateful or ungrateful." (Al-Insan: 1–3)

"[But only too often] man destroys himself: how stubbornly does he deny the truth!

[Does man ever consider] out of what substance [God] creates him?

Out of a drop of sperm He creates him, and thereupon determines his nature, and then makes it easy for him to go through life; and in the end He causes him to die and brings him to the grave; and then, if it be His will, He shall raise him again to life." (Abasa: 17–22)

"For [thus it is:] when affliction befalls man, he cries out unto Us, whether he be lying on his side or sitting or standing; but as soon as We have freed him of his affliction, he goes on as though he had never invoked Us to save him from the affliction that befell him! Thus do their own doings seem goodly unto those who waste their own selves." (Yunus: 12)

"And [thus it is:] whenever We let [such] people taste [some of Our] grace after hardship has visited them—lo! they forthwith turn to devising false arguments against Our messages.

Say: "God is swifter [than you] in His deep devising!"

Behold, Our [heavenly] messengers are recording all that you may devise." (Yunus: 21)

"And thus it is: if We let man taste some of Our grace, and then take it away from him—behold, he abandons all hope. Forgetting all gratitude [for Our past favours]. And thus it is: if We let him taste ease and plenty after hardship has visited him, he is sure to say, "Gone is all affliction from me!"—for, behold, he is given to vain exultation, and glories only in himself.

[And thus it is with most men—] save those who are patient in adversity and do righteous deeds: it is they whom forgiveness of sins awaits, and a great reward." (Hud: 9–11)

"NOW THERE IS a kind of man whose views on the life of this world may please thee greatly, and [the more so as] he cites God as witness to what is in his heart and is, moreover, exceedingly skillful in argument. But whenever he prevails, he goes about the earth spreading corruption and destroying [man's] tilth and progeny: and God does not love corruption. And whenever he is told, "Be conscious of God," his false pride drives him into sin: wherefore hell will be his allotted portion—and how vile a resting–place!

But there is [also] a kind of man who would willingly sell his own self in order to please God: and God is most compassionate towards His servants." (Al-Baqarah: 204–207)

Thus, the Islamic concept deals with man as a real being with specific attributes and characteristics, the subject and object of actions and effects, not as an abstract idea or a hypothesis unrooted in reality. It does not deal with humanity as an abstraction or as a deity worthy of worship,[46] nor does it deal with "absolute reason"[47] as a specific being, because "absolute reason" has no actual existence. All that exists is the individual reason, incapable of creating the universe or the spirit.[48]

---

[46] As seen by Feuerbach, of the positivist school of thought.

[47] As seen by Nietzsche, of the rationalist idealist school of thought.

[48] As seen by Plotinus, the foremost figure of Neo-Platonism.

The Islamic concept differs from rational idealism which is concerned only with purely mental categories that have no connection to the beings in the universe and life that both receive and exercise influence.

At the same time, it differs from the theory that takes nature as a god that creates the intellect and intellectual perceptions. According to the Islamic concept, it is God Who creates nature and man, and it is the human intellect that perceives the norms of the natural realm, learns its laws, and becomes acquainted with its potentials, having a positive effect upon it in a way that is both sensory and rational, balanced and moderate.

It seems that Islam anticipated the emergence, centuries later, of the various pollutions that would assail humanity at the hands of the "innovative" philosophers and thinkers who produced this welter of theories—rational idealism, dialectical materialism, and so forth. It formulated its concept with balance and equilibrium, perfection and comprehensiveness, in order to bestow tranquillity, stability, and certainty on the human mind:

> "VERILY, this Qur'an shows the way to all that is most upright, and gives the believers who do good deeds the glad tiding that theirs will be a great reward."
> (Al-Isra': 9)

> "And who could be better of speech than he who calls [his fellow-men] unto God, and does what is just and right, and says, "Verily, I am of those who have surrendered themselves to God?"
> (Fussilat: 33)

The second manifestation of the realism that marks the Islamic concept relates to the nature of the path which it offers to human life. The realism of this path consists of its compatibility with the nature of man, the circumstances that surround him in life, and the extent of his true capacities.

Man in the Islamic concept is man as familiar to us, with all of his strengths and weaknesses, his aspirations and longings, his flesh, blood and nerves, his body, mind and soul. He is not a being as willed by some extravagant fantasy or a floating dream derived from the operations of pure logic. He is also not the being depicted as the lowest of the low by those who regard him as the creation of dumb nature or of economic forces.

He is man whom God created to be His vicegerent on this earth, to act positively by creating and innovating in the material world and thus fulfilling the will of God.

He is man, the real, the actual, and the path that Islam traces out for him is therefore a realistic and actual one. Its limits correspond to the limits of man's own capacities and his nature as a creature of flesh and blood, with body, reason and spirit all intermingled in his being. Despite its loftiness, purity, idealism, and divine origin, the Islamic way of life is designed for a being living on this earth, one who eats food, walks through the market, marries and procreates, likes and dislikes, hopes and fears, and expresses all the traits of humanity that God has placed in him.

It takes into account his essential nature, his capacities and talents, his virtues and vices, his strengths and weaknesses. It does not demean him, belittle the role he plays on earth, or deny value to any aspect of his life. At the same time, it does not elevate him to the rank of divinity or depict him as a pure and translucent angel, devoid of all material aspect. It does not, therefore, despise his natural instincts and needs.

Since Islam alone takes into account all the aspects of man's humanity, it is also Islam alone that can raise man to the highest level and most perfect state attained in any time or place.

Let us now cite verses of the Qur'an which depict the realism of the Islamic path, its conformity to the actuality of human life, and the summons it proclaims to loftiness and purity, the utmost degree of perfection available to man within the limits of his created nature:

> "Yet they say: "What sort of apostle is this [man] who eats food [like all other mortals] and goes about in the market-places? Why has not an angel [visibly] been sent down unto him, to act as a warner together with him? Or: "[Why has not] a treasure been granted to him [by God]?" Or: "He should [at least] have a [bountiful] garden, so that he could eat thereof [without effort]!"
>
> And so these evildoers say [unto one another], "If you were to follow [Muhammad, you would follow] but a man bewitched!"
>
> See to what they liken thee, [O Prophet, simply] because they have gone astray and are now unable to find a way [to the truth]!

Hallowed is He who, if it be His will, shall give thee something better than that [whereof they speak]—gardens through which running waters flow—and shall assign to thee mansions [of bliss in the life to come].”   (Al-Furqan: 7–10)

“And so they say: “[O Muhammad,] we shall not believe thee till thou cause a spring to gush forth for us from the earth, or thou have a garden of date-palms and vines and cause rivers to gush forth in their midst in a sudden rush, or thou cause the skies to fall down upon us in smithereens, as thou hast threatened, or [till] thou bring God and the angels face to face before us, or thou have a house [made] of gold, or thou ascend to heaven—but nay, we would not [even] believe in thy ascension unless thou bring down to us [from heaven] a writing which we [ourselves] could read.

Say thou, [O Prophet:] “Limitless in His glory is my Sustainer! Am I, then, aught but a mortal man, an apostle?”   (Al-Isra’: 90–93)

“God does not burden any human being with more than he is well able to bear: in his favour shall be whatever good he does, and against him whatever evil he does.

“O our Sustainer! Take us not to task if we forget or unwittingly do wrong!

“O our Sustainer! Lay not upon us a burden such as Thou didst lay upon those who lived before us! O Our Sustainer! Make us not bear burdens which we have no strength to bear!

“And efface Thou our sins, and grant us forgiveness, and bestow Thy mercy upon us! Thou art our Lord Supreme: Succour us, then, against people who deny the truth!”   (Al-Baqarah: 286)

“AND THEY will ask thee about [women’s] monthly courses. Say: “It is a vulnerable condition. Keep, therefore, aloof from women during their monthly courses, and do not draw near unto them until they are cleansed; and when they are cleansed, go in unto them as God has bidden you to do.”

Verily, God loves those who turn unto Him in repentance, and He loves those who keep themselves pure.

Your wives are your tilth; go, then, unto your tilth as you may desire, but first provide something for your souls, and remain conscious of God, and know that you are destined to meet Him. And give glad tidings unto those who believe.”   (Al-Baqarah: 222–223)

"FIGHTING is ordained for you, even though it be hateful to you; but it may well be that you hate a thing the while it is good for you, and it may well be that you love a thing the while it is bad for you: and God knows, whereas you do not know."   (Al-Baqarah: 216)

"ALLURING unto man is the enjoyment of worldly desires through women, and children, and heaped—up treasures of gold and silver, and horses of high mark, and cattle, and lands. All this may be enjoyed in the life of this world—but the most beauteous of all goals is with God.

Say: "Shall I tell you of better things than those [earthly joys]? For the God-conscious there are, with their Sustainer, gardens through which running waters flow, therein to abide, and spouses pure, and God's goodly acceptance."

And God sees all that is in [the hearts of] His servants."
(Al-'Imran: 14–15)

"And vie with one another to attain to your Sustainer's forgiveness and to a paradise as vast as the heavens and the earth, which has been readied for the God-conscious, who spend [in His way] in time of plenty and in time of hardship, and hold in check their anger, and pardon their fellow-men because God loves the doers of good; and who, when they have committed a shameful deed or have [otherwise] sinned against themselves, remember God and pray that their sins be forgiven—for who but God could forgive sins?—and do not knowingly persist in doing whatever [wrong] they may have done.

These it is who shall have as their reward forgiveness from their Sustainer, and gardens through which running waters flow, therein to abide: and how excellent a reward for those who labour!"
(Al-'Imran: 133–136)

"MEN SHALL take full care of women with the bounties which God has bestowed more abundantly on the former than on the latter, and with what they may spend out of their possessions. And the righteous women are the truly devout ones, who guard the intimacy which God has [ordained to be] guarded.

And as for those women whose ill-will you have reason to fear, admonish them [first]; then leave them alone in bed; then beat them; and if thereupon they pay you heed, do not seek to harm them. Behold, God is indeed most high, great!"   (An-Nisa': 34)

"Hence, let them fight in God's cause—all who are willing to barter the life of this world for the life to come: for unto him who fights in God's cause, whether he be slain or be victorious, We shall in time grant a mighty reward.

And how could you refuse to fight in the cause of God and of the utterly helpless men and women and children who are crying. "O our Sustainer! Lead us forth [to freedom] out of this land whose people are oppressors, and raise for us, out of Thy grace, a protector, and raise for us, out of Thy grace, one who will bring us succour!"

Those who have attained to faith fight in the cause of God, whereas those who are bent on denying the truth fight in the cause of the powers of evil. Fight, then, against those friends of Satan: verily, Satan's guile is weak indeed!"   (An-Nisa': 74–76)

"O YOU who have attained to faith! Be ever steadfast in your devotion to God, bearing witness to the truth in all equity; and never let hatred of anyone lead you into the sin of deviating from justice. Be just: this is closest to being God-conscious. And remain conscious of God: verily, God is aware of all that you do."   (Al-Ma'idah: 8)

"O CHILDREN of Adam! Beautify yourselves for every act of worship, and eat and drink [freely], but do not waste: verily, He does not love the wasteful!

Say: "Who is there to forbid the beauty which God has brought forth for His creatures, and the good things from among the means of sustenance?"

Say: "They are [lawful] in the life of this world unto all who have attained to faith—to be theirs alone on Resurrection Day."

Thus clearly do We spell out these messages unto people of [innate] knowledge!

Say: "Verily, my Sustainer has forbidden only shameful deeds, be they open or secret, and [every kind of] sinning, and unjustified envy, and the ascribing of divinity to aught beside Him—since He Has never bestowed any warrant therefor from on high—and the attributing unto God of aught of which you have no knowledge."
                                                        (Al-A'raf: 31–33)

The more we delve into the Qur'anic texts that define the precepts and duties of the Islamic life, the more we are impressed with the realism of this system, its congruence with the actuality of human nature and the limits of human powers and capacities; it neither suppresses any capacity man has or dissuades him from using it, nor does it impose on him anything beyond his capacities or alien to his nature.

This realism becomes particularly clear when we examine what Brahmanism requires of its adherents, namely that they should refrain from whatever strengthens their corporeal selves, so that their spirits hasten to liberation from bodily thrall and deliverance from the darkness and evil of non-being, returning thereby to perfect, virtuous and luminous being.

Likewise, the concepts of the Church which have come to color Christianity suggest that the compounding of the human out of matter and spirit was a grievous error; man must be delivered from it by separating the realm of the spirit from the realm of the body and despising whatever is corporeal. This results in demanding of man what lies beyond his capacity, as for example cohabiting with a wife whose company he cannot endure, or separating from her without the possibility of divorce or being able to cohabit thereafter with any other woman. There are many similar matters relating to the teachings of the Church which are in conflict with man's essential nature.

Islam is a religion of realism, a religion for life and movement. It is a religion for work, production and development, a religion whose imperatives conform to human nature, enabling all man's capacities to function for the purpose for which they were created. At the same time, man is able to reach his highest levels of perfection through movement and effort, through responding to his aspirations and longings and not by subduing or suppressing them.

The Islamic mode of life laid down for mankind is thus realistic, in the same way that the Islamic concept is itself realistic, with respect to God, the universe, life, and man. Creedal concept and practical action are in perfect harmony in Islam.

Man is thus launched with all his capacities on the task of making the earth flourish, bringing about change, growth and development, creating in the material world whatever God wishes him to create. No creedal barrier or practical obstacle confronts him, for his creed and his practice are both realistic, in conformity with the actualities of his life and the actual circumstances surrounding him. Both arise from the same source as man himself, the source that provided him with his capacities and talents.

It thus becomes possible for one who believes in this creed and perceives the truth of the Islamic concept and the way of life springing from it, to create real and actual effects upon earth, to create and innovate within the material realm in perfect conformity with morality, with ethical loftiness and purity.

> "AND SO, set thy face steadfastly towards the [one ever-true] faith, turning away from all that is false, in accordance with the natural disposition which God has instilled into man: [for,] not to allow any change to corrupt what God has thus created—this is the [purpose of the one] ever-true faith; but most people know it not."
>
> (Ar-Rum: 30)

9

THE ONENESS OF GOD

"We sent no Messenger before you without revealing to him, "There
is no God but Me, so worship Me alone."   (Al-Anbiya': 25)

The Oneness of God is the primary constituent of the Islamic concept, for it is also the fundamental truth in the Islamic creed.
It also counts, however, as one of the characteristics of the concept,
insofar as the Islamic concept distinguishes itself from all other creeds
and philosophies on earth by the pure monotheism it teaches. We will
therefore now speak of the Oneness of God as a characteristic of the
Islamic concept, explaining how it stands utterly apart from all other
creedal and philosophical concepts.

We begin by stating that the Oneness of God was the principal
characteristic of every religion brought from God by His Messengers
and at the same time its main constituent. In a general sense, therefore,
Islam was the religion brought by every Messenger, for the sense of
"Islam" is submission to God alone, adhering to the path He has prescribed in every area of life, serving Him through following His laws,
and worshipping Him both in ritual devotion and in the actualities
of life. However, the deviations and distortions that afflicted the concepts of the followers of those Messengers, together with the revolt of
paganism against religion, left no authentic religious concept in place
except that brought by the Prophet Muhammad, upon whom be peace
and blessings. God guarded its principles from all distortion and it was
spared the onslaught of paganism.

There is also another consideration which causes us to assert that
the Oneness of God is a characteristic of the Islamic concept: namely,

the vast area covered by monotheism in the creed of Islam and the way in which it extends to man's awareness, his ethics and conduct, and the organization of his practical life. It extends to the way in which the Muslim sees the universe and his own active role within it, to the ordering of every aspect of human life, the hidden and the visible, the small and the great, the petty and the portentous, ritual and law, belief and action, the individual and society, this world and the hereafter. In short, there is nothing left untouched by the comprehensiveness of monotheism.

The Islamic concept is based on the belief that there is divinity and servanthood, the former pertaining to God in exclusivity and the latter characterizing everything and everyone other than Him. Since divinity belongs exclusively to God, it is He alone Who possesses its attributes. Likewise, in the same way that all things and animate beings have servanthood in common, they are all utterly devoid of any of the attributes of divinity. There are, then, two distinct existences: the existence of God, and the existence of other than God; His servants. The relationship between the two existences is the relationship of Creator and created, of Lord and servant.

This is the basic principle of the Islamic concept, all others deriving from it or being based on it.

We have already mentioned that the Oneness of God was the foundation of every religion delivered by a Messenger of God. The Glorious Qur'an asserts this fact and repeats it in relation to every Messenger.

> "INDEED, We sent forth Noah unto his people, and he said: "O my people! Worship God alone: you have no deity other than Him. Verily, I fear lest suffering befall you on an awesome Day!"
>
> (Al-A'raf: 59)

> "AND UNTO [the tribe of] 'Ad [We sent] their brother Hud. He said: "O my people! Worship God alone: you have no deity other than Him. Will you not, then, be conscious of Him?"   (Al-A'raf: 65)

> "AND UNTO [the tribe of] Thamud [We sent] their brother Salih. He said: "O my people! Worship God alone: you have no deity other than Him. Clear evidence of the truth has now come unto you from your Sustainer.
>
> "This she-camel belonging to God shall be a token for you: so leave her alone to pasture on God's earth, and do her no harm, lest grievous chastisement befall you."   (Al-A'raf: 73)

"AND UNTO [the people of] Madyan [We sent] their brother Shu'ayb. He said: "O my people! Worship God alone: you have no deity other than Him. Clear evidence of the truth has now come unto you from your Sustainer. Give, therefore, full measure and weight [in all your dealings], and do not deprive people of what is rightfully theirs; and do not spread corruption on earth after it has been so well ordered: [all] this is for your own good, if you would but believe."   (Al-A'raf: 85)

"AND HAS the story of Moses ever come within thy ken?

Lo! he saw a fire [in the desert]: and so he said to his family: "Wait here! Behold, I perceive a fire [far away]: perhaps I can bring you a brand therefrom, or find at the fire some guidance."

But when he came close to it, a voice called out: "O Moses! Verily, I am thy Sustainer! Take off, then, thy sandals! Behold, thou art in the twice-hallowed valley. And I have chosen thee [to be My apostle]: listen, then, to what is being revealed [unto thee].

"Verily, I—I alone—am God; there is no deity save Me. Hence, worship Me alone, and be constant in prayer, so as to remember Me!"

(Taha: 9–14)

"AND LO! God said: "O Jesus, son of Mary! Didst thou say unto men, Worship me and my mother as deities beside God?"

[Jesus] answered: "Limitless art Thou in Thy glory! It would not have been possible for me to say what I had no right to [say]! Had I said this, Thou wouldst indeed have known it! Thou knowest all that is within myself, whereas I know not what is in Thy Self. Verily, it is Thou alone who fully knowest all the things that are beyond the reach of a created being's perception.

Nothing did I tell them beyond what Thou didst bid me [to say]: 'Worship God, [who is] my Sustainer as well as your Sustainer.' And I bore witness to what they did as long as I dwelt in their midst: but since Thou hast caused me to die, Thou alone hast been their keeper: for Thou art witness unto everything.

If thou cause them to suffer—verily, they are Thy servants: and if Thou forgive them—verily, Thou alone art almighty, truly wise!"

(Al-Ma'idah: 116–118)

"And [this despite the fact that even] before thy time We never sent any apostle without having revealed to him that there is no deity save Me, [and that,] therefore, you shall worship me [alone]!"

(Al-Anbiya': 25)

But this monotheism conveyed by all the Messengers was distorted by the incorporation into it of the myths propagated by various creeds, whether religions claiming a heavenly origin or idolatrous cults intermingled with the residues of various heavenly religions. We have already touched on this subject.

Before we survey the broad area occupied by this truth in the Islamic concept, let us—in order fully to appreciate this characteristic of the concept—examine some other concepts touching on the subject of divinity and servanthood, particularly those that posit two distinct beings or existences or profess the divine unity in one way or another.

Hinduism, for example, recognizes a single existent, Brahma, in which it discerns the attributes of exclusive perfection, exclusive virtue, and exclusive immortality. Everything else is non-being and non-existent; the universe and all it contains is pure non-being. However, Hinduism also has this unique and absolute being descend into non-being, into evil and deficiency, so that Brahma is dispersed into all the particles of the world, which nonetheless remains non-being. Everything including man is therefore compounded of being and non-being, of good and evil, of deficiency and perfection, of permanence and transience. The duty of the believing Hindu is constant exertion to liberate being, good, perfection and immortality from non-being, evil, deficiency, and transience, in order to become Brahma. Hence the desire for mortification of the body—which represents non-being—so that the being dissolved in it can escape, resulting in the state of nirvana, which represents salvation and return to Brahma.

However, this form of monotheism—quite apart from the incarnationism it implies—was blemished by trinitarianism, for Brahma came to be considered one of the three forms of the single god: Brahma, his form as creator; Vishnu, his form as preserver; and Shiva, his form as destroyer. Then they appointed Karma as the fate that has dominion over the gods and the heavens and causes the universe to repeat its cycle of creation and destruction. Not much remained, therefore, of monotheism.

The religion of Ikhnaton also contained a type of monotheism. Ikhnaton ascribed to his god Aton the attributes of unity and agency, by virtue of which he created, sustained and ordered the universe. This was the loftiest concept attained by humanity outside of the heavenly religions (although even here we must not overlook the influence of those religions on Ikhnaton). It was, however, polluted by idolatry, for the material sun was made a symbol of God, and its name was made synonymous with his. Monotheism thus became intermingled with traces of idolatry.

Aristotle made a distinction between the "necessary existent"—God—and the "contingent existent"—other than God. But he rendered this one God neutral towards the universe, for he neither created the universe nor entertains any relations with it. However, the universe moves toward the "necessary Being" by virtue of some ardor latent within it.

Monotheism was the religion of Abraham (peace be upon him), and he enjoined it on Ishmael and Isaac. Jacob, son of Isaac, also believed in the oneness of God and he enjoined the teaching on his offspring at the moment of his death, as narrated by the Qur'an.

> "And who, unless he be weak of mind, would want to abandon Abraham's creed, seeing that We have indeed raised him high in this world, and that, verily, in the life to come he shall be among the righteous?
>
> When his Sustainer said to him, "Surrender thyself unto Me!"—he answered, "I have surrendered myself unto [Thee,] the Sustainer of all the worlds."
>
> And this very thing did Abraham bequeath unto his children, and [so did] Jacob: "O my children! Behold, God has granted you the purest faith; so do not allow death to overtake you ere you have surrendered yourselves unto Him."
>
> Nay, but you [yourselves, O children of Israel,] bear witness that when death was approaching Jacob, he said unto his sons: "whom will you worship after I am gone?"
>
> They answered: "We will worship thy God, the God of thy forefathers Abraham and Ishmael and Isaac, the One God; and unto him will we surrender ourselves."   (Al-Baqarah: 130–133)

When Moses was sent as a Messenger to the Children of Israel, he called on them to embrace the Oneness of God, and in fact Judaism is still regarded as a monotheistic religion. But the Children of Israel, both before and after Moses, tarnished and perverted his message. They manufactured a special god for the Children of Israel, a national god to give them victory over the followers of other gods. Next, they slandered even this "god of Israel" by claiming to be his beloved sons, so that he would in no way punish them. Then they said that Ezra was the son of God, and that he had sons who married men's daughters and begat giants. This struck fear into the heart of their god lest they become gods like him, so he came down to earth and plagued their tongues with confusion. They said that once Jacob wrestled with their god, and he beat him and stripped off his loincloth. They said that their god walks in shady gardens to enjoy the cool breeze, and that he likes the smell of roast meat to the exclusion of others. Not to mention all the other myths with which they tarnished their creed of monotheism.

Jesus, peace be upon him, came with the message of the Oneness of God, but Christianity ended up as a trinitarianism asserting the existence of three hypostases: the father, the son and the holy ghost; opinions differed among the Christians concerning the hypostasis of the son and his will. The result was that Christianity's claim to monotheism, whichever of the separate churches be involved, became utterly baseless.

Thus we can state with assurance that the Islamic concept is the only one to remain firmly based on a solid foundation of pure monotheism. Monotheism is one of the characteristics of the Islamic concept that set it completely apart from all other beliefs prevailing in the world.

Let us now spell out concisely the nature and scope of this monotheism. As previously stated, the Islamic creed clarifies that there exists divinity and servanthood, divinity belonging exclusively to God and servanthood being the common denominator of all else. Similarly, all the attributes of divinity pertain exclusively to God and they are utterly lacking in other than Him. From this distinction arise all the consequences and demands of the Islamic concept for human life.

God, be glorified, is one in His being, exclusive in His attributes:

"SAY: 'He is the One God:
    God the Eternal, the Uncaused Cause of All That Being'.
    He begets not, and neither is He begotten; 'and there is nothing that could be compared with Him'."   (Al-Ikhlas)

"The Originator [is He] of the heavens and the earth. He has given you mates of your own kind—just as [He has willed that] among the beasts [there be] mates—to multiply you thereby: [but] there is nothing like unto Him, and He alone is all-hearing all-seeing."
                                                    (Ash-Shura: 11)

"Hence, do not coin any similitudes for God! Verily, God knows [all], whereas you have no [real] knowledge."   (An-Nahl: 74)

"Such is God, your Sustainer: there is no deity save Him, the Creator of everything: worship, then, Him alone—for it is He who has everything in His care."   (Al-An'am: 102)

"He to whom the dominion over the heavens and the earth belongs, and who begets no offspring, and has no partner in His dominion: for it is He who creates every thing and determines its nature in accordance with [His own] design."   (Al-Furqan: 2)

"Say: "Have you [really] given thought to what it is that you invoke instead of God? Show me what these [beings or forces] have created anywhere on earth! Or had they, perchance, a share in [creating] the heavens? [If so,] bring me any divine writ preceding this one, or any [other] vestige to knowledge—if what you claim is true!"   (Al-Ahqaf: 4)

"Say: "Unto whom belongs all that is in the heavens and on earth?" Say: "Unto God, who has willed upon Himself the law of grace and mercy."

He will assuredly gather you all together on the Day of Resurrection, [the coming of] which is beyond all doubt: yet those who have squandered their own selves—it is they who refuse to believe [in Him]."   (Al-An'am: 12)

"O men! Call to mind the blessings, which God has bestowed upon you! Is there any creator, other than God, that could provide for you sustenance out of heaven and earth? There is no deity save Him: and yet, how perverted are your minds!"   (Al-Fatir: 3)

"And how many a living creature is there that takes no thought of its own sustenance, [the while] God provides for it as [He provides] for you—since He alone is all-hearing, all-knowing."   (Al-'Ankabut: 60)

"And there is no living creature on earth but depends for its sustenance on God; and He knows its time-limit [on earth] and its resting-place [after death]: all [this] is laid down in [His] clear decree."   (Hud: 6)

"Verily, it is God [alone] who upholds the celestial bodies and the earth, lest they deviate [from their orbits]—for if they should ever deviate, there is none that could uphold them after He will have ceased to do so.

[But,] verily, He is ever-forbearing, much-forgiving!"   (Al-Fatir: 41)

"And among His wonders is this: the skies and the earth stand firm at His behest.

[Remember all this: for] in the end, when He will call you forth from the earth with a single call—lo! you will [all] emerge [for judgment]."   (Ar-Rum: 25)

"Verily, We shall indeed bring the dead back to life; and We shall record whatever [deeds] they have sent ahead, and the traces [of good and evil] which they have left behind: for of all things do We take account in a record clear."   (Ya Sin: 12)

God the Exalted is the Sovereign with dominion over all things:

"And He alone holds sway over His servants. And He sends forth heavenly forces to watch over you until, when death approaches any of you, Our messengers cause him to die: and they do not overlook [anyone]. And they [who have died] are thereupon brought before God, their true Lord Supreme. Oh, verily, His alone is all judgment: and He is the swiftest of all reckoners!"   (Al-An'am: 61–62)

"Say: "It is He alone who has the power to let loose upon you suffering from above you or from beneath your feet, or to confound you with mutual discord and let you taste the fear of one another.

Behold how many facets We give to these messages, so that they might understand the truth."   (Al-An'am: 65)

"Say: 'What do you think? If God should take away your hearing and your sight and seal your hearts—what deity but God is there that could bring it all back to you'

Behold how many facets We give to Our messages—and yet they turn away in disdain!"   (Al-An'am: 46)

"And He [it is who] applied His design to the skies, which were [yet but] smoke; and He [it is who] said to them and to the earth, 'Come [into being], both of you, willingly or unwillingly!'—to which both responded, 'We do come in obedience.'   (Fussilat: 11)

"And among His wonders is this: the skies and the earth stand firm at His behest.

[Remember all this: for] in the end, when He will call you forth from the earth with a single call—lo! you will [all] emerge [for judgment].

For, unto Him belongs every being that is in the heavens and on earth; all things devoutly obey His will."   (Ar-Rum: 25–26)

"For, before God prostrates itself all that is in the heavens and all that is on earth—every beast that moves, and the angels: [even] these do not bear themselves with false pride."   (An-Nahl: 49)

"The seven heavens extol His limitless glory, and the earth, and all that they contain; and there is not a single thing but extols His limitless glory and praise: but you [O men] fail to grasp the manner of their glorifying Him!
    Verily, He is forbearing, much–forgiving!"   (Al-Isra': 44)

Let these verses suffice as an indication of the scope afforded in the Islamic concept to monotheism, the profound truth that divinity belongs to God alone, that all else is in a state of servanthood, and that relations between the creation and the Creator are exclusively on the basis of their servanthood to Him, not lineage or marital connection, not partnership or similarity in essence, attribute, or characteristic.

But any discussion of the Oneness of God will remain incomplete until we discuss, however briefly, the implications for human life of this absolute, perfect, comprehensive, decisive and precise monotheism. These implications show how the Oneness of God is an important characteristic of the Islamic concept.

One of the implications is that God's exclusive possession of the attributes of divinity has consequences for the ordering of human life in all its particulars, just as it does for men's beliefs, concepts, ideas, and forms of devotion.

The Muslim believes that there is no god but God, that He alone shall be worshipped, that He alone is the Creator, He alone is the Sustainer, He alone is the source of benefit or harm, and He alone controls the affairs of the universe. It is therefore to Him alone that the Muslim addresses himself with his acts of ritual devotion, in neediness and hope, in reverence and awe.

He believes likewise that there is no sovereign but God, no legislator but God, and no orderer of human life, relationships and the universe in its entirety, but God. From God alone does he receive guidance and law, way and principles of life, and criteria of value and judgement.

To address oneself exclusively to God in worship and to receive from Him in exclusivity all that has just been mentioned—both are imperatives deriving from the Islamic concept, and both illustrate the broad range covered in the mind and life of the Muslim by the truth of the divine oneness.

The Noble Qur'an draws a close connection between the belief in the Oneness of God and its implications for life. It ties everything that it imposes as a duty on the Muslim—modes of thought and sentiment, acts of devotion, adherence to divine law—to God's Oneness and His nurturing exercise of sovereignty throughout the entirety of the universe. In one and the same context we find mention of the Oneness of God, the effects of His sovereignty in the universe, in this world and the hereafter, and a repeated command to follow the law of God as the necessary consequence of the divine oneness.

"AND YOUR GOD is the One God: there is no deity save Him, the Most Gracious, the Dispenser of Grace.

Verily, in the creation of the heavens and of the earth, and the succession of night and day: and in the ships that speed through the sea with what is useful to man: and in the waters which God sends down from the sky, giving life thereby to the earth after it had been lifeless, and causing all manner of living creatures to multiply thereon: and in the change of the winds, and the clouds that run their appointed courses between sky and earth: [in all this] there are messages indeed for people who use their reason.

And yet there are people who choose to believe in beings that allegedly rival God, loving them as [only] God should be loved: whereas those who have attained to faith love God more than all else.

If they who are bent on evildoing could but see—as see they will when they are made to suffer [on Resurrection Day]—that all might belongs to God alone, and that God is severe in [meting out] punishment!

[On that Day] it will come to pass that those who had been [falsely] adored shall disown their followers, and the latter shall see the suffering [that awaits them], with all their hopes cut to pieces! And then those followers shall say: "Would that we had a second chance [in life], so that we could disown them as they have disowned us!

Thus will God show them their works [in a manner that will cause them] bitter regrets; but they will not come out of the fire.

O MANKIND! Partake of what is lawful and good on earth, and follow not Satan's footsteps: for, verily, he is your open foe, and bids you only to do evil, and to commit deeds of abomination, and to attribute unto God something of which you have no knowledge.

But when they are told, "Follow what God has bestowed from on high," some answer, "Nay, we shall follow [only] that which we found our forefathers believing in and doing. "Why, even if their forefathers did not use their reason at all, and were devoid of all guidance?

And so, the parable of those who are bent on denying the truth is that of the beast which hears the shepherd's cry, and hears in it nothing but the sound of a voice and a call. Deaf are they, and dumb, and blind: for they do not use their reason.

O you who have attained to faith! Partake of the good things which we have provided for you as sustenance, and render thanks unto God, if it is [truly] Him that you worship."

(Al-Baqarah: 163–172)

Examining these verses of the Qur'an, we find that they begin by affirming the Oneness of God and His exclusive possession of Divinity. This is followed by the presentation of cosmic phenomena which display divine power. Next, scenes from the Day of Judgement are depicted, that day on which God stands indisputably alone in His possession and exercise of sovereignty. After this, man is ordered to obey God's law, its commands and prohibitions, and to disobey Satan; those who continue to follow the ways of Jahiliyya are condemned. Then the believers are commanded to eat of the good things that God has proclaimed licit and to shun that which He has forbidden, for it is He alone Who permits or prohibits, just as it is He alone Who is to be worshipped, Who disposes of the affairs of the universe, and Whose sovereignty becomes undeniably manifest on the Day of Judgement. In short, the Oneness of God involves necessarily exclusive orientation to Him in both ritual and law.

Such integrated, interconnected passages are numerous in the Qur'an, to demonstrate the meaning and scope of the Oneness of God. Let us provide one more example for the sake of clarity:

"[Thou art but entrusted with Our message:] and so We have revealed unto thee a discourse in the Arabic tongue in order that thou mayest warn the foremost of all cities and all who dwell around it—to wit, warn [them] of the Day of the Gathering, [the coming

of] which is beyond all doubt: [the Day when] some shall find themselves in paradise, and some in the blazing flame.

Now had God so willed, He could surely have made them all
one single community: none the less, He admits unto His grace him
that wills [to be admitted]—whereas the evildoers shall have none to
protect them and none to succour them [on Judgment Day].

Did they, perchance, [think that they could] choose protectors
other than Him? But God alone is the Protector [of all that exists],
since it is He alone who brings the dead to life, and He alone who
has the power to will anything.

AND ON WHATEVER you may differ, [O believers,] the verdict thereon rests with God.

[Say, therefore:] "Such is God, my Sustainer: in Him have I
placed my trust, and unto Him do I always turn!"

The Originator [is He] of the heavens and the earth. He has given
you mates of your own kind—just as [He has willed that] among the
beasts [there be] mates—to multiply you thereby: [but] there is nothing like unto Him, and He alone is all-hearing all-seeing.

His are the keys of the heavens and the earth: He grants abundant sustenance, or gives it in scant measure, unto whomever He
wills: for, behold, He has full knowledge of everything.

In matters of faith, He has ordained for you that which He had
enjoined upon Noah—and into which We gave thee [O Muhammad]
insight through revelation—as well as that which we had enjoined
upon Abraham, and Moses, and Jesus: Steadfastly uphold the [true]
faith, and do not break up your unity therein.

[And even though] that [unity of faith] to which thou callest them
appears oppressive to those who are wont to ascribe to other beings or
forces a share in His divinity, God draws unto Himself everyone who
is willing, and guides unto Himself everyone who turns unto Him.

And [as for the followers of earlier revelation,] they broke up
their unity, out of mutual jealousy, only after they had come to know
[the truth]. And had it not been for a decree that had already gone
forth from thy Sustainer, [postponing all decision] until a term set
[by Him], all would indeed have been decided between them [from
the outset]. As it is, behold, they who have inherited their divine writ
from those who preceded them are [now] in grave doubt, amounting
to suspicion, about what it portends.

Because of this, then, summon [all mankind]. And pursue the
right courses, as thou hast been bidden [by God]; and do not follow
their likes and dislikes, but say:

"I believe in whatever revelation God has bestowed from on high; and I am bidden to bring about equity in your mutual views. God is our Sustainer as well as your Sustainer. To us shall be accounted our deeds, and to you, your deeds. Let there be no contention between us and you: God will bring us all together—for with Him is all journeys' end."   (Ash-Shura: 7–15)

Examining these verses, we find that they begin by affirming revelation and prophethood, in order for the Messenger to warn men of Judgment in the hereafter. Next are mentioned the differing fates that await the believers and the miscreants in the hereafter, depending on the paths they have followed in this world, and God's exclusive sovereignty on the Day of Judgment. Then are mentioned the power of God, as manifested in His resurrecting the dead, and once again, His exclusive sovereignty. It is then stressed that man should place his reliance on God alone and turn to Him alone in repentance. This is followed by verses presenting the manifestation of His power in creating the heavens and the earth, mankind in pairs of male and female, and the beasts, all this with the reminder that "there is naught like unto Him." His sovereignty is unique, for "his are the keys to the heavens and the earth," and His provision of sustenance is unique, for "He grants abundant sustenance to whomsoever He wills in due amount." The verses then proceed to clarify that God alone is the legislator, not simply from the beginning of the Qur'anic revelation, but from the dawn of revelation as such. God thus ordains that what He has legislated constitutes religion and must consistently be followed, and He forbids men to follow their own whims. Finally, a sharp distinction is drawn between those believers who judge and rule according to God's legislation and all others, and a reminder is given that all return to God.

These two examples should suffice to show the interconnectedness, in the Islamic concept, of the Oneness of God with His sovereignty, to explain the meaning of monotheism and its scope in human life, and to demonstrate that monotheism, in this comprehensive sense, is indeed one of the characteristics of the Islamic concept. All that remains for us to say is that the effects of this concept on the mind and heart of man and in his life are unique. It creates a sense of cohesion unaffected by changing shapes and forms, of firm and unshakable values, of consistent and vigorous conduct.

He who understands divinity in this sense, and is cognizant also of his own servanthood, will be able to define his orientation and conduct in a firm and precise manner. "Who is he? What is the purpose of his existence? What are the limits of his power?"—he will have answers to all of these questions. He will know too the true nature of all that exists in the universe and the single force that determines all within it. He will have a correct basis on which to interact with all things within well-defined limits. This sense of cohesion and orderliness will extend itself to his intellect and the criteria by which it operates and to his heart and the values which it embraces. To the degree that he inter- acts with the divine norms everywhere manifest, he will find this sense strengthened and confirmed.

We realize this clearly when we compare the Muslim who deals with his Lord, the one God, the Creator, the Sustainer, the Powerful, the Vanquisher, the Sovereign, with the adherents of other visions and concepts, whether it be those who deal with two competing gods—the god of good and the god of evil; those who deal with a god that exists but dissolves himself in the non-existent; those who deal with a god who is not in any way concerned with his own affairs or those of the entire universe; or those who deal with a pseudo-god, matter, who nei- ther sees or hears nor posseses any degree of permanence.

The Islamic concept creates in the heart and mind consistency and steadfast. One who perceives the true nature of his Lord and His attri- butes and of his own relationship with Him is bound to be consistent and steadfast in his dealings with Him, in his heart and in his mind, without confusion or indecision. The Muslim knows what his Lord wishes for him and what He dislikes for him, and is firmly convinced that the sole path to gaining His pleasure is belief in Him, knowing Him and His attributes, and being steadfast in following the path He has laid down. He will not attribute to Him sonship or any other type of kinship, nor will he seek to approach Him with incantations or inter- cessors. Rather, he will worship Him exclusively by adhering to His commands and prohibitions, by following His laws and ordinances.

All this is in addition to the clarity, simplicity and ease inherent in the concept, as well as in the form of conduct it inculcates in the believer. This can easily be realized if we compare the Islamic concept based on the affirmation of God's oneness with the Church's trinitarian dogma, its doctrine of the sonship, and its claim that man's original sin can be expiated only by accepting Jesus as the son of God, not to mention a whole series of similar riddles.

The same can be said of those who deal with "nature," which does not hear or see, permit or forbid, demand of its devotees that they strive to be virtuous or instruct them to avoid evil and immorality. How could such persons have any path to follow consistently? How could their minds or hearts enjoy any stability? They lack all certitude concerning the true nature of their god, hoping each day to find out something new concerning him, to discover some attribute of his previously unknown to them. Experiment or chance are the only paths open to them.

We could continue to discuss the state of those who follow the various concepts we range under the heading of "wilderness and debris." None of them can inspire in their followers any cohesion of concept or consistency in conduct, marked as they all are by obscurity, complexity and confusion. By contrast, the first feature that the heart and the mind notices when it encounters the Islamic concept is straightforwardness, simplicity, and clarity. It is this feature that attracts contemporary Europeans and Americans who enter Islam; they always mention it as the first characteristic that aroused their attention. It is also this selfsame feature that has attracted to Islam primitive peoples in Africa and Asia in times ancient and modern, for it is inherently attractive to the innate nature of man, be he civilized or primitive.

This concept assures the integration of the personality and capacities of both the individual Muslim and the community, and it negates the disintegration and dissolution that are engendered by other doctrines and concepts.

Humanity, a single whole in its original creation, interacts with a single deity in every aspect of its activity, in belief and awareness, in worship and orientation, in legislation and social organization, in this world and the hereafter. Its belief is not diffused among various gods; differing elements within one and the same deity; various forces some of which are within the sphere of the deity to the exclusion of others, without any knowable law governing interaction with them; or the forces of nature, something lacking definable existence.

Similarly, man's attention is not directed in one way with respect to belief, awareness and worship, and in another way in matters of social organization. Man receives all of this from a single source, a source that governs his mind and his awareness, his motion and his labor, just as it governs the uiverse as a whole. Man's interaction with the universe is guided by this single source, without the slightest diffusion or dispersion.

This comprehensive integration creates an immense and insuperable force, a force wherein lies the secret of the wonders that the Islamic creed has accomplished in human life and history. This force is both integrated within itself and integrated with the forces of the universe, for both go back to a single source, are governed by its norms, and are oriented to God, the One.

Let us now come to the unique effect created by the Islamic concept in the consciousness of the Muslim and his life, as well as in the life of Muslim society, by virtue of the chracteristic of monotheism on which the concept is based. That effect is none other than the liberation of man, or to put it differently, the birth of man.

The exclusive possession of divinity and its attributes by God on the one hand, and the servanthood to God that is shared by all other than God, together with their lack of any share in the divine attributes, on the other hand, mean and necessitate thhat men should receive legislation for all aspects of their life from God alone. This is in exact parallel to their confining their devotional worship to God, for the exclusive possession of sovereignty is one of the attributes of divinity. No believer would deny this, nor would even a disbeliever dispute it.

Qur'anic verses underscore and define this meaning, in a manner that leaves no room for doubt or disputation:

"All that you worship instead of God is nothing but [empty] names which you have invented—you and your forefathers—[and] for which God has bestowed no warrant from on high. Judgment [as to what is right and what is wrong] rests with God alone—[and] He has ordained that you should worship nought but Him: this is the [one] ever-true faith; but most people know it not."   (Yusuf: 40)

"Is it that they [who care for no more than this world] believe in forces supposed to have a share in God's divinity, which enjoin upon them as a moral law something that God has never allowed?

Now were it not for [God's] decree on the final judgment, all would indeed have been decided between them [in this world]: but, verily, grievous suffering awaits the evildoers [in the life to come]."

(Ash-Shura: 21)

"Verily, it is We who bestowed from on high the Torah, wherein there was guidance and light. On its strength did the prophets, who had surrendered themselves unto God, deliver judgment unto those who followed the Jewish faith; and so did the [early] men of God and the rabbis, inasmuch as some of God's writ had been entrusted to their care; and they [all] bore witness to its truth.

Therefore, [O children of Israel,] hold not men in awe, but stand in awe of Me; and do not barter away My messages for a trifling gain: for they who do not judge in accordance with what God has bestowed from on high are, indeed, deniers of the truth!"

(Al-Ma'idah: 44)

"But nay, by thy Sustainer! They do not [really] believe unless they make thee [O Prophet] a judge of all on which they disagree among themselves, and then find in their hearts no bar to an acceptance of thy decision and give themselves up [to it] in utter self-surrender."

(An-Nisa': 65)

The Islamic concept makes no distinction between dedicating all devotional observance to God and accepting legislation from Him alone. For both are necessary implications of the Oneness of God and His sole possession of divinity, and to deviate from either results inexorably in the abandonment of Islam and religion. This can be deduced from the verses we have already cited.

It will also be instructive to cite another verse and the way in which the Prophet, upon whom be peace and blessings, interpreted it. This is the verse:

"They have taken their rabbis and their monks as well as the Christ, son of Mary—for their lords beside God, although they had been bidden to worship none but the One God, save whom there is no deity: the One who is utterly remote, in His limitless glory, from anything to which they may ascribe a share in His divinity!"

(At-Tawbah: 31)

The People of the Book to whom this verse refers considered Jesus Christ their lord and directed their devotional rituals to him. As for their priests and their monks, they also took them as lords, not in the sense of profeering them worship, but in the sense of adhering to the laws and commands they promulgated. The verse in question, however, mentions them both as taking Jesus as a lord and as taking their priests and monks as lords, affirming thereby that the two practices were equally repugnant to the worship of God. The Christians thus became tainted with polytheism. None of this can be disputed.

Quite apart from all else, the Prophet, upon whom be peace and blessings, has interpreted the verse in a fashion that ought to lay to rest any controversy.

Imam Ahmad, al-Tirmidhi and ibn Jarir have narrated concerning 'Udayy ibn Hatim that when he was informed about the mission of the Messenger of God, he fled to Syria, for he had converted to Christianity in the era of Jahiliyya. When his sister and a group of his people were taken prisoner, the Messenger of God had her released and sent her back to her brother, whom she then caused to become favorably inclined to Islam. 'Udayy came to Medina, and entered the presence of the Prophet wearing a silver cross. When he heard the Prophet reciting the verse, "They have taken their priests and their monks as well as the Christ, son of Mary—for their lords beside God," he objected, saying, "they have not worshipped them." To which the Prophet responded, "Indeed they have, for they [the priests and the monks] have forbidden the permitted and permitted the forbidden, and they [the Christians] followed them in that. This constitutes their worship of them."

Al-Suddi said in interpretation of the verse under discussion: "they sought advice of men and ignored the Book of God behind their backs. It is for this reason that God said, 'they were commanded to worship but one God.' That is to say, when God has prohibited a thing, it is prohibited, and when He has permitted something, it is permitted. Whatever He legislates is to be followed, and whatever He decrees is to be implemented."

By thus decisively settling the matter, the Islamic concept has effectively declared the liberation of man, or even the birth of man. For by this declaration men have been liberated from servitude to each other and instead made servants of God. Man, in the full sense of the word "man," will never exist on earth until the day comes when he is liberated from rule and dominance by others, in whatever shape or form, in his person, his life, his mind, and his belief.

By assigning legislation and sovereignty to God alone and making all men servants of God, Islam, and only Islam, liberates men from servitude to each other.

In all systems where legislation and sovereignty are in the hands of men, in one way or another, the result is that some men are the servants and slaves of others. This servitude is abolished in Islam, all men being equally the servants of God. This is the true meaning of the liberation of man, a liberation which might also be termed the birth of man, short of which man cannot enjoy a fully human existence. It is a divine gift, bestowed on mankind as a blessing:

> "Today, I have perfected your religion for you, and I have completed
> My blessing upon you, and I have approved Islam for your religion."
> (Al-Ma'ida: 3)

And this is the gift that the adherents of the creed of the Oneness of God can pass on to mankind in its entirety. It is something fresh and new for them to present to humanity today; let humanity receive it today as a gift from the Muslims, just as their own ancestors once did. Its appeal is irresistible, for it gives man what he previously lacked, something utterly different from all concepts and creeds, ideas and philosophies.

Rab'i ibn 'Amir was sent by the Muslim army as a messenger to Rustam, commander of the Persians, who asked him what had brought him to his lands. The few words he uttered in response conveyed the whole essence of the Islamic creed and the great historical movement that arose from it, and delineated, too, the conceptual world of the early Muslims and their understanding of their role. He answered: "God has sent us, to bring forth whoever wishes from servitude to men into servitude to God; from the narrow straits of this world into the broad expanse of this world and the hereafter; and from the oppression of existing religions into the justice of Islam."

In these few words are embodied the foundations of this creed and the nature of the movement to which it gave rise. It is to bring forth whomever God wishes from among His servants from servitude to men into servitude to God; to assign all their affairs to God, in life and in death, in this world and the hereafter; and to recognize God's exclusive possession of the attributes of divinity such as sovereignty and fitness to legislate that none would dispute except the stubborn unbeliever. There is no freedom for man, nor even a truly human existence, except in utter devotion to God.

When those who profess monotheism return fully to it and raise high its banner, they will be able to proclaim to humanity what once Rabi' ibn 'Amir proclaimed. For humanity today is, in a certain sense, in exactly the same condition as it was when Rabi' ibn 'Amir made his proclamation—sunk in the servitude of some men to others. It is the monotheism of Islam, in its comprehensive sense, that will bring men forth from this state into servitude to God. Then, and then only, will man be liberated, or indeed, be truly born.

When the adherents of monotheism return to the path with which God has favored them, they will be able to present humanity with something lacking in all systems of thought and social organization existing on earth. They have, therefore, a new role for today and tomorrow, a great, global role in the service of humanity, a role to lead humanity forward like the role once vested in the unlettered Arabs of the Arabian Peninsula, giving guidance and leadership to the world of humanity.

They cannot present humanity today with great scientific accomplishments or civilizational advances, surpassing what humanity already possesses. They can, however, present humanity with something else, something nobler and greater than scientific accomplishments or civilizational advances—with the liberation or true birth of man. They will be presenting humanity at the same time with a complete way of life based on the dignity of man; on the emancipation of his intellect, his conscience and his spirit; and on the emancipation of all the capacities he needs to fulfill his role as divine vicegerent on earth, as a free and noble being. Then man will be able to continue his scientific and civilizational advance in freedom and dignity, without being a slave to the machine or to other human beings.

May God grant us correct understanding, and praise be to God, Lord of the Worlds.

INDEX